ISLAMIC FEMINISM AND THE DISCOURSE OF POST-LIBERATION

This important study examines the cultural turn for women in the Middle East and North Africa, analyzing the ways they have adjusted to, and at times defended, socially conservative redefinitions of their roles in society in matters of marriage, work and public codes of behavior.

Whether this cultural turn is an autochthonous response, or an alternative to Western feminism, *Islamic Feminism and the Discourse of Post-Liberation: The Cultural Turn in Algeria* examines the sources, evolution, contradictions as well as consequences of the cultural turn. Focusing on Algeria, but making comparisons with Tunisia and Morocco, the book takes an in-depth look at Islamic feminism and studies its functions in the geopolitics of control of Islam. It also explores the knowledge effects of the cultural turn and crucially identifies a critical way of re-orienting feminist thought and practice in the region.

This new work from a highly regarded scholar will appeal to researchers, graduates, and undergraduates in North African studies; Middle Eastern studies; sociology; women and gender studies; anthropology; political science; and ethnic and critical race studies.

Marnia Lazreg is Professor of Sociology at Hunter College and The Graduate Center, CUNY, USA. Her research interests span constructions of otherness, colonial history, cultural movements, international development, women in the Middle East and North Africa, and postmodernist social theory. She has lectured extensively around the world and participated in radio and television programs. Her most recent publications include *Foucault's Orient: The Conundrum of Cultural Difference, From Tunisia to Japan* (2017), *Questioning the Veil: Open Letters to Muslim Women* (2010), and *Torture and the Twilight of Empire: From Algiers to Baghdad* (2017).

ISLAMIC FEMINISM AND THE DISCOURSE OF POST-LIBERATION

The Cultural Turn in Algeria

Marnia Lazreg

Routledge
Taylor & Francis Group

LONDON AND NEW YORK

First published 2021
by Routledge
2 Park Square, Milton Park, Abingdon, Oxon OX14 4RN

and by Routledge
52 Vanderbilt Avenue, New York, NY 10017

Routledge is an imprint of the Taylor & Francis Group, an informa business

British Library Cataloguing-in-Publication Data
A catalogue record for this book is available from the British Library

Library of Congress Cataloging-in-Publication Data
Names: Lazreg, Marnia, author.
Title: Islamic feminism and the discourse of post-liberation : the cultural
turn in Algeria / Marnia Lazreg.
Description: Abingdon, Oxon ; New York, NY : Routledge, 2021. | Includes
bibliographical references and index.
Identifiers: LCCN 2020032286 (print) | LCCN 2020032287 (ebook) | ISBN
9781138631441 (hardback) | ISBN 9781138631458 (paperback) | ISBN
9781315208855 (ebook) | ISBN 9781351804905 (adobe pdf) | ISBN
9781351804899 (epub) | ISBN 9781351804882 (mobi)
Subjects: LCSH: Feminism–Religious aspects–Islam. | Feminism–Algeria. |
Feminism–Africa, North. | Women–Algeria–Social conditions. |
Women–Africa, North–Social conditions.
Classification: LCC HQ1170 .L387 2021 (print) | LCC HQ1170 (ebook) | DDC
305.420965–dc23
LC record available at https://lccn.loc.gov/2020032286
LC ebook record available at https://lccn.loc.gov/2020032287

ISBN: 978-1-138-63144-1 (hbk)
ISBN: 978-1-138-63145-8 (pbk)
ISBN: 978-1-315-20885-5 (ebk)

Typeset in Times New Roman
by Taylor & Francis Books

To the memory of Aoued,
in gratitude

CONTENTS

ACKNOWLEDGMENTS

Without the cooperation and help of all the women and men I have interviewed or held discussions with, some of whom have preferred to remain anonymous, this book would never have come into being. I hope that all that is good in the interpretations I have provided herein is worthy of their trust as well as the time they spent with me, while everything else is my sole responsibility.

I would like to give special thanks to Louisa Ighilahriz; Bouabdallah Ghoulamallah; the murshidat at the Ministry of Religious Affairs and Waqfs; Noureddine Mohammedi; Nadia Bellal; Raja Rhouni; Nadia Zai; Fatma Lahouari; Cherifa Kheddar; and all the professors and graduate students from various disciplines who patiently answered my questions.

I am also indebted to Hayat Laouedj, Director of the Research and Publications Department at the Bibliothèque Nationale d'Algérie in Algiers, who unearthed invaluable bibliographic sources.

I am particularly grateful to the management, staff and researchers at the Centre de Recherche en Anthropologie Sociale et Culturelle (CRASC) in Oran for their welcome and willingness to share their views as well as research with me. At Routledge, Eleanor Catchpole Simmons's patience and support carried me through a long and slow process of writing.

This book has not been easy for me to write. It compelled me to confront issues I have yet to sort out in light of Algeria's unprecedented and peaceful mass movement for change initiated in February 2019. There were moments when I wanted to throw in the towel. It was thanks to Azizah Al-Hibri's willingness to hear my concerns that I finally brought myself to part with the manuscript. I greatly appreciate her generosity of spirit and intellectual openness.

INTRODUCTION

Why is it that women in the Middle East and North Africa (MENA) have adjusted to, and at times defended, socially conservative redefinitions of their roles in society in matters of marriage, work and codes of behavior in public in the name of cultural specificity? Why have women done so in an era of economic precariousness[1] and at the expense of relinquishing past claims for systemic change? These are the questions that led me initially to write this book. As I pondered them in interviews with women and through my research travels, another question nagged at me: why is it that even though women across the region have made progress, the societies in which they live have yet to be feminized? The feminization of a society does not mean that women have achieved absolute equality with men, that their lives are free of sexual violence and harassment, or that they no longer have to struggle to prove their humanity. It means a society in which women have entered the collective conscience as a reality that cannot be ignored, as an unavoidable reminder of a repairable tear in the fabric of the national ethos; a society in which there is a social and legal cost to denying women's humanity or the implementation of their rights; a society in which women's rights are not seen as a favor done by a government or a leader, but recognized as an indisputable and integral part of governance, the standard by which to assess the character, behavior as well as performance of men in leadership positions.

It soon became clear to me that these initial questions had to be further specified since they implied that women had a clear choice and that they somehow contributed to the failure of political systems to promote gender equality. Consequently, the overriding question shifted to an inquiry into the factors framing, facilitating, or fostering the cultural turn among women. The state is a key player in what at first glance looks like a women-initiated cultural trend, just as it is instrumental in the conflation of religion with culture—a move that erases the difference between constitutional right, and duty to a transcendental God. Interestingly, in facilitating the emergence of the cultural turn, the state further actively engages in a cultural policy, which plays a national as well geopolitical role in the "war on terror." Hence the state is at once a promoter and an agent of the turn using a variety of techniques in a departure from its past role of occasionally sponsoring women's rights primarily for domestic political reasons. Briefly, the "war on terror" is not only a hot war, which informed the United Sates invasions of Afghanistan in 2001, and Iraq in 2003. It is also a "war of ideas" centered on and targeting Islam.[2] As such it focuses on Islam as a source of violent strife[3] and devises strategies to promote a "moderate" modality of it. It seeks to transform its meaning through various interventions, directly or indirectly through the media, educational institutions, and civil society. The war of ideas requires and elicits the active cooperation of Muslim states just as it targets modernist and "secularist" Muslim intellectuals, youth as well as feminist advocates of gender equality as potential allies.[4] Hence the "war on terror" is not simply concerned with religious practices; it concerns itself with the very *idea* of Islam.

In thinking through the role of the state, taking as an example Algeria, I also had to confront my misgivings about "Islamic feminism"[5]—another modality of the cultural turn, most active in Morocco, Middle Eastern and Asian countries as well as among Muslims in Europe and North America. Islamic feminism is an umbrella concept encompassing a heterogeneous trend among women holding various views about the ways in which they could square their aspirations for change in an age of feminism with their identity as Muslims. It ranges from advocacy for women ranging from working with poor and vulnerable women in accordance with a Muslim ethic,[6] to exploring Islam's foundational texts to reveal their progressive contents, which had been passed over or misconstrued, using a contextualist methodology.[7] Invaluable to women whom it enlightens about the positivity of their religion, the contextualist current in Islamic feminism contributes to the production of knowledge of Islam. Importantly, it signals women's empowering themselves to read and interpret foundational texts, a task traditionally carried out by men. However, the contextualist current in Islamic feminism lends itself to critical scrutiny for its method and claims when a version of it, herein referred to as Quranic attributor contextualism, makes it clear that it is an alternative to "secular" feminism, which it declares dead; aims for a "liberation" of women through revised religious texts; and on occasion joins in a state's policy of establishing a normative Islam in cooperation with European and North American powers in their prosecution of the "war on terror." These are the claims about which I am skeptical. The skeptical posture I assume in this book is not synonymous with "secular" in the narrow sense of the term (although there would be nothing amiss with being secular); it is a posture that permits me to resist a monistic approach to change that evades a (needed) critique of the very structures that have enabled this trend in Islamic feminism to become an ascendant and popular mode of "liberation" of women to which one must bow for fear of going against the grain, or being taxed with collusion with neo-imperialism.[8] My skepticism is born out of a concern that Quranic attributor contextualism, no matter its claims to align itself with "social justice," uncouples the struggle for women's rights from the search for a restructuring of political and economic systems without which change in the political culture that sustains gender inequality may not occur.

Although at times it denies its feminist roots, this trend of Islamic feminism is an heir to academic postfeminist knowledge from which it derives its theoretical legitimacy and to which it owes its positive reception.[9] This trend shares features with Biblical and Christian feminist contextualism, albeit its goals transcend the domain of religion. When viewed from the standpoint of the prevailing empiricist and functionalist knowledge production, women's Quranic attributor contextualism threatens to make building a feminist theory more, not less difficult. Indeed, its unacknowledged postfeminist background knowledge distances it from the universalistic emancipatory ideals of women's liberation against which academic postfeminism asserted itself.[10]

In focusing on Algeria, the book first intends to trace the process through which culture and religion become fused to culminate in the constitution of an engineered *wasatiya* Islam[11] with geopolitical ramifications. The conflation of religion with culture is at times perceived as a manner of combatting secularization understood as the privatization of religion in a society purportedly bereft of moral values grounded in religion. Yet the dichotomous view of secularization as hostile to religion disregards the continued influence of religion in "secular" societies,[12] just as it ignores the evolution of the notion of secularization in Western societies.[13]

Algeria provides a concrete example of how *wasatiya* policy seeks to shepherd women by structuring and managing the cultural turn. The book first examines from a historico-critical perspective the roots, method, and effects on women of *wasatiya* Islam. Although ostensibly tailored to Algeria, *wasatiya* Islam policy meshes with and shares in the objectives of the global "war on terror." This war incorporates states on the Islamic periphery (among whom Algeria and Morocco) within its logic of distinguishing between "moderate" and "radical" Islam.[14] The Algerian modality of the cultural turn reflects the manner in which the Algerian state positions itself towards France and/or the USA,[15] architects of the "war on terror," and reveals the degree to which it is willing to assume the moral cost of promoting an Islam designed as an antidote to "terrorism." The comparative geopolitical role of the state helps to distinguish the modality of the cultural turn in Algeria from "Islamic feminism" in neighboring Morocco or other countries in the Middle East.[16] In Algeria, women's engagement in the cultural turn is more situational and less institutionalized than in Morocco, in spite of both countries' commitment to a *wasatiya* Islam.[17] It expresses itself in behaviors and attitudes, rather than a militant cultural activism.

Conceptually, to adapt Michel Foucault's analytical concepts, *wasatiya* Islam policy reveals the overlapping characteristic forms of state power as "disciplinary" in its establishment of an educational, training, and administrative apparatus with a specialized staff, including *imams and murshidat* (religious guides), to disseminate a normative Islam in mosques and centers of learning; "juridical" in its participation in a global combat against "radical" Islam through a militarized security system; and surrogate *irshadi* in its shepherding women, guided by *murshidat* and *'alimat* (women theologians) to an avowedly moderate Islam through targeted intervention in health, reproduction, mothering, and carceral rehabilitation.[18] The Foucauldian notion of "pastoral power" in the context of a Muslim country strikes as anachronistic as it is evocative of Christian symbolism, although the history of the term reaches back to ancient Greece.[19] By surrogate *irshadi* power, I mean a technique of governance through which the state acting as a substitute of religious authorities establishes an apparatus intended to guide individual women and men through a normative religious model aligned on a geopolitical policy of restructuring Islam. The Arabic root of *irshadi* is *"rashada,"* which means to guide or orient a person towards the right path. Early Islamic history refers to the *"al khulafaa' ar-rashidun,"* or the rightly guided caliphs.[20] In contemporary Algeria, the state attempts to orient individuals towards a conception of Islam, which it alternately deems civilizational, one that harks back to Islam in the Iberian Peninsula, and indigenous. By contrast, in Morocco, the monarch poses as a latter-day emulator of the rightly guided caliphs albeit implementing the terms of Western powers' policy of restructuration of Islam.

Metaphorically, the state acts as a guide in order to rationalize an Islam seen as insufficiently determinate, open to interpretations threatening to state power, and escaping state political control. Since the late 1990s the state (whose management of religion has oscillated between strategic control and acquiescence) has entered a different phase, one that is more rationalized and aims for a degree of systematization that reaches across borders. Algeria and Morocco exercise the same *irshadi* power to various degrees. However, they differ in the extent to which each enlists women either as willing participants or mostly yielding. One of the consequences of the normalization of this form of governance through *wasatiya* Islam is to occlude or screen out the non-religious discourse of rights.[21] This perspective allows an understanding of the state as a collaborator of the liberal European and North American state in its strategy of promoting a deradicalized Islam in the Muslim world without transforming itself into a liberal secularizing state. In reality the positioning of the state in Algeria (as well as in Morocco) toward religion is not fundamentally different from the French or American states, especially in times of crises. France (in its battle against the veil and for *laïcité*)[22] as well as the United States (as exemplified by Republican support for evangelicals) involve themselves directly in the religious domain all the while asserting the principle of secularity.

Second, the book further explores from a sociological perspective, the central role played by the emergence of Quranic attributor contextualism in the legitimation of *wasatiya* Islam. However, since the policy in Algeria includes women as more yielding than active agents, it is fruitful to compare it to Morocco's policy, which gives women advocates of Quranic attributor contextualism a prominent role. The comparison helps to determine whether in Algeria a space between religion and culture is preserved in which change that is not subordinated to Quranic exegesis could occur. Indeed, in spite of everything as an analyst put it, "women are less inhibited than in the past; they enter new spaces."[23]

Third, the book analyzes the conceptual patterns in the academic theoretical discourse originating outside of Algeria and the Middle East that wittingly or unwittingly lend support to the normalization of women's Quranic attributor contextualism as a new mode of liberation. It specifically identifies the effects of the migration of American (and global) postfeminist concepts, their adaptations, transformations, or distortions in justifications of the cultural turn. It traces the assumptions as well as effects of the academic postfeminist discourse in order to understand how they hamper the elaboration of a theoretical counter-discourse of resistance to the cultural turn. In addition, the book enquires into the conditions of possibility of a feminist thought that would rekindle the liberatory ideal of liberal feminism while disrupting its Euro-centered practice.[24]

Islam is at the heart of the cultural turn. The policy of promoting a "moderate" Islam is the rationale behind "deradicalization" programmatic actions which Algeria in the past five years, and Morocco for more than a decade have embarked on. In Algeria (whose program is less elaborate than in Morocco) deradicalization evokes a recent past, the war of decolonization (1954–1962) in which brainwashing was used as a method of "turning" an Algerian combatant into a docile colonial subject.[25] Although deradicalization and brainwashing may not be synonymous, they both involve behavior modification either in confined settings as practiced in French (and Middle Eastern) jails, or in teaching and preaching about one perspective on Islam aimed at ensuring the stability of a political system, local or global. Deradicalization is invasive and not free of coercion, not the least that of the soul.[26] The manualized, professionalized, and institutionalized method of deradicalization used in Morocco is also exported to other countries as a packaged method of eradication of "radical" Islam. It is ironic that Algeria, whose population was denied citizenship rights in 1830–1962 because of its religion, would find common ground with France's own war against Islam. The Moroccan method specifically enlists women advocates of Islamic feminism in its policy.[27]

The "cultural turn" as a concept used in this book originates in the social science literature. It refers to a trend in research that emerged in the late 1980s as a result of a waning of metanarratives such as Marxism or grand theory as exemplified by Talcott Parsons's systems theory.[28] Although it appears in various modalities, the trend questioned the scientific claims of social research that did not always give its due to the importance of culture in the construction of its methodology, especially in its historical sociology. Practitioners of the cultural turn[29] sought to restore the balance by focusing on culture, defined in broad terms as encompassing not only symbols and rituals but also ways of thinking and constructing meaning.[30] Gradually, culture appeared as the bedrock of values and norms that inescapably shape individuals' perceptions to a degree that not only makes any scientific claim to the study of social beings impossible, but irremediably hampers (or prevents) cross-cultural understandings.

The cultural turn as studied herein is not synonymous with another phase of political Islam, although the two are intertwined. Nor is it identical to Islamic feminism although the two frequently borrow the same channel, religion. Moreover, the cultural turn is not an unrecognized pathway to a woman's conscious search for spirituality through piety.[31] Evidence indicates that the latter occurs in the absence of what is viewed as the cultural turn in this book. If the cultural turn is not identical to political Islam, Islamic feminisms or a personal yearning for piety and spirituality, what is it? How can it be studied?

I propose to define the cultural turn among women in this book as an attitude born out of juridical, political, and social discourses, alternately contradictory, ambiguous or indeterminate. It is an attitude that implicitly rests on and finds its justification in the academic feminist theoretical knowledge. It is an attitude towards the self as well as its positioning vis-à-vis the family, community and polity in managing the intricate web of relationships that tie the self to a real or imagined identity in a situation of systemic crisis. The cultural turn is examined as evolving in the *present*, although it did not emerge ex-nihilo. In other words, it is not a process of retrogression, of turning back the clock to the way things were, which in Algeria would be before 1954 when the war of decolonization was launched, although some of its characteristics unmistakably hark back to a past women thought they had left behind. Shepherded by the state, the cultural turn presents itself as the assertion of an adaptive mode of being, the validity of which is grounded in a value system steeped in religion seen as indistinguishable from culture, although it spills over into other areas of life (such as politics and economics). More, by dint of iteration and under the weight of the collective conscience and its moral density, the cultural turn proceeds in capillary manner to refashion, re-arrange, or re-articulate the experience of the self in a process of re-subjectivation that normalizes re-activated cultural practices. The restructuring of the experience of the self has all the trappings of the discovery or re-discovery of a latent identity, a retrieval of an identity that has been questioned, belittled, and at times hounded as happens among Muslims in European and North American countries. Hence the cultural turn is part of a complex intermeshing of endogenous as well as exogenous events. By the same token, the cultural turn also conceals an aspect of identity that is less evident yet omnipresent: sexuality. The study of the cultural turn lends itself to an archeology that encompasses structural, cultural, social psychological as well as ideational components.

An analysis of the cultural turn is delimited by three state strategies,[32] juridical (family codes), political (*wasatiya* Islam policy), social (*murshidat* acting as social workers), and ideational (women's Quranic contextualism). These heterogeneous strategies produce the object "culture" in the cultural turn: they form it and express it in various modes depending on the country studied. Out of this heterogeneity[33] emerges a constant referential domain (gender/women), which gives all discourses a degree of homogeneity. Nevertheless, implicitly or explicitly, strategies refer to, or appeal to, religious values as their ultimate justification, if not truth. Whether it is family law in its broadest conception (that includes not only marriage, divorce, inheritance but also a wide array of issues pertaining to the everyday management of parental activities); state policy regarding women's participation in political life; the popular Sufi orders' pronouncements; the state's own discourse on an Algeria-specific Islam; or political Islamic parties, Islam, no matter how defined, is the referential par excellence. The challenge is to determine how the multiplicity of cultural practices, many of which escape the purview of the sacred, are brought under a unitary referential (Islam) which in itself is not unitary but subject to equally multiple interpretations. However, these strategies originating in different institutional sources are further stratified; they overlay one another, at times overlapping, at others intersecting. The heterogeneity and stratification of strategies in which a specific notion of culture and cultural identity is formed has an anthropological referential, women (or woman). Women as a referential are either identified as such or allowed to "float," although they are always present, and without them the religious referential would lose its coherence as well as its raison d'être.[34] Hence two referentials, one discursive-strategic, the other anthropological, characterize the cultural turn, its constitution as well as the modes of its functioning. The relationship between the two referentials varies with each strategy just as it is experienced differently. For example, the juridical strategy of the family code forms the notion of culture out of concepts such as family, dowry, inheritance, second wife etc. without specifically mentioning religion, and refers to women as spouses, daughters, or girls, thus as roles. Similarly, the state's religion policy forms the notion of culture out of the concept of "*wasatiya* Islam," a religious referent, by establishing a division between "us" and "others," "moderate" and "extremist" Muslims, without specifically identifying the characteristics of an empirical woman conforming to the ideal of this kind of Islam. It is social situations such as inheritance, battery, incarceration, literacy, child-rearing that anchor the floating referent of women. How the two strategies, religious and juridical, contribute to forming a homogeneous cultural identity out of disparate arrangements of concepts, practices, roles, and expectations determines the degree to which women (and men) adopt the turn to culture, are ambivalent towards it, or resist it. This view differs from a common Foucauldian assertion that discourse is constitutive of the self. There is a great deal of evidence that women are aware of the social power of political or juridical discourses, and although appearing to adjust their behavior to them also distance themselves from them. Consider the case (hardly unique) of a middle-aged woman wearing a *hijab* who suddenly opened the window of her car in which I was also riding and stopped long enough to loudly congratulate two young women walking on a sidewalk, hair blowing in the wind. She exclaimed, "bravo! bravo!" She then turned to me "we (meaning herself and women like herself wearing a *hijab*) are doing it for our children."[35]

The study of the cultural turn among women is expansive, not only because of its complexity, but also because to be complete it should also include how the turn affects men. This book interprets the state conception of *wasatiya* Islam as the groundwork that informs various manifestations of the cultural turn among women. It identifies the cultural turn as the outcome of a slow and discontinuous evolution of the relationship between politics, religion and culture. The foundational text of the Algerian republic, the Tripoli Program, formulated in 1962, a few weeks before the independence of Algeria, listed the cultural problems besetting Algerian society on the eve of its independence, and suggested ways of dealing with them. It specifically singled out customs and distorted religious practices as hampering the development of a *scientific* culture. Half a century later, the state would revisit and restructure these practices in developing its *wasatiya* Islam policy. The restructuring proceeded through the revival of popular Sufism now endowed with a political legitimation function; support of Quietist Salafism; a professionalization of imams tasked with disseminating *wasatiya* Islam; the creation of a corps of *murshidat*, a functional equivalent of *imams*, to tend to women; and routine intervention in a broad religious field to keep a balance between competing religious sects and associations. But the whole edifice is also oriented towards the geopolitics of the deradicalization strategy of the global "war on terror."

The aspirations behind the upheavals referred to as the "Arab Spring" as well as the ensuing repression throughout the region with the exception of Tunisia had been prefigured in Algeria by the events of October 5, 1988, a decade after the demise of socialism as the political-economic orientation of the country. What were referred to in the English language press as "riots," and "*émeutes*" in French, were spontaneous uprisings that spread from major cities to small towns among students (many of whom in high schools), state employees as well as the unemployed, and gained sufficient momentum to cause the state to call the military to crush demonstrators. The use of the Internet was in its inception at the time and so neither the demonstrators' demands for political freedoms and social justice, nor the scale of the repression were given the coverage they deserved. To a large extent, the significance of the uprisings was dismissed abroad as just another episode in Algeria's chaotic socio-political life. However, in retrospect October 5, 1988 has had long-lasting consequences internally, just as it has acquired the value of a historic marker dividing the perception of political life into a before and an after, or at times, a since "1988." Indeed, October 5, 1988, ushered in political liberalization as a multi-party system was established, which nevertheless would not erase the memory of thwarted hopes and loss of life. By the same token, October 5, 1988 acted as a catalyst for the emergence of political Islam and was a harbinger of what will become the cultural turn. The rise of opposition parties tested the capacity of the old leadership to accept the play of the new democratic rules as the government aborted the impending victory of the main opposition party, the Front of Islamic Salvation (FIS), in the parliamentary elections of Fall 1991. The ensuing Civil War (also referred to as "The Black Decade") began barely four years after the uprising, and ended in 2002. A remarkable feature of the Civil War was its targeting of women as symbols of a moral order gone awry. Rape, forced "marriages" with self-styled "guerillas," prohibition to work outside the home, banning of the occupations of hair stylist and cosmetologist, and mandated veiling became the norm. By 2002, as the War drew to an end (although sporadic fighting continues), and life slowly returned to normal, some patterns of behavior established in wartime persisted and a number of cultural practices were revived in an adapted form: these include, religious marriage (*fatiha/'urf* marriage); propensity to forsake work as frequently stipulated in marriage contracts; widespread veiling (often at the behest of a fiancé)[36] or advocacy for it; and an apparent acquiescence to the notion that religion and culture are co-extensive, if not the same. In spite of gains women made since the 1990s, and sustained militancy from feminist groups, the cultural turn has hardened in some areas.

The book reveals the slow development of the cultural turn, which in retrospect had already manifested itself in the adoption of the family code in 1984 and its timid amendments in 2005. Indeed, it permits a close-up look at the historical configuration of events (some of which have not been given sufficient attention) that frame the emergence and normalization of the turn. In many ways, the cultural turn in Algeria in its current form is a sort of microcosm of the complex and intricate institutions and pathways through which the turn is constituted and evolves. The Algerian experience brings together political, economic, social, social-psychological, as well as ideational practices spanning a period of three decades. While the modalities of the turn differ from country to country, its Algerian incarnation yields insights into the normalization process of the turn that have a trans-historical value.

Last but not least, as the research for this book was reaching its end, a mass movement of protests, named the *hirak*, started on February 22, 2019. Every Friday,[37] enormous crowds of demonstrators draped in flags, among them countless women, took to the streets throughout the country to demand the departure of the then president, Abdelaziz Bouteflika who, even though in failing health and unable to speak, was running for a fifth term. He was forced to resign on April 2, 2019, and some of his closest advisers, including his brother Said, as well as cabinet members were arrested, tried, and sentenced to jail terms. This was a seismic change in Algeria since the Civil War of 1992–2002.[38]

Remarkably, the movement (which suspended its demonstrations in March 2020 as a result of the COVID-19 pandemic) has been peaceful, leaderless, and civic. It has not been claimed by any religious group or party. I observed demonstrations in three cities in May–July 2019 and January 2020, interacted with the demonstrators, interviewed women (one of whom was one of the organizers of the movement) as well as young male marchers. At times there was an occasional scuffle between a marcher displaying signs of Islamic militancy, but the marchers were largely tolerant of one another's views and discussed them extensively in the streets. There were no statements made by the popular Sufi institutions which play such a big role in the state *wasatiya* policy. It looked as though *wasatiya* Islam might become redundant. Yet, in the midst of COVID-19 pandemic, the new government, elected in December 2019, issued a statement declaring "haram" (not permitted) the act of not reporting the infection of a relative. Hence, the insertion of a religious concept laden with significations is invoked in lieu of a clearly worded health statement that would explain the medical consequences of neglecting to report or shielding the identification of an infected individual. That a change in *wasatiya* Islam would not occur after the fall of the previous government is not surprising considering that the policy is also tethered to geopolitical interests.

To study the cultural turn, I have used discourse and content analysis methodology supplemented by structured interviews. The fieldwork for this book was carried out over a period of four years. It includes interviews with three *murshidat* and two directors from the Ministry of Religious Affairs and Waqfs; the head of the Haut Conseil Islamique; a consultant and trainer of *murshidat*; professors of anthropology, sociology, economics, history from the university of Algiers, Oran, Constantine, and Mostaganem; six researchers from the Center for Research in Social and Cultural Anthropology (CRASC) in Oran; two graduate students in the social sciences, the humanities as well as engineering at the University of Oran. In addition, I have examined the social spaces of everyday life in which women speak of their positioning in the normalization of the cultural turn, and the spaces in which individual men take it upon themselves to set normative limits to women's comportment as guardians of a religious-qua-cultural order. This phenomenology of everyday life as lived is captured through discussions with women in various settings such as hair salons, cab-sharing, informal chats after formal interviews, waiting in line in a courtroom or a bakery, exchanging views while on a long-distance train etc. Bits and pieces of life caught on the fly give a glimpse of how the cultural turn, out of the academic frame, but lived in purposive and episodic activity is played out in the flow of life, unordered by guided data collection, or staged focus groups. When examined in its totality, such a phenomenology of everyday life reveals patterns of agreements between individual women and men, unknown to one another, on some fundamental changes that have affected their existence caught in the web of the cultural turn. It is a precious adjuvant to the analysis of documents and theories.

Structure of the book

The chapters that follow reflect the complex task the book set out to accomplish as they unravel the historical, cultural, and theoretical matrix out of which the tun to culture among women emerged. Chapter 1 traces the history of the state's use of culture and religion to the Tripoli Program, a foundational document of the newly formed Algerian republic. The main socio-cultural issues, which the Program identified and called for their resolution were partially addressed by the Boumédiène government but abandoned afterwards. They re-emerged in a modified form as the bedrock of *wasatiya* Islam under the government of Bouteflika. Chapter 2 analyzes the construction of *wasatiya* Islam and describes how it incorporates women. *Wasatiya* Islam enlarges the field of intervention of the state in Islam which it seeks to rationalize by fixing its meaning. The state had created an autonomous domain, the family code, in which it allowed religious values to suspend the application of the egalitarian principle of the constitution to women. The *wasatiya* policy represents the state's direct intervention in what constitutes Islam—a momentous act. Chapter 3 focuses on one crucial pillar of *wasatiya* Islam policy, popular Sufism, whose political functions are studied through the analysis of the revival of anachronistic practices and the social abuses they inflict on women. Chapter 4 examines the second pillar of *wasatiya* Islam, Salafism. The state seeks to ensure the hegemonic character of its religious policy by keeping ascendant sects or groups off balance, playing one against the other. It favors quietist Salafism over others while at the same time professionalizing the position of *imam* in *wasatiya* Islam. However, the relative freedom enjoyed by Salafis allows for Salafi women to gradually develop their version of Islamic feminism. Chapter 5 describes the meanings of Islamic feminism from a critical perspective, and identities its limitations as it explores its role in *wasatiya* Islam's deradicalization objective. Chapter 6 explores the unacknowledged academic postfeminist theoretical underpinnings of Islamic feminism, which it identifies as Quranic contextualism. It further points to the effects that this theory has on the liberatory ideal of second wave academic feminism. Chapter 7 describes the limitations of Quranic attributor contextualism as the only viable avenue for reform, and formulates the principles of a theory of gender which would articulate change as the outcome of political will rather than re-interpreted religious texts.

Throughout this book, I have attempted to preserve transcriptions of Arabic terms as they are used in the contexts in which they occurred in order to keep their originality. In addition, to protect their confidentiality, I have assigned initials of my choice to respondents, unless they authorized me to identify their names.

The ultimate objective of this book is to contribute to debates on how to bring about long-term change in women's lives though a critical praxis that upholds the rights of women as citizens who may be "believers," and whose freedom to be "believers" should be protected from the interference of the state or other actors operating either in the name of religion or through religion.

Notes

1 World Bank, "The World Bank in Algeria," www.worldbank.org/en/country/algeria/overview (accessed June 17, 2016).
2 Angel Rabasa, Cheryl Benard, Lowell H. Schwartz and Peter Sickle, *The RAND Report: Building Moderate Muslim Networks* (Santa Monica: CA, The RAND Center for Middle East Public Policy, 2007), iii, www.rand.org/content/dam/rand/pubs/monographs/2007/RAND__MG574.pdf (accessed June 20, 2020).
3 Rabasa et al., *RAND Report*, xi acknowledges that there are material and political causes of extremism, such as "the prevalence of authoritarian political structures" and "dissatisfaction with the prevalent political, economic and social conditions."
4 Rabasa et al., *RAND Report*, ch. 5. Guidelines and strategies for refashioning Islam are contained in several policy documents in addition to the *RAND Report*. See, for example, National Commission on Terrorist Attacks Against the United States, "What to Do? A Global Strategy," 2004, http://govinfo.library.unt.edu/911/report/911Report_Ch12.pdf (accessed June 20, 2020), which in paragraph 12.3 recommends that the USA should "engage the struggle of ideas"; and Peter Mandaville and Melissa Nozell, "Engaging Religion and Religious Actors in Countering Violent Extremism," United States Institute of Peace, Special Report 473, www.usip.org/sites/default/files/SR413-Engaging-Religion-and-Religious-Actors-in-Countering-Violent-Extremism.pdf (accessed June 20, 2020). For a discussion focusing on the secular component of the United States Islam strategy see Saba Mahmood, "Secularism, Hermeneutics, and Empire: The Politics of Islamic Reformation," *Public Culture* 18:2 (2016): 330–335.
5 For a lucid definition of the term see Ziba Mir-Hosseini, "Beyond 'Islam' vs. 'Feminism'," *IDS Bulletin* 42, no. 1 (January 2011): 68. For a good analysis of the debates over Islamic Feminism in Iran, see Valentine Moghadam, "Islamic Feminism and Its Discontents: Towards a Resolution of the Debate," *Signs*, 27, no. 4 (2002): 1135–1171.
6 A good example is provided by Sherene Hafez in *An Islam of her own: Reconsidering Religion and Secularism in Women's Islamic Movements* (New York: New York University Press, 2011). Hafez reveals that although the women in her interviews did not claim to be feminists or secularists, some of the views they held overlapped with both in so far as they aspired to women's advancement in a non-theocratic state.
7 In this broad designation, I wish to avoid the (unwarranted) exclusion of women who work within the framework of Islam, which they interpret as gender egalitarian, but do not call for its reformation on feminist grounds, from the referent "Islamic feminism."

8 For example, in defending her view against her "secular" critics, Asma Barlas quotes Saba Mahmood to doubt their political goals. See Asma Barlas, "Secular and Feminist Critiques of the Qur'an: Anti-hermeneutics as Liberation?" *Journal of Feminist Studies in Religion*, 32, no. 2 (Fall 2016), 17; Saba Mahmood, 323–347. Although Mahmood's article suggests a "convergence" of interests between Muslim modernists and "secularists" with the United States policy of transforming Islam from within, it inexplicably remains silent on the role of Islamic feminism in the policy. Nevertheless, her critique of the hermeneutic method when applied to Islam is insightful.

9 Haideh Moghissi has noted that in Iran the relationship between feminism's adaptation of fundamentalism in Iran had been mediated by postmodernism's orientation towards relativism as a specious conception of cultural difference. Although it overlaps to an extent with Moghiss's general view, the analysis offered in this book is different. See Haideh Moghissi, *Feminism and Fundamentalism: The Limits of Postmodern Analysis* (New York: Zed Books, 1999), ch. 3.

10 I am taking American feminist theory as a marker of the second wave of liberal feminism on the grounds that it is more varied and more elaborate than in European countries. Furthermore, its dissemination has also been more widespread than other feminist theoretical schemes. Finally, a number of advocates of Islamic feminism live, write, or are associated with universities in the USA, and thus engage directly or indirectly with academic feminism.

11 Derived from *wasat, wasatiya* means middle. The term is used in the Quran in *sura* 2.143 "We have appointed you a middle nation that ye may be witnesses against mankind, and that the messenger may be a witness against you" (*The Glorious Qur'an*, trans. Muhammad Marmaduke Pickthall). An interpretive effort is needed to turn this term into a programmatic view of an Algerian-qua-Maghrebin Islam.

12 The literature on the resilience of religion is vast. Sigmund Freud posed the question of the staying power of religion in spite of the advancement of science cogently even if his explanation may not be convincing. See *The Future of an Illusion* (New York: W. W. Norton & Company, 1989).

13 Jürgen Habermas gives a clear summary of this evolution in his "Notes on a Postsecular Society," *signandsight.com*, June 18, 2008. It is true, however, that in "secular" societies, Muslim minorities have availed themselves of the notion of cultural rights to demand recognition for their identity as Muslims. This is a double-edged sword since religious traditionists or political Islam advocates have taken advantage of this right, which "secular" societies afford, to conflate religion with culture by controlling religious practice in order to curb the rights Muslim women enjoy as citizens. See Mohammad Magout, *A Reflexive Islamic Modernity: Academic Knowledge and Religious Subjectivity in the Global Ismaili Community* (Baden-Baden, Germany: Ergon, 2020), 132–136. The author argues that among Ismailis in the West the distinction between Islam as culture and civilization and Islam as theology and law enables them "to challenge fundamentalist understanding of Islam" which depicts them as a heretical sect (ibid., 35–36).

14 For an overview of "radicalization" in North Africa see Alison Pargeter, "Localism and Radicalization in North Africa: Local Factors and the Development of Political Islam in Morocco, Tunisia and Libya," *International Affairs*, 85, no. 5 (Sept. 2009): 1031–1044, www.jstor.org/stable/40388922 (accessed Aug. 1, 2017).

15 The USA has never had as close a relationship to Algeria as it has had with Morocco, which it considers an ally essential to its Middle Eastern policy. After 9/11 the USA secured Algeria's cooperation in the "war on terror," which former president Abdelaziz Bouteflika was eager to provide. See Yahia H. Zoubir, "Algeria and U.S. Interests: Containing Radical Islamism and Promoting Democracy," *Middle East Policy*, IX, no. 1 (March 2002): 64–81.

16 The cultural turn has also made its appearance in Tunisia where some women advocate for change within Islam. See Amal Grami, "Islamic Feminism: A New

Feminist Movement or a Strategy by Women for Acquiring Rights?" *Contemporary Arab Affairs*, 6, no. 1 (January 2013), 102–113.

17 Zakia Salime, *Between Feminism and Islam: Human Rights and Sharia Law in Morocco* (Minneapolis, MN: Minnesota University Press, 2011).

18 In his analytic of power, Michel Foucault identified juridical power, the power of the sovereign (as illustrated by Leviathan), which established the legal obligation to obey; disciplinary power which, without superseding juridical power, displaces its goals from domination to "normalization" through techniques of dressage informed by social scientific knowledge. See Michel Foucault, *Society Must Be Defended: Lectures at the Collège de France, 1975–1976*, eds. Mauro Bertani and Alessandro Fontana, trans. David Macey (New York: Picador, 2003), esp. lecture of January 14, 1976. The heuristic adaptation of Foucault in this text does not include his notion of biopower as a phase in which power targets "populations" rather than individuals, and coincides with the rise of (neo)liberalism.

19 See Michel Foucault, "Pastoral Power and Political Reason," in *Michel Foucault, Religion and Culture*, ed. Jeremy R. Carrette (New York: Routledge, 1999), 135–152.

20 I am indebted to Falih Hassan for this etymology of the concept of *rashada*. It must be noted that *murshida* (guide) is derived from the same root.

21 The euphoria surrounding the Moroccan 2004 family code (Mudawwana) must be understood against the background of severe restrictions on women's rights in the previous code. Although greatly improved, the new code has yet to unequivocally establish equality between women and men in the family. See, among others, Rachid Touhtou, "Gender Codification in the Family Code and the Constitution of Morocco: Social Movements and Feminist Approaches," in *Promoting Women's Rights and Gender Equity in the Middle East and North Africa* (Brussels, Belgium: Foundation of European Progressive Studies, and SOLIDAR, February 2014), 21–31.

22 A discussion of *laïcité* appears in Chapter 2.

23 Interview with a female professor of sociology, University of Algiers, Ben Aknoun, 9 July, 2018.

24 Marnia Lazreg, "Theorizing the Median Space between Power and Feminism in MENA," paper presented at a conference on "Theory and Feminism in the Arab World," University of Zurich (Switzerland), March 17–19, 2016.

25 For a description of the brainwashing method used during the Algerian War see Peter Paret, *French Revolutionary Warfare from Indochina to Algeria* (New York: Frederick A. Praeger, 1964). See also Marnia Lazreg, *Torture and the Twilight of Empire, from Algiers to Baghdad* (Princeton, NJ: Princeton University Press, 2008), ch. 3.

26 For a description of methods of deradicalization (outside of jails) in a number of European countries see Angel Rabasa, Stacie L. Pettyjohn, Jeremy J. Ghetz and Christopher Boucek, "European Approaches," ch. 5, in Deradicalizing Islamist Extremists (Santa Monica, CA: RAND, 2010). Agents of deradicalization vary from country to country. Some are recruited among Muslim communities in Europe. See in particular the British method (ibid., 124–138). Consultations with "moderate" Muslim associations are generally sought. A leader of an Algerian Sufi order revealed in a private conversation with me that he had counselled the French government on the deradicalization method it uses in jails.

27 Parenthetically, the critical view expressed in this book about deradicalization does not countenance acts of terror. It seeks to demystify the notion that religion produces them, and that the prevention of their occurrence requires imparting different meanings to religious texts or rehabilitating customs inimical to women.

28 Talcott Parsons, *The Social System* (Glencoe, IL: The Free Press, 1964).

29 A leading figure is Clifford Geertz, *The Interpretation of Cultures: Selected Essays* (New York: Basic Books, 1973). The cultural turn initially appeared in a linguistic

form as formulated by Claude Lévi-Strauss. See his *Structural Anthropology*, trans. Claire Jacobson and Brooke Grundfest Schoepf (New York: Doubleday Anchor Books, 1963).

30 For a description of the cultural turn and its evolution see Victoria E. Bonnell and Lynn Hunt, eds, *Beyond the Cultural Turn* (Berkeley, CA: University of California Press, 1999), esp. Introduction.

31 The literature linking aspects of the cultural turn (although it is not defined as such) to women is vast. It spanned a wide array of positions towards religion, Islamic feminism, and political Islam. For example, Saba Mahmood, *The Politics of Piety: The Islamic Revival and the Feminist Subject* (Princeton, NJ: Princeton University Press, 2005), focuses on the emergence of a trend among women towards religiosity/piety in the region that allows for the cultivation of a new subjectivity. Azza M. Karam, *Women, Islamisms and the State: Contemporary Feminisms in Egypt* (New York: Palgrave Macmillan, 1998) equates the turn to culture with the emergence of Islamic feminism. The latter is hailed as a new opportunity for women, regardless of their attitudes towards religion, to bring about change. See Ziba Mir-Hosseini, "Muslim Women's Quest for Equality: Between Islamic law and Feminism," *Critical Inquiry*, 32, no. 4 (Summer 2006), 629–645. See also Margo Badran, *Feminism in Islam: Secular and Religious Convergences* (Oxford: OneWorld, 2009). In the same vein, Islamic feminism is further perceived as expressing a new form of feminist practice, or a new method of resistance to political Islam, see Leila Ahmed, *A Quiet Revolution: The Veil's Resurgence, from the Middle East to America* (New Haven, CT: Yale University Press, 2012); Nawar Al Hassan Golley, "Is Feminism Relevant to Arab Women?" *The Quarterly*, 25, no. 3 (2004), 521–536; Stacey Philbrick Yadav, "Segmented Publics and Islamist Women in Yemen: Rethinking Space and Activism," *Journal of Middle Eastern Women's Studies*, 6, no. 2 (Spring 2010), 1–30. See also Faegheh Shirazi, *Velvet Jihad: Women's Quiet Resistance to Islamic Fundamentalism* (Gainesville, FL: University of Florida Press, 2009).

32 I limit the use of the concept of "discourse" in this analysis as it connotes a static approach to what is essentially a dynamic process, often in flux.

33 I am borrowing the notion of heterogeneity (as in "discursive heterogeneity") from Michel Foucault, *La sexualité. Cours donné à l'université de Clermont Ferrand, 1964 suivi de Le discours de la sexualité. Cours donné à l'université de Vincennes, 1969* (Paris: Gallimard Seuil, 2018), 156.

34 It goes without saying that women are also an object of discourse. However, this book is focused on the constitution of culture as an object of discourse with its implications for women.

35 Nacéra, interview, Algiers, July 11, 2020. Nacéra was driving me part of the way to my home after the interview. Her comment indicates that she would have preferred not to have taken the cultural turn. Once a woman wears a *hijab*, it is difficult for her to remove it. She intimated that there is social pressure on children too. She also pointed out that her daughter *wanted* to wear the *hijab*.

36 CIDDEF (Centre d'information et de Documentation sur les Droits de l'Enfant et de la Femme), "Connaissance des droits des femmes et des enfants en Algérie," especially "le choix de l'habillement," (Algiers: CIDDEF, 2007), 25–32.

37 Students demonstrate every Tuesday morning.

38 For personal accounts of the movement see Acherchour et al. *La révolution du sourire* (Algiers: Editions Frantz Fanon, 2019). See also Amel Hadjadj, "Le Hirak et la citoyenneté des femmes: opportunités et obstacles," *Revue du CIDDEF*, no. 40 (November 2019): 12–16.; and Amin Allal and Farida Souiah, "Hirak: l'an I? Interview with Belkacem Benzenine and Cherif Driss," *La Découverte*, no. 102 (2020): 57–69, www.cairn.info/revue-mouvements-2020-2-page-57.htm.

1

GENEALOGY OF THE CULTURAL TURN

The turn to culture, no matter how defined, as an instrument of control, contestation of power, or form of power in its own right, occurred in Algeria at a point of convergence of a number of events: political, geopolitical, demographic, and economic. The transition from ("Islamic socialism") to a fledgling neo-liberal orientation of the economy was initiated in a guarded manner upon the death of president Houari Boumediène in 1978. However, the gradual privatization of state-owned economic enterprises, loosening of national control over oil and gas fields, liberalization (albeit partial) of imports and trade took place in the context of diminished oil revenues and the mounting debt of the late 1980s. Structural adjustment programs, devised by the IMF albeit with the cooperation of the state, signaled a reduction, and in some cases elimination, of subsidies. After a few years of relative wealth, the cycle of high and low social spending in accordance with the fluctuations of the oil market began again in 2014. Fluctuating national income aggravated social problems, including unemployment and an ever-increasing demand for housing, a result of a pro-natalist policy practiced in the 1970s, and made more acute by incipient changes towards the conjugal family.

The October 5, 1988 uprising was to a large measure a response to the transition from socialism to a form of dependent capitalism, which the common people experienced as a worsening of their material life. The effective collapse of socialism in the former Soviet Union no doubt empowered the state in its change in economic orientation, and abandonment of an autonomous development project aimed at "catching up" to industrial countries. However, to the state, the uprising was a reminder that social unrest was a clear and present danger that needed to be kept in check. Liberalization of the political system, perceived as one method of forestalling unrest, demonstrated the depth of social discontent instead. The ensuing Civil War (1992–2002), fought with remarkable ferocity on all sides resulted in a sort of social fatigue, as families and individuals sought to repair their lives after the violence subsided. However, the memory of the Civil War has acquired a significant symbolic value. To the state, it provides a powerful reminder, dredged out at strategic moments, such as presidential elections, that political continuity, not change, must be secured if another civil war was to be avoided. To the people the experience of the Civil War became a filter through which to receive the spectacle of well-publicized strife in countries such as Libya, Syria, Yemen, or Egypt. The memory of the Civil War and its aftermath contributed to a distrust of politics and a sense that genuine change (political or economic) is beyond reach, that the system is beyond the pale. So, why bother? In a climate of social despair, adaptive coping mechanisms must be sought. Briefly, these include frequent flash riots focused on specific social demands, including housing (a burning issue in light of demographic pressure and change towards the nuclear family), water shortage, and at times education, although usually the object of strikes. Targeted and short-lived riots are but the most visible coping mechanism. Another one, far more pernicious and pervasive, affects the moral fabric of social life and compounds the sense of diffuse social despair. It is the adaptation to a regular or sporadic engagement in a complex array of normalized actions aimed at circumventing the law, best seen in paying or receiving bribes, cheating on exams, or plagiarizing. Such behavior denotes a most important erosion of the belief that personal effort, merit, and ethical standards are not rewarded, but can even become an obstacle to personal progress. Hence a "culture" of deceit and moral expedience takes hold of everyday life as these patterns of behavior become pervasive.[1]

Engaging in asocial conduct of this sort is hardly synonymous with not knowing the difference between right and wrong. Nor does it mean contentment with a disjuncture between conduct dictated by material life and aspiration to the very values that have been eroded. These are mobilized in one form or another, through official iteration of the culture that grounds them, appeals to ritualistic forms of spirituality, or assertion of a religious sectarian lifestyle. In the midst of the changes that have affected the social fabric of society, women stand out as a category of people that has become at once more visible than in the past, and more contested. Oddly, their public visibility as workers (even if in smaller numbers than men), achievers in educational institutions, or objects of occasional remedial legislation (such as that against sexual harassment) singles them out as symbols of injustice done to men. Furthermore, diffuse resentment of the relative success of ethnic-based social demands made by Berberists compounds the perception that the universalistic vocation of the state that emerged from the Revolution has eroded, and that the state has become privatized at the expense of the individual citizen. That women are not a special group, but constitute half of the population is beside the point. What matters is the symbolic value attached to their accession to public spaces. It is not uncommon, for instance, for a disgruntled taxi driver to rail against working women "when men need jobs." Comments such as these abound, and although they may be dismissed as passing and thus inconsequential, they are signs of a diffuse malaise that fastens itself to women as presumed bearers of a gendered normative cultural order either out of kilter or threatened with destruction. Perception of change in a habitual cultural environment problematizes one's entanglement in it. Indeed, where does one locate one's self if the cultural ground on which one stands is no longer firm, if it starts to shake?

It is this cultural ground which, not only the taxi driver, or the Court usher, who decides on his own to establish a gender norm of propriety by directing women to one side of the waiting room and men to the other, but also the state and religious institutions, seek to restore, preserve, defend, or amend just enough to prolong its survival. How the struggle over the preservation or change of this cultural order is carried out, the channels through which it evolves, and the agents of its execution, sheds light on the centrality of women to the cultural turn. To understand such events, this chapter will follow a double procedure: first, analyze practices, behaviors, and attitudes towards change as they are defined and regulated in the political and the juridical discourses. It will subsequently determine how implicitly or explicitly these rules and concepts produce a certain notion of culture and cultural identity that has a constraining effect on behavior and (ironically) calls up past behavior.

The foundational political discourse

Foundational texts of the future independent state, such as the Soummam Platform of August 1956, or the Tripoli program of June 1962 indicate a concern for breaking with the political and economic past. In the Soummam Platform, a text explaining the rationale for the launching of the war of decolonization and assessing progress, culture is obliquely evoked as forming on of the thick "roots" of the Front de Libération Nationale (FLN), described as reaching into the depth of the entire people (in French, "*les couches du people*").[2] A hint that behavior was changing towards greater freedom for women is mentioned in passing as attributable to the spirit of the incipient revolution: "the example of a young Kabyl woman who turned down a marriage proposal because it was not offered by a combatant illustrates beautifully the sublime spirit that animates Algerian women."[3] In this fleeting cameo of change, the cultural practice of arranged marriage requiring a woman to consent to the choice of her spouse by her father or his surrogate is broken. The text does not define culture, it superimposes an image of change on it. The anonymous woman apparently *chose* the kind of man she would marry. The right of refusal for political reasons, not for age or character of the spouse, stands out for its singular departure from the past. That the example needed to be cited bespoke an aspiration to a different future. The specificity of the example contrasted with the nebulousness of the future seen primarily as political. Perhaps it could not be otherwise as the Platform was elaborated barely two years after the launching of the war of decolonization.

By contrast, the Tripoli Program, intended to provide policy guidelines to the newly independent state when it took over in July 1962, offers critical concepts and describes attitudes that foreshadow the contradictions at the roots of the cultural turn. Remarkably, this political discourse draws a picture of an Algeria divided within and against itself. There is the Algeria of the people, particularly the peasantry, animated by a revolutionary spirit nurtured by the struggle for decolonization, and an FLN leadership cut off from the people and already displaying signs of a counter-revolution. The two major political and cultural deficiencies or weaknesses that threatened to prevent revolutionary change were identified as the "feudal mindset" ("spirit" in the text) and the "petty-bourgeois mindset."[4] The economic and social organization of feudalism, "a stage in humanity's development,"[5] which characterized pre-colonial Algerian society started to erode during the colonial era, although the colonial system relied on feudal chiefs as allies in maintaining society in a state of "stagnation" and fostering "obscurantism."[6] Colonial capitalism (not referred to as such) transformed Algeria into a "semi-feudal" country, one in which the indigenous population was marginalized economically and maintained in a state of social and cultural retardation. The text strenuously distinguishes the defunct feudal mode of production, which underwent a transformation under colonial capitalism from its "ideological survivals as well as its social vestiges."[7]

The "feudal mentality" found its extension in the equally nefarious institution of "*maraboutisme*" or popular Sufism. Although some Sufi orders resisted the colonial invasion of Algeria in 1830, as did the Qadiryyia order of Emir Abdelkader who waged a war against France, many collaborated with the obscurantism induced by colonial power. Subsequently, they "partially turned into an administrative feudalism" serving as a force of cultural pacification of the population for the benefit of the colonial system and with its support. Thus, "in the framework of the obscurantist character of colonialism, it [*maraboutisme*] has not ceased to exploit, through superstition and the crudest practices, religious sentiment."[8] The evocation of religion in 1962 as a casualty of the feudal mentality supported by *maraboutisme* acquires special significance in light of the Civil War as well as the juridical discourses of family law. Indeed, here, as early as 1962, religion, Islam, or a particular practice of it, appears as an effect rather than the bedrock of life prior to the independence of Algeria. Indeed, the "vestiges" of feudalism as a social practice "have contributed to alter the spirit of Islam and have led to the stagnation [in French, '*immobilisme*'] of Muslim society."[9] The characterization of Algerian society as Muslim but practicing an Islam whose "spirit" was altered encapsulates what was wrong with the society as well as with its beliefs. Culture in the Tripoli Program connotes mental attitudes, one feudal, the other religious. Both attitudes operate together with a third one, the "petit bourgeois spirit." If the feudal mentality with its adjuvant, *maraboutisme*, were outgrowths of the colonial society, the "petit-bourgeois spirit" was fostered by the FLN's lack of commitment to the Revolution, and its lack of "ideological development" (in French, "*formation*").[10] The "petit-bourgeois" mentality, affects not only a number of cadres of the FLN, but is also present among youth which makes it that much more worrisome. It is expressed in "easy habits," careerism, profit-making, an avoidance of the real "due to a lack of revolutionary development," as well as a jejune pride. Besides, the petit-bourgeois mentality fosters a prejudice against the peasantry and the rank-and-file of the Revolution (in French "*militants obscurs*").[11] Finally, the petit-bourgeois mindset, suffers from a "pseudo-intellectualism, which unwittingly recycles the most harmful and fallacious [in French, '*frelatés*'] concepts of the Western mentality,"[12] in addition to "formalism."[13] The intellectual deficiencies feed into "an unwarranted romanticism," and a "taste for a reckless and inflated heroism,"[14] which contrast with the "discreet temperament of the people."[15]

The lingering feudal mentality, popular Sufism, and the petit-bourgeois spirit combine to reinforce and sustain the "backwardness," "retrogression," and "stifled culture" of Algerian society in 1962. At the political level, the three attitudes towards self and others account for "an abusive conception of authority, the absence of rigorous criteria, and lack of political culture."[16] The abuse of authority results in a "paternalistic" conception of political responsibility. All these attitudes and mindsets which impede the revolution's goals to bring about a profound social and economic change stem from two main reasons: structural and ideological. Structurally, the location of the political leadership of the FLN outside of the country (as a result of France's radical anti-guerilla warfare bent upon isolating and destroying combatants) made communication with operatives in the field more difficult. Hence there appeared "a gap between the leadership of the FLN and the masses."[17] To this structural issue must be added a recurring one: insufficient or lack of grounding in a political ideology. In other words, as the war of decolonization unfolded, leadership became increasingly rudderless, "depoliticized," and thus vulnerable to a return of attitudes and practices that threatened to lead the independent state astray. Noteworthy is the Tripoli Program's insistence that, cut off from the people, the leadership of the FLN, local or external, lagged behind the people in commitment to the revolution.

Among the remedies the Program proposed to stamp out the socio-political ills it identified, culture figures prominently. The Program advocates a redefinition of culture specifically to counter "erroneous mental attitudes."[18] Culture must be "national, revolutionary and scientific." The re-valuation of Arabic as a language and a vehicle for the rediscovery and transmission of a classical and modern humanistic heritage will "combat cultural cosmopolitanism and Western acculturation (in French, '*imprégnation occidentale*'), which helped to inculcate in many Algerians contempt for their national values."[19] However, national culture must not be closed on itself; it must be revolutionary by getting rid of feudal, retrogressive and conformist attitudes.[20] National culture will be scientific in so far as it will stress rationality, research, and technology, all characteristics necessary to overcome "obscurantism" as well as "anti-intellectualism."[21] The Program advocates an "elevation" of the cultural level of the FLN cadres, the peasantry and workers—categories of people that had suffered the most from cultural stagnation in the colonial era. Importantly, a scientific culture would guard against the use of Islam for political demagoguery: "it goes without saying that we belong to the Islamic civilization [...] but, it is doing a disservice to this civilization to believe that its renaissance rests on some simple and self-styled behavioral formulas or religious practices."[22] The Program calls for an "Islam cleansed of all its excrescences and superstitions that stifled or altered its [character]."[23] This kind of Islam must be reflected in the culture as well as the "personality" of the Algerian viewed as open to modernity without relinquishing its past. Women appear in the Program's guidelines under the caption "Meeting Social Aspirations," after sections on housing and public health. The "liberation of women" must be secured through the Party's permanent struggle against all the social prejudices and "negative mentality" that promote the "inferiority" of women. After hailing women's contribution to the war of decolonization, the text notes that "women themselves share in this secular belief [in their inferiority]."[24]

The critical discourse of the Tripoli Program weaves culture, religion, and politics into a matrix that imbricates the past into the present. In its characterization of culture, women are alternately named as its virtual casualties, or float as a silent referential. The emphasis placed on culture foretold a recurring conundrum in later political discourses and practices that will pit state against its opposition, women against men. However, and perhaps more important, the critical Tripoli political discourse builds an image of a culture in the throes of feudal and colonial vestiges that affect the mental and behavioral attitudes of swaths of the population, including cadres of the FLN, youth, the peasantry, and workers. The lack of emphasis on women as the population that experiences firsthand the effects of the cultural attitudes denounced by the Program reveals the very problem at the heart of the Program's own discourse: the culture that produced the Program's political discourse. If the tone and economic orientation of the critical discourse reveal a left sensibility, the hypomnesia of the gendered nature of the culture that sustains it betrays the limits of its criticism. The formalism the Program denounced among the FLN cadres applied to its authors too. Indeed, the Program itself suffers from an (liberatory) ideological insufficiency where women are concerned. However, the discourse is silent on what the political ideology it bemoans exactly is. If some of the economic measures the Program adopted are borrowed from a socialist agenda, the Revolution is defined as national, democratic and people's oriented. These are objectives rather than a "doctrine" and their implementation is cast in the global framework of Third World struggles against imperialism and injustice. If some of these objectives resonate with the Western left, or with Marxism, they are framed as part of other contemporary revolutionary movements (without specifying which ones). Among the revolutionary movements of the time, the Vietnamese and the Cuban, figured prominently. However, whereas communism was the ideology of the Vietnamese Revolution, the Revolution of the Tripoli Program has no philosophical or doctrinal foundation. It is "not a collection of practical recipes applied lazily or bureaucratically. There is no ready-made ideology; there is only a constant and creative ideological effort."[25] Two factors make this effort at "creating a new thought" necessary: the challenge of the profound "disruptions" (in French, "*bouleversements*") caused by the War; and the establishment of a new "political regime." State-building requires a "scientific" assessment and analyses of the new reality arising out of the War, with its revolutionary and anti-revolutionary features. The anti-revolutionary trends include, the tendency towards "subjectivism," and "moralism." The subjectivist tendency is defined as a form of "intellectual laziness" characterized by a lack of realism and an inability to see beyond the spectacular and the uncouth. As for moralism, it is an attitude that stresses moral values as a solution to complex societal problems.[26] Implied in this definition of "moralism" is a critique of the notion that political problems can be resolved with a reassertion of religious values.

At first glance, the emphasis on building a "scientific culture" that would get rid of the feudal and colonial mental attitudes and practices but within the framework of an undefined ideological doctrine allows for flexible and innovative methods. The implicit counter-posing of "science" to "ideology" (a familiar trope in political, as well as academic discourse) notwithstanding, it means that the postcolonial government could invent itself, unhampered by the strictures of an ideological doctrine such as, for example, socialism or communism. It would preserve the "originality" of the Algerian revolutionary situation. By the same token, the repeated reference to a deficiency in ideological development is also a call for a need for one. The antinomy between wanting an ideology and rejecting one is the hallmark of the Tripoli discourse. It appears to be an outcome of its opposition to communism. In its brief review of the political background that led to the Revolution, the Tripoli Program notes the failure of the pre-war Algerian Communist Party (mostly comprised of French members) to support the Revolution due its rigidity and lack of analytical perspicacity.[27] Indeed, it is unlikely that lingering feudal mental attitudes, surviving colonial norms, subjectivism, or moralism could be remedied without a clearly defined socio-political orientation, or detailed plan of action no matter what philosophy undergirds it. In this sense, the lack of an identifiable ideology may have played to the detriment of women. Indeed, socialism, for example (and this is not a personal preference), specifically addresses gender even if imperfectly. If a foundational text, such as the Tripoli Program, acknowledged gender inequality as well as the mental attitudes that sustain it, its silence on serious remedial action on behalf of women (except for a vague entreaty to give women access to positions of responsibility) speaks volumes. Indeed, this silence reveals a contradiction between the Program's critique of the ideological and behavioral weakness of the incipient state, but also its own ambivalence towards women as a category of people. In this sense, women emerge in the Tripoli Program discourse as the core of its contradictions as well as its political weakness. Summoned up in a critique of feudal attitudes, women are made to disappear as a category of people with needs different from those of classes of people such as "peasants," "cadres," or "youth." They are subsumed under one of the "movements" the future state will mobilize. Cultural change is perceived as occurring through language and the development of scientific technology. Implicitly, were the development of the Arabic language to fail and technology to remain limited, "national culture" would not materialize.

The portrait drawn of Algerian society on the eve of the establishment of the newly independent state serves as a comparative basis for understanding change since then. Noteworthy is, however, the continuity between the Tripoli Program and the 1964 Charter of Algiers, a left-leaning discourse, which in its essentials repeats the critical analysis formulated by the Tripoli Program about the condition of women, and the survivals of feudal structures as well as practices.[28] Algerian socialism in the 16 years following the Tripoli Program was not grounded in an identifiable philosophy or theory. For a brief period, in the first three years of its existence, the government (under President Ben Bella) included Marxists or members of the Communist Party, some of whom Frenchmen acting as advisers. Until 1989, the state showed sustained hostility towards the left, no matter how small it was, banned the Communist Party and its main publication *Alger Républicain*. In other words, ideas promoting civil law and gender equality where from the start of the newly independent republic viewed with suspicion as part of a communist agenda. Consequently, the Yugoslav model of socialism was perceived as more suitable to a post-colonial *economic* development, as it permitted the state to formally turn over to rural workers (generally men) the management of the estates formerly owned by settlers in fulfillment of the promise of the Revolution to return landless peasants (some of whom descendants of Algerians dispossessed in the early years of the colonial era) to the land they aspired to, and which they now theoretically "owned" collectively. In other words, socialism was understood as a shortcut for achieving rapid economic development through state control of the means of production; an extensive program of social expenditures on education, healthcare, transportation, as well as subsidies of food staples.

The Tripoli Program's emphasis on creating an ideology and culture that would preserve the specificity of Algeria, subsumed under the concept "national," gave the newly formed state a symbolic cover for economic and social policies which in hindsight had little room for women except as agents of demographic growth. The ideological creativity that the Tripoli Program advocated fell short as the development policy of rapidly catching up with industrialized countries was uncoupled from its social context and oblivious of its social consequences. Hence, economic modernity through technology was not universalistic, but essentially a de facto male preserve. Excluded from the discursively gender-neutral economic development sphere, women were re-inscribed in the juridical discourse of the family. Hence, the paradox of this binary conception of governance of the post-colonial state, whereby the juridical sphere became a compensatory mechanism for the insertion of women in a field in which culture is defined independently of the economy or the political discourse of the constitution. In other words, "culture" resurfaces as in need of preservation (not development) in the juridical discourse regulating the family. The relatively autonomous juridical discourse of the family becomes the field in which a view of "culture" is formed through prescriptions of the roles, obligations, as well as expectations of women as wives, mothers, and daughters. Such expectations run parallel to the rights of men (and their obligations) as husbands and fathers. Said in passing, an oft-noted paradox of the post-colonial state in 1962 was the disjuncture between its avowedly socialist political orientation and its tinkered family law, a combination of *shari'a* and timid reforms brought about by the colonial government in its waning years. The 1984 Family Code (amended in 2005) passed as socialism was being dismantled, marks a retreat from the cultural ideal of the Tripoli Program; it squarely placed women in the codified discourse of *shari'a*, as the bearers of an Islamic identity shielded from the legal universalistic discourse of the Constitution, which had declared them equal to men in rights and obligations.

That, in the long run, the democratization of education might result in women's aspirations for freedoms at odds with the gender imbalance characteristic of family law, was hardly apparent at the time. Nevertheless, the incompatibility of socialism with a socially restrictive family law goes to the heart of what became the cultural turn. The discourse of socialism was articulated in such a way that it countenanced a law that contradicted its very foundation, equality regardless of sex. Ironically, the more the state emphasized its socialist character, the more it denied it and contradicted it in practice. In the end, it was not development, or the economy that was at stake, it was whether women could or could not be equal to men, and whether the Revolution was male only.

How was this struggle carried out discursively? Through what concepts, images, inventions or re-inventions of the past? These questions will be answered in the second chapter. Suffice it to say that the effects of the juridical discourse of the family of 1984 and 2005, cannot be understood without a brief analysis of the impact of the Civil War on women.

The experience of the Civil War

The Civil War was not, as if often portrayed, caused by the cancellation of the second round of parliamentarian elections, which the Front of Islamic Salvation (FIS) was poised to win in December 1991. The interruption of the electoral process was but the catalyst of a long simmering discontent that had already erupted on October 5, 1988 and which found in the Front of Islamic Salvation's acerbic critique of the government comfort and solace. The FIS, formed as a result of the political liberalization initiated after the social upheaval of October 5, 1988, articulated people's aspirations for change in the language of culture. Hence, the problems people encountered in their material life were defined in cultural terms. And culture was reduced to religious values and norms. For instance, poverty, unemployment, or prostitution, were blamed on the state's purported abandonment of Islamic values and the adoption of secular-qua-French norms of governance and behavior. Yet, the state had done no more than institute coeducation in grade schools. In fact, it had passed a family code in 1984 that legalized gender inequality in marriage, divorce, child custody, and inheritance, in violation of the constitution's principle of equality between citizens regardless of sex. The 1984 code (as well as its 2005 revision), based as it was on a codification of the *shari'a*, could hardly be construed as a violation of Islamic values. But, for the FIS as well as socially conservative groups, a codified *shari'a* may very well constitute a violation of the *shari'a* itself because it was codified by a state perceived as having lost its moral compass. That classical *shari'a* might have been relatively more liberal than it is in its codified form was obviated by the FIS's outright rejection of the family code. In support of the FIS's view, some of those affiliated with the party, staged a demonstration against the family code when it appeared in 1984.[29]

The Civil War, however, revealed the extent to which rising expectations, sustained by the rhetoric of socialism as well as the spread of education, could be framed as demands for cultural authenticity, and channeled into concrete actions to establish a purportedly new social order in which women emerged as the softest yet crucial target. Without veils women are visible. Hence, they became the immediate symbols of a socio-political order in need of reform. Interestingly, along with women, drinking habits were also targeted as needing to conform to an Islamic code of behavior. The focus on women, however, was twofold. On the one hand, they were the embodiments of sex that needed to be concealed; on the other hand, they also represented laborers competing on the job market with men. Restrictions under threat of harm spread by word of mouth that occupations such as those of beautician, hairdresser, or clairvoyant did not fit in the new moral order. Gradually, work for women came to be presented as unjust to unemployed men. More, a working woman further disrupts the moral foundation of the family in which man is the breadwinner. Indeed, the 1984 family code unequivocally defined the role of the husband as that of the head of the family who supports his wife. Consequently, the role that the FIS assigned women in its vision of an Islamic cultural order was in keeping with the prescriptions of the 1984 family code. Oddly, the FIS echoes the Tripoli Program call for the elaboration of a "national" culture. The FIS's view of such a culture (although the party was not referring to the Tripoli Program) was one that removed women from the public domain and reinforced their role as agents of the stability of the family. That women's work was necessary to the economy of the family in a changing society was elided. Cultural authenticity, was subsumed under Islam, implicitly perceived as resistance to a government deemed culturally and politically alien to society and to its ethos.

The FIS's advocacy of a society based on religious values also symbolized opposition to the state's appropriation of Islam. There has been, since the inception of the postcolonial state in 1962, an ambivalent and contradictory attitude towards Islam. On the one hand, the constitution stipulates that Islam is the state religion. Hence imams are salaried functionaries and their Friday lectures are supervised by the state. On the other hand, the state bows to religious scholars by passing family laws that contravene the constitutional rights of women. In essence, the state cedes to religion the socio-cultural domain, in return for preserving control over politics. Hence the state sets boundaries between the religious and the political. However, where the boundary is blurry at the points where women (who are also citizens theoretically protected by the constitution) stand the state deems the blur inconsequential to its control of the political sphere. Therefore, the oft-repeated notion that the state in the Middle East and North Africa nationalizes religion is not entirely accurate. The state carves out a space in which it allows religious leaders and opponents to operate with relative autonomous secured through episodic negotiation and renegotiation. As long the political space where the political discourse unfolds is not infringed upon, the state would even allow marked (in the sense of socially vulnerable) categories of people to be symbolically managed by religious leaders in the religious space it has created. Women are the prime example of such categories of people because traditionally it was taken-for-granted (and thus self-evident) that their social roles were to be defined and managed by their male relatives within the family. Hence the "feudal attitudes" denounced by the Tripoli Program, which included attitudes towards women, find their acceptance in the family code. The relatively autonomous space the state cedes to religion-as-law becomes a zone of exception in which women emerge as subjects of a religious creed. Their rights as citizens are suspended, and subjected to a law based on faith and belief.[30] In other words, they cannot be citizens as well as Muslims. Consequently, family law is constructed on a conception of culture that excludes customary as well as new norms of behavior that have started to appear in the post-independence era which, although not always opposed to those inscribed in the family code, are nevertheless different. These include the notion of a career for a woman, new lifestyles resulting from women working outside the family in proximity of male colleagues, women traveling alone for work or leisure, gradual change towards the conjugal family, etc.

The reduction or equation of culture to religious norms enforced in the years leading up to the FIS's dissolution persisted through and after the Civil War. Women's apparent acceptance of the conflation of religious values with new social norms lends itself to several interpretations. At first glance, it appears as a sign of protest against a government that had neglected women in its economic development strategy and failed to promote their employment or political participation. Although this explanation is plausible, it overlooks the effects of women's acquiescence to the conflation of values and norms on the direction of change they seek in their status. While veiling, one of the dominant norms that became widespread since the 1990s, may not be in and of itself essential, its symbolic significance cannot be minimized. It feeds into the gender order presumed to be rooted in religion. It symbolically re-inscribes women in a social space in which they appear as bearers of religious norms as they discharge their non-religious activities. Since religious values do not rest on the notion of equality, women shoulder a moral burden in the taken-for-granted world within which their daily activities unfold. This analysis does not presume an opposition between "religious" and "secular." Rather, the reduction of culture to religious values restricts the very domain of religious culture. Indeed, in everyday life, Islam incorporates practices that fall squarely in the domain of the sacred, practices that are accepted yet fall outside of the sacred, and still others that do not contravene the sacred but enlarge the cultural domain. Hence the conflation of culture with religion limits cultural development by excluding new values or norms which may not contravene religious norms. Furthermore, the restrictive equation of religious values with cultural values does not allow for a questioning of practices that sustain an unequal gender order. It predisposes a woman for instance to accept religiously sanctioned forms of marital union (such as *'urf*), which she would not otherwise if culture had not been defined as synonymous with religious values. The codification in law of religious values compounds the morally constraining power they have on women. Consequently, the only way to enlarge the domain of culture is to position one's self in the restrictive space of religious culture, argue the details of law and traditions, and point to the difference between the spirit and the letter of the sacred texts, in order to redefine the *meaning* of the rules and regulations of the juridical discourse on the family. This is the path taken by Islamic feminism, which will be covered in a separate chapter.

What this brief chapter has shown is that women have been a recurring theme in the political discourse of the incipient postcolonial state as well as the faith-based party. They have been so as a category of people representing symptoms of a culture in need of renovation. The Tripoli Program, the most detailed policy program defining the orientation of the new state, clearly identified the salient mental attitudes and practices prevalent in the waning years of the war, which sustained gender inequities. More important, and although it clearly spelled out the deficiencies of Algerian culture, the Program further advocated a "national" culture. Admittedly, a nation in the process of building a new culture needs to identify itself as Algerian in contradistinction to the French-colonial culture. However, the qualifier "national" was not given a specific content. Hence it remained a hollow concept amenable to being infused with different meanings depending on the conjuncture. Similarly, by approaching culture as the domain of science and technology that somehow would resolve lingering feudal attitudes, gender inequality, and even misinterpretations of Islam, the Program gave little substance to the renovation of culture it advocated for; it remained a rhetorical exhortation. It is no wonder that the faith-based discourse seized upon women as the embodiments of a political culture gone awry that threatened the national character of a society perceived as misled by a government that had lost its Islamic moral compass. Hence women as well as Islam, two pillars of a national culture, were to be saved from the state which presumably used Western-qua- "scientific" knowledge to move away from Islam. Ironically, the state's juridical discourse will also adopt an attitude similar to the faith-based party in its discourse of the family, which it shields from the rationality of its political and economic systems. Consequently, the state cedes the domain of "culture," decried by the Tripoli Program, to the very people who would give it its own religious contents in violation of the constitutional discourse of rights. Paradoxically, the state will also try to compensate for the domain it ceded by normalizing a heterogeneous conception of Islam which it qualifies as *wasatiya*, or moderate Islam.

Notes

1 I hesitate to adopt the Durkheimian language of anomie because, in the Algerian case, "anomie" is not situational but systemic as it affects institutional as well as individual behavior. Furthermore, anomie presumes the existence of a norm that is valued by all. Where political, economic, and social norms are contested, it is unclear how the concept of "anomie" would reflect the specificity of such a situation. However, as I was writing this note, protests have erupted since February 23, throughout Algeria against a fifth term which the ailing president, Abdelaziz Bouteflika, sought.
2 Plateforme de la Soummam, in *Les textes fondamentaux de la Révolution* (Alger: Editions ANEP, 2005), 40.
3 Ibid., 51.
4 Projet de programme pour la réalisation de la Révolution démocratique et populaire (adopté à l'unanimité par le CNRA à Tripoli en juin 1962) in *Les textes fondamentaux de la Révolution*, 86–87. The CNRA was the Conseil National de la Révolution Algérienne. The Program was debated and adopted in the city of Tripoli, Libya.

 5 Ibid., 93.
 6 Ibid., 86–87.
 7 Ibid., 95.
 8 Ibid., 94.
 9 Ibid., 95.
10 Ibid., 88–89.
11 Ibid.
12 Ibid., 89.
13 Ibid., 88.
14 Ibid., 88.
15 Ibid.
16 Ibid., 87.
17 Ibid., 89.
18 Ibid., 104.
19 Ibid., 105.
20 Ibid., 105.
21 Ibid., 105–106.
22 Ibid., 107.
23 Ibid.
24 Ibid., 121.
25 Ibid., 103.
26 Ibid., 103–104.
27 Ibid., 23.
28 *La Charte d'Alger: Ensemble de textes adoptés par le premier congrès du parti du FLN* (Alger: FLN, Commission Centrale d'Orientation, 1964), especially 81–82.
29 For a discussion of the family code see Marnia Lazreg, *The Eloquence of Silence: Algerian Women in Question* (New York: Routledge, 2019, revised edition), 142–150. See also Feriel Lalami, *Les Algériennes contre le code de la famille* (Paris: Sciences Po, 2012).
30 Even though *shari'a* was not elaborated on the basis of the Quran only, but also on the traditions, methods of reasoning, as well as the consensus of legal scholars, its purpose was to order gender relations according to a perceived equitable justice steeped in values either inscribed in, or inspired from the word of God as revealed.

2

NATIONAL RELIGIOUS CULTURE

The notion that Algerian culture should be "national" in the sense of reflect-
ing historically specific features that survived the cultural erosion it sustained
under colonial rule serves as a subtext in the various political-juridical discourses. The Tripoli Program identified the revalorization of the Arabic language, and the development of science as the main instruments for building a
new culture. Although language is a vehicle of cultural development, its construction of concepts, images, and meanings is not ex-nihilo but occurs in an
evolving historical, political, and social context that shapes its creative capacity. The state's policy of instituting Arabic as the official language was elaborated in such a way as to hamper rather than facilitate the achievement of a
renovated culture. By limiting the domain of Arabic to primary education,
law, and the social sciences, the policy implicitly defined Arabic as inimical to
the scientific culture, which the Tripoli Program advocated for. The consequences of such an ambivalent linguistic policy are beyond the scope of this
book. Suffice it to say that the unstated view that the French language is the
language of science and technology is a source of social conflicts between
those who were schooled in Arabic and received limited instruction in French,
and those who favored French, which they learned in private schools or in the
family.

The intrinsically contradictory linguistic policy, challenged internally by
social groups opposed to it, and undermined by the continued use as well as
valorization of French (actively supported by the French government eager to
retain its linguistic preeminence in its former colonies), turned out to be an
inefficient instrument of the creation of a new culture. Hence, religion
emerged as a more viable instrument, especially in the aftermath of the Civil
War. The peculiarity of the Algerian case lies in the state's paradoxical attitude towards religion: on the one hand it created a relatively autonomous

space in which religious groups could assert their power over the definition of cultural values in matters of family law in contravention of the constitution. On the other hand, the state also intervenes as an interested actor in the relatively autonomous field it created, producing its own version of what Islam is about. In this it not only competes with other religious forces in the field for control over religious values and symbols, it also seeks to supplant them. Hence, the state will establish a structured religious apparatus with its own functionaries, pedagogical programs, and social services.

The state religion

Scope and pathways of a culture of religion

Once the state selectively cedes its constitutional commitment to ensuring the juridical equality of its citizens to a field of competing religious actors, how does it manage the conflicting demands of its traditional political and religious roles? The natural institutional context within which a state religion is produced would ordinarily be the Ministry of Religious Affairs and Waqfs which was formed in 1962 to adjudicate issues arising out of the *waqf* form of property,[1] oversee the traditional corps of imams, manage conversions, etc. However, the emergence of an engaged form of religiosity prior to and during the Civil War led to an interpretation according to which faith-based groups held religious views and even practices that had been imported from Middle Eastern societies. Therefore, the government felt the need to create a separate structure focused on the promotion of an Algerian Islam. Implicitly, Islam as practiced in Algeria and the Maghreb in general is not amenable to political interpretation, and certainly not conducive to the singular violence that characterized the Civil War. On the face of it, this was a plausible response to a chaotic situation. On close examination, the interpretation shifted the focus of analysis of the causes of the Civil War from its social-economic and political framework onto religion presented as distorted by outside influences—a cause of social strife. By the same token, imputing local problems to outside forces helped the state to justify its own violence against individuals whose grievances were grounded in real life problems, albeit their solutions were expressed in the language of religion.[2] At any rate, the government under Liamine Zeroual[3] formulated a decree creating the Haut Conseil Islamique (High Islamic Council; HCI) implemented in 1998.[4] Initially, the HCI focused on "cultural issues arising in society in general." However, since 2016 it addresses "social problems such as *khul'* divorce, national language, and Islamic education."[5] A review of the HCI intervention in these three areas is instructive:

The intervention of the HCI in *khul'* divorce reveals a determination to correct what this institution considers an abuse of a right women received under the 2005 amended version of the family Code. The HCI believes that women abused this right in order to "get rid of a husband." It is concerned that judges are too lax and do not pay sufficient attention to children as casualties of divorce. Having "little patience to counsel women against divorce, judges simply allowed them to get rid of a husband. The woman keeps the children and the house." Furthermore, the HCI was alarmed that young people who "marry themselves directly" (meaning without parental approval or input), and in the name of "emancipation" abuse *khul'*. "We asked that this situation be remedied [because] children should not be sacrificed."[6] Although concern for the children of divorce is laudable, curbing women's (still) limited right to divorce is a throwback to the status quo ante when a husband had a broad right to divorce a wife except for five specific (and restrictive) reasons. It must be remembered that *khul'* divorce is contingent upon a woman's relinquishing part of her dowry and/or marital property. Nevertheless, the HCI's intervention to limit, presumably through a restrictive interpretation, a woman's right to divorce transforms it into a de facto rights-monitoring body that curbs rather than enhances what the religion-based law prescribes.

The Ministry of Religious Affairs and Waqfs echoes the HCI's position on this and other matters of significance. Hence it frowns upon any attempt to change inheritance law on the grounds that it is clearly spelled out in the Quran. In the words of a director, "no one can change it; there are things that cannot be changed. Besides, there are cases where a woman inherits more than a man." When told that Tunisia had amended its inheritance law, the director explained that women would not go along with the amendment because it goes counter the sacred text.[7] From the HCI's perspective, change in the economic situation of women in the long run will make the issue of inheritence redundant. As science and technology develop, "women's productive capacity will increase so that in the next 10 to 15 years women will earn more than men." However, it is not clear how a daughter would be able to inherit her mother's wealth if she has a brother who is entitled to twice her share. Admittedly, the HCI simply meant that focusing on inequality in inheritance obscures what it perceives as women's progress in economic participation, or that it obliquely intimated that progress in women's material life will render a crucial provision in Islamic law inapplicable. This, of course, would mean that religion itself would become less central to the state. It is unlikely that the HCI's leader would endorse such a view. However, this was one of those moments when a personal musing connotes meanings one may not have intended.

However, at times the HCI interprets religious texts in a more liberal manner as is clear in the assertion that in the case of an unwed mother, her right to life and dignity is preserved through appeal to the appropriate hadith. For example, the head of the HCI noted, Prophet Muhammad said that a woman who had left her cat alone and without food deserved to go to Hell; but a woman who gave water to a thirsty dog should go to paradise. Hence, the case of the unwed mother could be assimilated to the woman who showed kindness to a dog. Besides, sparing an unwed mother punishment follows the example set by Caliph Omar, "who did not punish a pregnant woman." In addition to protecting unwed mothers, the HCI further tackles practices inimical to women yet presented as empowering women. Specifically, the HCI noted that in some universities, female doctoral students are "urged by Islamists to propose marriage to a professor seeking a second wife or to a fellow student [apparently] in application of the Sunna."[8]

The second focus of the HCI, language, reveals the state's view of Arabic as the language of religion. Admittedly, this is a fact. By the same token, by entrusting the development of Arabic to the care of the HCI as well as the Ministry of Religious Affairs, even if partially, the state implicitly admits that the justification of its linguistic policy according to which Arabic is the official language of the land is religious. Arabic could also draw its legitimacy from other sources, such as history and use. However, the state's move must be placed in the context of the Berberist claim, often made to implicitly de-legitimize Arabic, to parity between Arabic and the Amazigh language.[9] Nevertheless, the purpose of the HCI is religious literacy, which it carries out in the language of the Quran. The HCI acknowledges linguistic pluralism and notes the interdependence of languages in literacy classes. It also noted women's enthusiasm for religious literacy, especially knowledge of the Quran. The HCI as well as the Ministry of Religious Affairs and Waqfs[10] point, without some admiration, to women over 60 years old who learned the 60 *hizb* comprising the entire Quran. Some of these women lived in rural areas and did not speak Arabic. One such woman in a literacy class in Bouira, a city about 60 miles southeast of Algiers in the Kabylie, who even though had no interest in Arabic as a language, insisted on learning the Quran in Arabic. From his perspective, the woman's reaction stemmed from her generation's cultural heritage, "neither western, nor oriental." She only spoke a Kabyl dialect, but wished to "valorize her prayers" (through learning the Quran in its original language). Such women have "no feminist complex. They are very free; they act as citizens." Similarly, at the Ministry of Religious Affairs, the staff marveled at the capacity of illiterate women to memorize the Quran.[11] What this otherwise genuine admiration denotes is the extent to which women's depth of commitment to their religion and their faith might have been underestimated. In reality, women from all walks of life express interest in their religion and seek to increase their knowledge of spiritual as well as ethical matters. Perhaps the realization of women's enthusiasm for expanding their knowledge of Islam led the HCI to deplore the unsatisfactory level at which Islam has been taught in Algeria. It is also part of a debate among Muslim countries as exemplified by the April 2018 International Congress on Islamic Education in which the HCI took part.

The third focus of the HCI, the economy, enlarges the domain of its action. Commenting on the scope of the informal sector in Algeria (which according to the press accounted for 70% of the economy in 2019), the HCI explained that operators of this sector were reluctant to place their ("illicit") money in banks because of the Islamic prohibition against usury. They preferred instead to invest in mosques. Consequently, the HCI thought of "Islamizing banks." It planned to hold consultations at a forthcoming conference on Islamic banking and finance. In the spirit of *ijtihad*, it further undertook to devise ways of putting the Islamic obligation to give charity (*zakat*) to productive use. Hence, it issued a *fatwa*[12] that channeled *zakat* into the creation of income generation schemes. The fatwa was based on the Quranic prescription that *zakat* should be given to the poor and the needy, and that according to the Islamic tradition it can even be used to free a prisoner. Although this did not mean that jails were mandated to free prisoners, it did mean that one could give the part of charity intended to free a prisoner to someone who needs it, or to invest it in a socially useful project. "Out of the eight parts of *zakat* mandated by the Quran, three could be used to create microenterprises for the unemployed." In this way, the HCI wishes to enlighten the public about more creative and sustainable ways of fulfilling their religious obligation. It also intends to counteract the Salafi practice of giving the poor charity in kind (semolina, flour, or other staples), which from the HCI perspective has no long-lasting effect on the poor or the needy.

The *zakat* fatwa requires that *zakat* be given to its beneficiary. Hence, "if I give a young woman 500,000 DA [about $5,000] to start a business, I'll tell her, 'I am lending you this money but you will return it to me within an agreed upon period of time.'" Recounting his time as Minister of Religious Affairs and Waqfs, the president of the HCI pointed out that in using this logic he was able to create 9,000 microbusinesses.

In all its interventions, the HCI aims for interpreting religious texts, or resolving social issues in the context of Algerian culture, which it insists is rooted in Maghrebin Islam. Developed in centers of learning such as the Qarawayn and the Zitouna in Tunisia, as well as Mazouna, Adrar and Biskra in Algeria, Maghrebin Islam, according to the HCI, is characterized by tolerance, respect for liberty, and individual choice. Hence, the solution to contemporary social problems need not be imported from outside cultures, which may not be adapted to local practices and understandings. The local culture invoked is synonymous with religion, Maghrebin Islam. The emphasis placed on local Islam reflects the HCI's concern about the spread of Salafism, which it notes "was born in Najd, Saudi Arabia," and consequently is a foreign import. Given that Islam arose out of the Arabian Peninsula, the HCI is careful to point out that Islam as such is "general" in its orientation. It allowed each country or region, such as the Maghreb, to adapt it to its own needs. Hence, Salafism, being a specific sectarian system of beliefs that had few adherents in Algeria, is presumably alien to Maghrebin Islamic practices. Yet, where women are concerned, within Algeria, in the region of the M'zab, the gender order is just as constraining to women as that of the Salafists.

At any rate, the Islam that the HCI wishes to encourage is implicitly one that defines itself against trends of religiosity and practices that have emerged since the 1970s to challenge governments throughout the Middle East and North Africa, through the revival or dissemination of sectarian interpretations of religious texts. If one starts with the notion that "man in the Quran is the substitute of God on the earth in order to develop [its resources], to colonize it, fill it [through procreation]," it follows that "God has entrusted us with the earth in order to fructify not destroy it. It is science and technology that [help man to carry out] his substitution to God. This is the meaning of living together." This last phrase has become the focus as well as motto of a Sufi order, *zawiya al 'Alawiya*, based in the city of Mostaganem, in Western Algeria. The president of the HCI was planning a trip to Mostaganem to attend a conference on how to promote "living together ['*le vivre ensemble*'] through the teaching of mathematics due to open a few days later organized by the *zawyyia al 'Alawiya*.

Hence the HCI represents the state's paradoxical role as: (a) subverting the rights of women *it* spells out in the constitution; (b) overseeing as well as re-interpreting the rights religious law grants women, which it orients in a socially conservative direction. Consequently, it is hardly accurate to see the family code simply as the product of the state's acquiescence to pressure from religious groups—a commonly held view. In fact, the state intervenes through its own machinery to orient the religious interpretation of a right, such as *khul'* which Islamic law grants women. It could just as easily expand this right to gradually blur its boundary with a civil law that would grant women the same right to divorce as men. However, it does not, as it appears to set a limit to the practice of *ijtihad* (or freedom of interpretation), which it claims to uphold.

The murshidat

The principal task of educating women about their religious duties (*wajibat*) as well as rights (*huquq*) in the context of a "national Islam"[13] is carried out by a corps of women especially trained in religious matters, the *murshidat* (sing. *murshida*). *Murshidat* came into being in the aftermath of the Civil War, "after the FIS was defeated." Their role is to promote "the *diniya wataniya* (national religious culture), the culture of yesteryear, which erases the negative effects of the FIS [Front of Islamic Salvation]."[14] They teach women Quranic exegesis, the hadith, Arabic, and literacy. In addition, in keeping with their mission to be "in touch with society," they also provide assistance in three areas, reproductive health (in cooperation with the Ministry of Health and the centers for the Protection of Mothers and Infants), work, and the family (especially children).[15] Hence, through them, the Ministry of Religious Affairs has an input in, and provides assistance to, various ministries seeking to reach the population. The social scope of the *murshidat* also extends to centers for delinquent youth (where they initially began their outreach) as well prisons in which violence is rife. Reaching female inmates through God with lectures and education (*tarbiya*) has met with a measure of success as some women "repent."[16] *Murshidat* are trained by consultants on how to approach, counsel, and orient women in solving problems as sensitive as reproductive health and contraception. A *murshida* gives her own lecture (*khutba*) at the mosque (just like the *imam* does), which she nevertheless coordinates with her male counterpart. Unlike the *imam*, she cannot lead the Friday prayer; she prays alongside other women. The message she or the *imam* conveys is "national" as it is sponsored by a national commission within the Ministry in keeping with the principle that "Islam is the religion of the state."[17] Not all mosques have a *murshida*. Where there is none a *mutatawi'a*, a volunteer working part-time, fulfills the function for a period of six months (generally a *murshida* works 18 hours per week). The volunteer receives guidance before carrying out her function. A *murshida* listens to women's concerns and where she cannot resolve an issue, she brings it to the attention of the *imam* who will include it in his Friday *khutba* (lecture). Some of the issues a *murshida* deals with are delicate, such as domestic violence, and land disputes as happened in a town in the south of the country.[18]

Before acquiring a legal status by government decree on March 2, 2002, *murshidat* were quasi-volunteer teachers in Quranic schools, with no specific title, who received a nominal wage. Seeking to normalize their role, Mr. Ghoulamallah, then Minister of Religious Affairs, created the post of "*imam-usted*" (literally professor-imam),[19] which ensured that *murshidat* received the same pay as *imams*. Recruitment to the post requires a candidate to have a degree in Islamic sciences, either a certificate obtained after the sixth year of study or an MA after the eighth year, in addition to passing an exam. A higher post of *murshida diniya ra'isiya* or principal *murshida*, was created on December 8, 2008,[20] one of whom practices in each *wilaya* (or administrative regional division). Her functions include "participation in the drafting and codification of *fatawa* (pl. of fatwa); lectures and scientific research activities undertaken by the scientific council for the establishment of mosques; and taking part in the program for the protection of the family."[21] Clearly, the functions of this category of *murshidat* are similar to those of a *'alim*, or religious scholar.

The concept of *murshida* means in Arabic spiritual "guide" or "adviser." The official description of these women's function transcends the role of religious guide since they include participation in the formulation of legal opinions, research, and protection of the family. In the hierarchy of *murshidat*, the highest post is occupied by a *murshida mufattisha*, or inspector. The administrative structure of *murshidat* and *imams* is decentralized. There are offices of *shu'un diniya* (religious affairs) in the 48 *wilayat* throughout the country. Each *wilaya* has a *majlis 'ilmi*, a commission of religious scholars dispensing religious information and advice when needed. In general, *imams* constitute the bulk of the membership of these commissions. Said in passing, the Ministry of Religious Affairs enjoins *imams*, as civil servants, to refrain from incitation to violence under penalty of law.[22]

The number (over 5,000)[23] of *murshidat* has been increasing, although it has yet to catch up with the number of *imams*. In addition to teaching and fulfilling their social roles, they also provide assistance to the training of personnel in various state and business venues. *Murshidat* note with pride that initially, the ministries requesting their assistance were skeptical about the quality of their work. In due time, they expressed satisfaction with their professional performance.[24] After the function of *murshida* was professionalized, women entered into competition with *imams*, all of whom are males. The *murshidat* superior qualifications were a source of conflict with *imams* before they too received training to upgrade their skills. Implied in discussions with *murshidat* is the notion that to do the same work as a man, a woman needed to have greater qualifications. When asked why a woman could not become *imam*, the Director at the Ministry of Religious Affairs explained that "the *imamat* is for men only. The [divine] law cannot be changed. Our religion cannot be changed." *Murshidat* too agree that they cannot become *imams* because "God willed it."[25]

At any rate, the creation of the corps of *murshidat* answers women's need for privacy. Women prefer to talk about their personal problems with a *murshida* rather than an *imam*. *Murshidat* point out the importance of their work especially in view of the increased attendance of women in mosques during Ramadan, a month of heightened religious observance. They note in passing that some of these women are not *hijab* wearers albeit they wear the proper attire for the occasion. They also point out that men from all professions too seek their help in acquiring more knowledge about their religion, especially religious ethics.

To return to the issue of what can or cannot be changed in the Quran, I asked three *murshidat* to list what can be changed. Based on their experience with women, they cited polygamy. They encountered married women who, for one reason or another, no longer wish to have sexual intercourse with their husbands, and as a result urge a husband to take another wife. Traditionally, it is a husband who decides to take a second wife. *Murshidat* explain that such women wish to spare a husband recourse to "illicit sex;" they are also eager to retain the security of a home (which they might lose in case of divorce) for themselves and their children while acknowledging that they can no longer fulfill their "obligation" as wives. Conversely, there are cases of older men who have "strong sexual desires, which they seek to satisfy with a new wife."

Murshidism and Islamic feminism

Are *murshidat* facilitators of Islamic feminism understood as the search for change in gender relations within the framework of a historicized re-interpreted Quran and Islamic law? Both the director and his collaborator, a *murshida ra'isiya*, who also trains *murshidat*, answered negatively. They both pointed out that there are international conventions concerning gender which their Ministry abides by and which they attempt to bring to women's attention. They both explained away the *sura* (4:34) that is frequently inter-preted as empowering men over women.[26] They argue that its misinterpreta-tion is based on a selective reading focused on part of the *sura* only. They further noted that regardless of the *sura*, gender equality has been progressing in the areas of education, work, and politics. Besides, they stressed that the role of *murshidat* was to expand women's autonomy "within the limits of Islam in our society, *din wa watanna*."[27] Parenthetically, this reading of pro-blematic *sura* 4:34 (which is not uncommon outside of Algeria among Islamic feminists) is what a consultant, hired by the Ministry to train *murshidat,* found enlightening. She argued that the *murshidat's* task to enlighten women about their rights and obligations within Islam helped her to place western feminism in its proper perspective by sensitizing her to different paths women can take to achieve the same goals which western feminists pursue. As a result, she started lecturing in Europe about the rights women have in Islam. Undeniably, this consultant had discovered something she did not know about her religion. To the question, why couldn't Algeria follow the example of Tunisia and reinterpret inheritance law so as to make it egali-tarian, the answer was that women themselves would not accept a change in the law laid down in the Quran, and that Tunisia's reform will not succeed. One *murshida* thought that it is the women who do not attend mosques who clamor for "rights." In explaining away Islamic feminism, another *murshida* stressed that *murshidat's* work focuses on "national religious unity" not "division and *fitna* [conflict]; for us Islam means women and men working together … If a woman, in respect for her brother, allows him to take her inheritance from her, should we follow a Western solution or act according to local conditions?"[28] At any rate, from this perspective, Islamic feminism appears as "the will to destroy the *shari'a*." The question raised, however, is crucial to understanding the Ministry's view of Maghrebin Islam. In prac-tice, the problems *murshidat* uncover in the discharge of their functions illustrate the power of customs over religion, of inegalitarian gendered practices over the spirit, if not the letter, of Islam. Hence the official view of retrieving and promoting a Maghrebin Islam as an antidote to "extremism" does not distinguish between customs and belief just as it does not take into account the dysfunctions resulting from the conflation of custom and reli-gion. It rests on a reassertion of customs inimical to women that jeopardize the very "equilibrium" of the family it seeks to preserve. Besides, the cus-toms upheld by commission or omission (such as physical abuse, or disin-heritance) violate the law. In the autonomous sphere the state created in which to enforce "Maghrebin Islam," it actively violates the constitutional rights it is meant to protect.

It is true that part of a *murshida*'s task is to enlighten women about common cultural explanations of behavior as "*haram*" (prohibited by Islam). As professionals knowledgeable in religious matters, *murshidat* explain to women when an action is "*haram*" and "how not to accept blindly" what they are told is "*haram*." Admittedly, questioning taken-for-granted definitions of behavior is a method of warning women against self-styled preachers because "we cannot let anyone who wants to control a mosque [preach the way he wants]."[29] The dissemination of religious knowledge which *murshidat* under-take among women includes providing individual or group preparation of young brides-to-be; assistance with questions such as how to live as a couple; lecturing at weddings; or counseling women about to engage in *fatiha* mar-riage. The solution to some of these problems such as depriving a mother or a sister of her inheritance is related to Quranic injunctions and thus requires at a minimum upholding the right of a woman to her share of inheritance as the Quran prescribes.

When asked to characterize the kind of Islam they learned and advocate for, *murshidat* emphatically rejected the notion that there is an Algerian, or "Ottoman" Islam:

> Our Islam is that of the Prophet; it draws its roots from the Prophet. We cannot abandon these roots to adopt another country's Islam, which is [in reality] inspired from the same roots. These are the four *madahib* [schools of law]. We studied Islam as a religion of moderation (*wasatiya* or middle) and justice, not extremism. The Islam of Ibn Badis.[30]

This Islam of the "middle" ground is contrasted with the one that brought about the Civil War of 1992–2002.

That by dint of hearing and dealing with women's abuse, *murshidat* might become actively involved in asserting women's rights against accepted "tradi-tional" practices is not impossible, although at present this appears to lie beyond the political orientation of their mission.

The limits of Wasatiya *Islam*

There is a paradoxical aspect to the role that the Ministry of Religious Affairs has defined for *murshidat*. On the one hand, *murshidat* educate women about their rights in Islam, and increase literacy among them. On the other hand, they take on the task usually discharged by the non-religious branches of the government, such as the Ministry of National Solidarity, the Family and Women's Condition. Admittedly, their extra-religious role speaks of an expansive conception of religion according to which Islam is both a religion and a culture. However, the state operates in its various branches in a civil-technical manner that is not grounded in, or oriented toward religious prin-ciples, or values. To reiterate, the institution of *murshidat* was put in place to act as the socio-religious arm of the state's policy of combating "extremism," including Salafism (which ironically it also supports). It is true that in the aftermath of the Civil War, Salafism has made inroads quietly, advocating a strict form of religiosity with a distinctly rigid code of conduct for women who must adopt full *niqab* veiling. By the same token, news in the media and Internet about the Islamic State in Syria's (ISIS) treatment of women—appearing dressed like Salafi women—after their recruitment in its ranks, point to the potential of women as both agents and victims of extremism, and convey a diffuse fear of Salafism.

There is a ceiling *murshidat* reach in the discharge of their social functions. The Ministry provides a call-in service answered by *imams* or *murshidat*. Women callers who prefer not to go to the police or court, usually call to seek help. While I was in the call-in office, an older woman caller reported that her son, urged by his father (her husband), beat her and threatened her life unless she signed over to him her inheritance. But she was standing firm. The *murshida* on duty told her that her son's as well as her husband's behavior was a violation of Islamic principles. She further pointed out the seriousness of the caller's situation and urged her to approach the nearest police station. The caller explained that she did not feel good about involving the police in a family matter. After a long back and forth, the call ended. The caller had received sympathy and advice, but perhaps more important she was able to speak in confidence to someone who did not know her. However, her abuse would in all likelihood continue at least for a while. The *murshida* (who had been in her functions for 14 years) explained that the abuse women suffer daily is so intense and severe that at times she cannot shut it out of her mind when she goes home. Even there her neighbors knock on her door or call her to seek her advice. Women callers are typically unwilling to involve the law because of social pressure to keep abuse by family members within the family. The woman who brings charges against a husband is subjected to more abuse for having involved the police. A *murshida* is not allowed to call the police on behalf of a caller. By the same token, since her role is to listen and orient victims of abuse or those seeking information, she is not liable for any physical harm a caller might incur after she had called a *murshida* and brought severe abuse to her attention.[31] Nevertheless, according to the *murshidat*, women prefer to call the Ministry rather than seek the help of one of the domestic abuse call-in centers because *murshidat* do not urge them to bring charges against their abusers as women centers do. From the *murshidat*'s perspective, their service is "popular" precisely because "people feel safer" in the sense that they prefer to "stay within the tradition of Islam" based on reconciliation and fear of God. A *murshida* may advise a woman to bring her husband or father to her office for counseling. If all attempts at reconciliation fail, women (and men) are advised to go to court. Hence, *murshidat* take on "a sociological as well as psychological role."[32] That *murshidat*'s work is socially useful goes without saying. For one thing, it brings to the attention of the ministry (even though anonymous, all calls as well as their purpose are registered) the breadth and depth of the myriads of problems women encounter in their daily lives. However, by seeking to reconcile women to their condition, it also fails them. By insisting that women's family problems should be dealt with within the "tradition of Islam," it assumes an idealized conception of traditional values seen as in need of iteration; it also precludes a reflection on why and how these traditional values had lost their grip on husbands, fathers, or sons in the first place. Indeed, why is it that "tradition" did not prevent a son from beating his mother, or a husband from urging his son to bully his mother? Acts of this kind violate the spirit if not the letter of Islam but are the stuff out of which traditions draw their gendered staying power. As the Ministry acknowledged, society has changed as have women's roles in it. However, it does not question its subordination of women's right to freedom from abuse, for example, to the "tradition" of preserving the status of the family in the community, or sparing a man the embarrassment of a visit from the police. The calculus at the root of the maintenance of a "traditional" solution to women's abuse occurs at the expense of women. Oddly, this ostensibly benign view that privileges local traditions over right draws its power from the strong belief (or internalization of professional duty) exhibited by the *murshidat* I interviewed: they were convinced that God willed women to be different from men in a way that makes them more oriented towards home-making and family-building. Although women may have careers, their vocation is to care for the family:

> For example, when a spouse in a career couple needs to travel, it is the man who leaves on a mission. The wife wants to stay home. It is a matter of equilibrium [of the family]. God gave us equality in some specific areas. During pilgrimage [to Mecca], women pray before men. In the *haram* [the sacred mosque were pilgrims pray], a wife prays alongside her husband. Our religion values women, but practices violate it.

Unwittingly, this understanding of women helps to explain away abuse if not justify it in the name of the preservation of the "equilibrium" of the family. It opens the door for the acceptance of multiple forms of gender inequality such as the prohibition against a woman serving as *imam* (even if the audience is comprised of women only) "because there are times [such as during menstruation, or maternity leave] when a woman would not be able to fulfill her function as *imam*."[33]

In the end, the scope of *murshidat*'s functions obscures the difference between engaging in religious literacy and tackling the social problems women encounter in their daily lives as wives, mothers, sisters, or daughters. The imperative of maintaining *diniya wataniya* (national religion) as the framework within which social problems must be resolved proves to be divorced from the complexity of the concrete reality women experience. In other words, some of the problems encountered by women call for the defense of their rights as equal citizens regardless of the state's conception of an idyllic family that must be protected against women. Thus, the operative *diniya wataniya* framework acts as a screen that conceals the systemic nature of the concrete problems women encounter in their daily lives, which it sublates and presents as requiring a necessary adjustment in an ordained and orderly existence. By the same token, the pre-requisite of *murshidat*'s function to uphold a *diniya wataniya* in cases calling out for civil intervention, acquires a ritualistic character that hampers rather than facilitates raising women's consciousness of their rights. Hence, the avowed goal of combatting "extremism" and "Salafism" founders on the woman question since it reasserts the power of customs albeit with a wistful recognition that it may violate Islamic precepts.

In addition to *murshidat*, the state's advocacy of a national religion further rests on the revival, support and development of popular Sufism as will be discussed in the next chapter. The strategy itself is inscribed in a broader, international context, in which Algeria is an active player. Nevertheless, *murshidat*'s experience with the staggering problems women encounter in everyday life is echoed by a senior attorney who confided that "at times I think our society has lost its soul."[34] The loss of soul is an apt metaphor for the reality which the normalization of *wasatiya* Islam conceals, or covers over. A journalist and stage manager explained that women are exposed to various religious messages from self-styled preachers, which "cause them" to put up with unhappy marital situations. She also attributed women's staying in unhappy marriages to the "value" they place on marriage.[35]

Paradoxically, Algeria's *wasatiya* policy attempts to blur or erase the relative boundary between faith and culture, *din* and *dunia* (by reducing socio-economic issues to an expansive conception of a national Islam), yet it also acknowledges that women's progress is and can occur outside of its normative framework. Two young male graduate students referred to this situation as "hypocritical." They argue that "the instrumentalization" of religion, the "closure" that faith presupposes makes for a number of contradictions. For example, even though there are signs of a "softening of masculinity among young couples, man is still man, a man's word is never equal to a woman's word."[36]

Deradicalization

Islam between Algeria and France

Since the war it waged against the Front of Islamic Salvation (FIS), the state has acted as a relay on the side of the United States as well as Europe in the "war on terror" they have been actively pursuing in the aftermath of 9/11. Algeria ritually invokes its experience of the Civil War as a motivation for combating "extremism." Yet the event that precipitated the Civil War was not an attack staged by a "radical" Islamic group, but the state's decision to cancel parliamentary elections that the Front of Islamic Salvation- a Sunni Islamic party- was poised to win, and arrest its leaders. This act paved the way for several factions of the faith-based movement to engage in violence. Although it is true that in the course of the War, sectarian groups emerged and engaged in egregious acts of violence, it does not mean that the Front of Islamic Salvation was in and of itself a sectarian party. Its leading *imams*, Abbasi Madani and Ali Benhadj were home grown Algerians, practicing Muslims, who used their power of oratory to mobilize youth in an attempt to bring about political change through the ballot. At any rate, the Civil War has acquired the power of a politically mobilizing myth through which the state has been able to justify domestic or foreign policies to maintain the status quo and eschew meaningful reforms.

On December 18, 2014 the Minister of Religious Affairs and Waqfs, Mohammed Aïssa, signed a convention with France for the training of Algerian Imams assigned to mosques in France. These *imams* would be taught French (implicitly so as to teach religious matters in French), as well as [the functioning of] "French institutions as concern their *laïcité* and its spirit. They will specifically be trained in the requirements of the 1905 law which states the separation of Church and state."[37] Coordinated by the Institute Al Ghazali sponsored by the Paris *Grande Mosquée*, the training of *imams* takes place in upward of ten French universities. In 2008, French universities had refused to take part in training *imams* in "'laïcité French style' in the name and in defense of a strict *laïcité*."[38] The Catholic Institute of Paris took up the task as a "sort of pilot project." The idea of training imams had been proposed to the Algerian state in 1995 by the then French Minister of the Interior, Charles Pasqua. His successor, Manuel Valls, had signed a convention with the Algerian government during a visit for teaching French to *imams* as well as a brief introduction to "*laïcité à la française*" at the French Institute in Algiers.[39] Subsequently, it is the Algerian government, which revived Pasqua's proposal to train *imams* in France. There are 15,000 imams in Algeria, 120 of whom are sent each year to officiate in France in rotation. Noting that "times have changed," a veiled reference to the worsening of political events in Syria, Yemen, as well as the rise of ISIS, the French Minister of the Interior, Bernard Cazeneuve, noted that Algeria wished to combat "the radicalization of Islam." Remarkably, speaking in the name of Islam, Cazeneuve asserted that "We need to do what we should and what we could to prevent the perversion of Islam by sectarian terrorist groups who have nothing to do with Islam or its texts." Convinced that ignorance fosters "obscurantism," Mr. Cazeneuve evoked the enlightened knowledge yielded by "the Islam of Cordoba, the Islam of the middle ground (in French *juste milieu*) [founded on] tolerance, love of the other, respect, peace, and brotherhood, which the Algerian Minister of Religious Affairs promotes." Echoing the French Minister, Mr. Aïssa added that the joint action between France and Algeria intended to bring about "a practice of Islam steeped in citizenship, republican in character, and respectful of laïcité. This is what the Algerian *imams* on (temporary) assignment to France must strive to do ... in order to facilitate integration [of Muslims in France] ... and promote an Islam of the middle ground, [characterized] by conviviality, respect, and love of the other." From Mr. Cazeneuve's perspective, France shares in these values in the context "of our own history, our guidelines, and our principles."[40] *Imams* would be taught "the history of religions and laïcité, the foundational principles of law, or even the method to create and manage a cultural association at the universities which had started offering a 'university diploma' modeled after that of the Catholic University of Paris."[41] Perhaps more concerned than his Algerian counterpart about potential criticism, Mr. Cazeneuve explained that France did not intend to teach *imams* theology. Rather, the point was to involve academics and intellectuals in the struggle against the lies and manipulations deployed by terrorist groups.[42] In total agreement with France, the Algerian Minister of Religious Affairs, wishing to "immunize" his country against the religious views attributed to "terrorists," revealed that the training of *imams* in Algeria proper would be revised. Indeed, in addition to holding a higher education degree in Islamic sciences, an *imam* will be required to undergo training (sponsored jointly with the Ministry of Higher Education) "for one semester, and pass an exam before he could practice."[43]

It must be noted that Algeria is not the only supplier of *imams* to France. Turkey and Morocco too assign imams to France as paid civil servants in the absence of a financially independent body among French Muslims or Muslims in France. Said in passing, there is at first glance nothing wrong with raising the level of *imams* and teaching them French. Algeria invokes its experience of the Civil War as a motivation for combating "extremism," yet the state's rejection of violence obscures the egregious acts of violence it too committed in the name of fighting "radicalism."

Algeria's cooperation with France in ensuring that *imams* partake in a program of preventive "deradicalization" of young French Muslims mirrors the Algerian state's own policy of creating a national Islam. For example, the state screens *imams* before recruiting them to make sure that they "submit to the national religious orientation" (in French, "*référence religieuse nationale*"). Ostensibly, the training of *imams* is meant to counteract the preaching of Salafist *imams*, who having higher university diplomas than state *imams* often achieved the rank of "*imam* professor."[44] The state fears that the degree would allow Salafi *imams* to disseminate their beliefs more effectively than traditional *imams*.[45] Salafi *imams* too, however, receive additional training in the state's religious policy. The friction between *imams* with different levels of education frequently takes on political overtones as some *imams* identify with the state religious policy whereas others (and not only *Salafists*) demand greater freedom and independence.

Murshidat were not mentioned as part of this training in *laïcité*. Besides, when asked on my first visit to them about the *imams*' training in *laïcité* (*intidab* in Arabic), *murshidat* did not appear to be aware of it. On my second visit, they indicated that they did not know the exact contents of the *laïcité* training program, which they thought had taken place ten to 15 years ago. However, they recalled that three *murshidat* (one each from the Kabylie, Oran and Algiers) had made a trip to France.[46]

Presumably, although not plausibly, *murshidat*'s social role overshadowed their religious role thus disqualifying them from training. Yet training them in *laïcité* like imams would be beneficial to them, given that one of their missions is to enlighten women about "their rights." For this to happen, the state would have to ensure that whether officiating in France or in Algeria, *imams* as well as *murshidat* should understand that national Islam must be respectful of "citizenship" as the former Minister of Religious Affairs who signed the convention with France, Mohammed Aïssa, declared. At any rate, three factors emerge from the Algero-French convention, which shed a new light on the Algerian state's religion policy at home: the selection of a specific type of Islam, "deradicalization," and a "catholic" method of *laïcité*. To recall, in Algeria the state spearheads a conception of Islam deemed Maghrebin. It does not refer to a "Cordoba Islam," nor does it attempt to "secularize" Islam (for lack of a better word) in the manner that it advocates the teaching of *laïcité* to its *imams* in France. Yet, the objectives of the state in its management of religion are the same as those of the French state. The creation of the function of *murshidat* and the raising of the level of knowledge of *imams* were born out of a desire to prevent the re-emergence of Islamic militancy experienced during the Civil War, as well as put an end to the spread of Salafism. However, France engaged in a multi-pronged project of "deradicalization," based on the production and dissemination of knowledge, which brings together universities, research institutes, new institutions such as the *Fondation de l'Islam de France* (Foundation of French Islam), created on December 5, 2016,[47] as well as a legal machinery for the implementation of its secularizing objective. Hence the French response has breadth and depth, and is aimed though a combination of laws, education, and training to bring about new discursively constituted French Muslim subjects. By comparison, the Algerian management of an Algerian-qua-Maghrebin Islam is more modest (albeit no less determined), and less interested in bringing Islamic practices in conformity with citizenship rights. Furthermore, the French insistence on *laïcité* incorporates women as well as men. By contrast, and even though the Algerian Ministry of Religious Affairs endorses the notion that Islam in France must be steeped in citizenship, it violates this principle at home. Besides, the state's engagement in the management of religion rests on a literal reading of the Quran, which enables it to either limit some of the rights the *shari'a* accords women such as *khul'* divorce, or justify inequality between women and men in inheritance.

The inevitable question is how could the state act as an advocate of secularity in the practice of Islam in France, but as an orthodox interpreter of religious texts in Algeria? Besides, how is it that it refrains from proposing to the French state the training of *murshidat* in the principle of *laïcité* as it did for men, or promote their participation in teaching Islam in France as *imams* do? Imams serving temporarily in France eventually return to Algeria. How would they interpret citizenship rights in teaching about Islam in Algeria? Would they become agents of change? Such questions can be answered only after research is carried out among returning *imams*.[48] In the meantime, the state's dual religion policy, one for Muslims in France, the other for Muslims in Algeria, casts doubt on its integrity and reveals the deliberateness of its gendered view of Maghrebin Islam. If emphasis on respect for citizenship shows deference to France's *laïcité,* the suspension of women's citizenship entitlement in the formulation and defense of family law in Algeria reveals the expedient nature of the state's insistence on a tolerant form of Algerian Islam. Admittedly, the state is merely pointing to two different, albeit related, modalities of Islam, one from a long-gone Cordoban experience that is more appropriate to France, the other born out of the Algerian-qua-Maghrebin experience that reflects a national culture. But, if combating Salafism and "terrorism" is the overarching goal of the state's management of Islam at home and abroad, the methodological principles it advocates for its *imams* in France should also be the ones that guide its policy in Algeria. Why should there be two models of Islam, one deemed enlightened, erudite, tolerant as befit French values, and another popular, somehow adapted to Maghrebins' own traditions and customs? Implicitly, the state recognizes that such customs do not fit the principle of "tolerance" it seeks to put forth. Neither the HCI nor the Ministry of Religious Affairs evinced awareness that the customs in which Islam in Algeria is embedded have traditionally supported an inegalitarian gender system. Neither institution described the lingering mental attitudes inimical to women, which the Tripoli Program had described and denounced. Perhaps what is singular in the Ministry of Religious Affairs' endorsement of the French policy of "deradicalization" of Islam is its silence on gender. The signing of the convention immediately preceded the attack of January 7, 2015, on the satirical paper, Charlie Hebdo, by two French-born brothers, Saïd and Chérif Kouachi, children of Algerian immigrants. The Algerian Minister of Religious Affairs of the time, M. Abbas, remarked defensively that the two brothers "had never been in Algeria" and that "the fact they are of Algerian origin does not mean that Algerians are responsible [for their act]."[49] Finally, the policy of "deradicalization" of Muslims in France is a policy of state intervention (French or Algerian) in the definition of Islam, a classification of types of Islam (Cordoban and Algerian-qua-Maghrebin) according to criteria selected in one case by an essentially Catholic State, in the other by a state that defines itself as Muslim. Hence, it is a political institution, with its education, legal and social apparatuses, which selects and decides what kind of Islam should be suited to its political system and its geopolitical interests. In the case of France, this is an act that violates its own conception of *laïcité*. Indeed, the latter becomes the trope for selecting, deliberatively, the kind of Islam it can control politically. The selection is naturally laden with historical meanings, such as those pertaining to France's colonial policy of management of Islam in Algeria, which partially rested on France's nineteenth-century view that the colonization of North Africa signified the (triumphant) return of Christianity to a land that had been "Islamized" by "Arabs."[50]

The convention signed in 2014 between France and Algeria on the teaching of Islam reflects an on-going concern among politicians, which it did not allay. On May 31, 2016, the Algerian ambassador to France was invited by the Senate to be heard about a number of issues, including the "organization, role, and financing of Islam in France."[51] The president of the Senate commission, Corinne Féret noted the special relation that Algeria has with the *Grande Mosquée de Paris*, its "demographic" ties with Algerian immigrants; its financial influence over mosques, and "the presence of 120 imams [employed] as Algerian civil servants."[52] In addition to questions about Algeria's participation in the organization of Islam as a religion, and the criteria for disbursement of funding, Ms. Féret wished to know more about the selection of the imams sent to France, "the prospects of training French imams in Algeria," and "whether Muslims of Algerian origins have special cultural expectations, which the Algerian government seeks to meet."[53] A senator explained that France's goal to create "a homogeneous Islam" was thwarted by the French Muslims' countries of origin, which include not only Algeria but also Morocco, Tunisia, and Turkey. The latter plays an important financial role among Franco-Turkish Muslims, which it also supplies with imams called "social workers." The point was to determine whether, from the standpoint of the ambassador, "French people having ties to Algeria and Algerians living in France would accept an Islam cut off from their country of origin." This question goes to the heart of the convention signed between Algeria and France. Training imams in French *laïcité* and insisting that they learn and master French may very well be one method to gradually distance from Algerian culture the Algerian immigrant community as well as French Muslims of Algerian origin. Although on the face of it, mastering French makes sense, the insistence on it renders it less banal. However, historically, during the colonial era, France had pursued a policy of supplanting Arabic with French. The French language was used as a method of alienating natives from their identity as well as isolating them culturally from Middle Eastern countries were Arabic was spoken. When read in this context, the insistence on training *imams* in French *laïcité* in the French language acquires another meaning. After disposing of the notion that Algeria somehow impeded a French project of creating a French Islam separate from Algeria's Islam, the ambassador reminded the senators "it was at the urging of associations representing our community in France that we are making this effort [to help]." He added that Algeria works in tandem with the French ministry of the Interior and that it behooves everyone to make sure that mosques do not become empty, as "such a vacuum would be dangerous to our community as well as the host country." This was an oblique reference to young Muslims leaving institutional mosques for alternative ones offered by various sects, or groups eager to interpret Islam differently from what the ambassador described as Algerian Islam, an "Islam of the middle ground, empathetic, open to research and questioning, in brief to modernity."

Questions from senators open up a window into their concerns about Islam in France but also its future in Algeria. Senator André Reichardt wished to know the details of the convention between his country and Algeria, particularly whether the French language was required of imams sent to France (something he should have known). Most important the senator inquired about the effect that officiating in France (clearly after being trained in *laïcité*) had on imams after they returned to Algeria. "Is Islam practiced differently in Algeria than in France? Do you believe we could establish a French Islam [as an antidote to] religious extremism, the appeal of Daech[54] to which far too many Internet surfers succumb?" Although stemming from different concerns, the last two questions are relevant to understanding Algeria's management of Islam at home. Speaking candidly, the ambassador noted "our *imams* in Algeria are trained for Algeria. They are civil servants just like priests and pastors [in France], although in Algeria Islam is the religion of the state. Besides, the government provides for the upkeep of churches as well as mosques." Finally, "our *imams*' conduct of prayers is regularly monitored by [other] *imams* or by professors." As for the French language, conceding that this issue was a problem, the ambassador asked pointedly: "should we send to France imams knowledgeable about Islam or imams who know French? Both of course. This is why a crash course in French is offered in collaboration with the French embassy ... Beginning this year [2016] *imams* who need it are required to register for a university diploma offered by 13 French universities where they study not only exegesis, but also philosophy and religion." Although attending these courses would "improve the *imams*' knowledge of France," the ambassador cautioned: "let's be clear: speaking French does not simply mean to be able to live normally; imams must also be able to engage in philosophical debates, which is more difficult than communicating about material questions." The ambassador did not specify or ask which religious "exegesis" was taught the *imams* in the French universities involved in their training, but wished to reassure the senators about the seriousness with which Algeria was taking the language question: "French is an essential subject on the national exam that the forty or so religion studies graduates must take to be selected for France." Casting doubt on the French senators' project to create "an Islam of France or a French Islam," he preferred "to speak of a tolerant Islam that teaches love and living together":

Instead of organizing a religion, which you do not feel obligated to do
with other religions, you could perhaps—and I say this in all humility—
ensure that Muslims in this country [France], who are also French citizens, are able to practice their religion decently and with dignity.

With this jab, the ambassador wished to implicitly convey to the senators that
the roots of the Islam they seek to eradicate may lie in their obliviousness to
the conditions under which Muslims practice, which include not only a lack
of decent space in which to pray, decried by Muslims, but implicitly a socio-
political as well as an economic climate hostile to Muslims. In other words,
before France could think of changing Islam, it should think of changing how
it deals with Muslims.

To a question concerning the payment of imams, the ambassador revealed
that salaries vary with the level of qualification of an imam: "an imam principal professor," who holds a doctorate is paid 2, 898 euros a month; "a
principal imam," who holds an MA earns 2,697 euros; and "an imam mou-
derrès" (or teaching imam), whose qualification is not defined, earns 2,324
euros. Other *imams* are adjuncts and thus paid according to the number of
prayers they lead, and earn between 740 and 1,481 euros a month. All *imams*
receive health benefits paid by the Algerian state. Interestingly, the ambassador explained that Algeria, being an oil-producing country with a fluctuating
revenue, was experiencing difficulty keeping its funding even at its present
level, unlike Morocco which finances the building of mosques as well as their
management through a foundation. To the senator's insistence on knowing
whether Algeria controls the contents of the *imam*'s "sermons," the ambassador remarked:

Jihadists did not come from Algerian, Moroccan, Tunisian, or Turkish
mosques. Look elsewhere: in the improvised places of worship, in garages,
on the Internet, in brief wherever anonymous and dangerous people take
advantage of young people's credulity. It is in these places that the cancer
that is currently eating up at French society has started to spread.[55]

This description of the exchange between the French senate commission of
information on the nature and extent of Algeria's role in the management of
Islam in France reveals two significant perspectives on the issue: on France's
side, extremism and the political "radicalization" of young Muslims is fostered by Islam. Algeria, even if it agrees with the senators' assessment may
not be trusted. However, it might contribute to the establishment of a French
Islam that would be under the control of the French government. Eliciting
Algeria's cooperation in training *imams* in French and in the language of
laïcité is not simply seen, from the senators' perspective, as a prelude towards
establishing an Islam that does not breed extremism, but as a way of influencing the practice of Islam in Algeria proper. Hence, even though Algeria is a

partner in the task of influencing the practice of Islam among Muslims in France, it potentially offers a terrain in which to bring about a different kind of Islam that would be in agreement with the one France wishes to establish.

The senators' question seeking to determine the impact of training imams in the French version of *laïcité* on Algeria after their return home, resonates with, but also transcends, president Emanuel Macron's ambitious program to create "a French Islam" ("*un Islam de France*"—literally "an Islam of France"), or more properly speaking an Islam *for* France. Macron's program is multi-pronged yet deployed on two axes: the "organization of Muslim worship in France;" and "the challenging relationship between Islam and the Republic."[56] The former involves the systematic training in *laïcité*, French history, and law of "all those in charge of [Muslim] worship." These include *imams* and chaplains in prisons and the military, Muslims servicing hospitals, and representatives of Muslim communities.[57] Furthermore, the teaching of religion (in French, *le fait religieux*, or "the religious fact") in school, which traditionally the Republic does not offer in its public schools, must be revisited and developed. As for the second axis of the project, it consists essentially in making the new French Islam independent of the country of origin through the elaboration of a "theology" for its practitioners, "adapted to the French context and not after that of the countries of [Muslims'] origin." This is the task the state farmed out to the *Fondation de l'Islam de France* (The Foundation of French Islam), though it was slow to materialize. Importantly, it consists of the development of a system of knowledge about Islam as well as its dissemination, including research on "Islamology," guiding "Muslim scouts of France," etc. Parenthetically, Muslim scouts of France are organized by an Algerian NGO, a branch of the Algerian *'Alawi* Sufi order, based in the city of Mostaganem. If training represents the technical side of the project of bringing about a French Islam—a system of knowledge of Islam, its articulation, what it leaves out and what it includes—its development and promotion aim for the constitution of Muslim subjects. The new Muslim subjects will think of themselves not as French Muslims, as both Muslims and French, as French Catholics are,[58] but as French secular Muslims, or possibly French reform Muslims. Their Islamicity will have been sanitized and structured to fit the needs of the French Republic. This means according to a commentator, engaging in "identity hygiene."[59] Interestingly, this new Muslim subject will have been constituted, according to Macron, with the help of French academics, as well as "representatives of all religions for I strongly believe that we must take our inspiration from our history, the history of Catholics and that of Protestants."[60] The French president may be clumsily taking the Church as a model for the mosque. However, the French Republic did not attempt to rewrite the New Testament as French politicians have proposed be done with the Quran. Furthermore, the French Republic protects the free exercise of religion, whereas it is actively involved in the interpretation and practice of Islam, if not the very idea of Islam.

Revealing of the confusion as well as the high-pitched climate in France in its combat against "radicalization," is Macron's assertion that through his program, France itself will be able "to *rediscover* [emphasis added] what is at the heart of laïcité, to believe or not to believe, in order to preserve *national cohesion* [emphasis added] and the possibility of freedom of conscience." This begs the question whether freedom of conscience is ensured through the teaching of a new theology, which normally is the task of a Church or a mosque, not the state. Although this de-structuring and rebuilding of ortho-dox Islam is frequently presented as a program of saving an ideal Islam from distortions, it occurs in an intellectual as well as political milieu that is hostile to the notion that Islam, as it is known, cannot be tolerated without being rewritten. For instance, a group of 300 notable political figures as well as artists, among whom were singer Charles Aznavour and actor Gérard Depardieu, using the trope of anti-semitism, called for the rewriting of a *sura* in the Quran.[61]

On the Algerian side, the management of Islam for the benefit of the French Republic is fraught with problems, symbolism, and laden with his-torical significance. The ambassador's annoyed reaction to whether a "French Islam" was possible, was captured by his choice of word "this interminable [in French, "*sempiternelle*"] question." This indeed was a burning question in France's colonial history with severe consequences on Algerian culture.[62] However, in practice, when individual Algerians in the past wished to become naturalized, they encountered numerous obstacles that revealed the purely ideological character of secularity. The policy failed to create an Algerian Islam suited to colonial rule since its practical purpose was containment and control, not the protection of the freedom of worship, an obligation of a republican state.

It is noteworthy that the Algerian state did not oppose the French decision to train *imams* in *laïcité*. On the one hand, it had to comply with the new French law. On the other hand, it could not relinquish its role in the Algerian immigrant Muslim community. Since other countries, Morocco, Tunisia, and Turkey are actively involved in the organization of their Muslim community, Algeria as the country of origin of two million immigrants could not simply bow out. However, Algeria shares with France the view that acts of violence committed in the name of Islam find their source in Islam.

Algeria's accord with France is perhaps the most extensive in its scope, but is not the only one. Algeria has also passed an agreement in February 2016, with the United States, "to present its deradicalization experience." A dele-gation of seven *imams* from the Berkeley Center for International Relations at the University of California, Los Angeles, came to Algeria for a study tour. Apart from attending a "workshop on religious dialogue," and leading pray-ers in a mosque, the American imams visited a number of mosques in the capital city as well as the *zawiya* Belqaidia in the city of Oran.[63] The inclu-sion of a *zawiya* in the visit speaks of the role that the state has played in encouraging centers of popular Sufism as a force of social quietism. Algeria was also discussing an agreement for experience-sharing with Italy in 2017, which ultimately signed one with Morocco.[64] Although Morocco borrowed from Algeria the idea of forming a corps of *murshidat* (albeit for a more expansive purpose), it has led Algeria in its active policy of advocating a view and practice of Islam aimed at preventing what it perceives as extremism.

The Algerian state cooperation with France in its program of organizing a "French Islam" is strategic but also intrinsically contradictory. On the one hand, Algeria seeks to cooperate with France, a country on which it has increasingly relied for cultural, economic, and security matters. On the other hand, by participating in the French program, it also gives itself free rein in its multi-pronged management of Islam at home as described above. Importantly, it gives short shrift to the functional equivalent of *laïcité*: the promotion and protection of citizenship rights. While the Algerian state violates the principle of equality of all citizens regardless of sex inscribed in its own constitution, it stresses a popular conception of Islam, even if it is inimical to women. To reiterate, in France, the Algerian state actively supports the French view that Islam must be taught in the political framework of *laïcité*, in Algeria it undermines women's citizenship (a civil notion) in the name of cultural specificity. Notably, the accord between the two countries obviates the question of women entirely. In France, the veiling policies clearly indicate, even if mistakenly, that the French state prohibits expressions of religious cultural identity. In Algeria, the state promotes religious cultural identity as its de facto justification for creating and protecting a religious cultural sphere in which the constitutional right to women's equality with men as citizens is suspended. The difference between the two states, the Algerian and the French, is "culture." In France, culture must be protected from Islam, in Algeria, culture must be protected from the constitution at the cost of infringing upon the rights of women.

The Algero-French convention reveals the deliberateness with which the Algerian state adopted a domestic policy specifically aimed at advocating for and safeguarding a religious culture in which women must be contained. The state's gendered cultural decision is reflected in the occasional police response to violence against women. During Ramadan 2018, a woman in *hijab* was jogging before the break of the fast near Algiers. A man passing by assaulted her physically and derided her for her purportedly irreverent religious act. He reminded her that "your place is in the kitchen." When she complained to the police, she was blamed for her plight. She subsequently posted her experience on the Internet, igniting a storm of indignation from women as well as men. Within days, women (and men) in a number of cities staged group jogging in solidarity with the aggrieved woman.[65]

Referring to this incident, a lawyer and activist interpreted it in light of the constitution's principle that "Islam is the religion of the state." From her perspective, the dual nature of the individual's status in the constitution as "subject-citizen and believer" is fraught with problems. As a carrier of rights, "the subject is responsible [before the law] as an individual":

> However, the believer is accountable to the community [of believers] to which she belongs. The passage from the believer to the free citizen is also the passage from a diffuse responsibility [in French *diluée*, meaning "diluted"] to the community to a non-diffuse responsibility.

For women their situation is further complicated since they have a "dichotomous status as objects (under the tutelage of men) in the family code, and subjects-qua-free citizens in the constitution. The subject [in the constitution] is transformed into an object [in the family code]." Hence women are doubly objectified. Returning to the jogger, the man who assaulted her drew his empowerment from the state's definition of itself as having a religion. The alienation of "women as 'objects' [meaning objectified subjects]" also explains "the family code's acceptance of *fatiha* marriage (religious marriage), derived from Islamic law, which gives primacy to religious over civil marriage under the cover of civil law in order to diminish women's [legal] capacity."[66] Although insightful, such an interpretation ignores the quasi legal status of *fatiha* marriage. It is religiously permissible, but is not registered in a civil court, and thus the law does not give it primacy. To be recognized by a civil court, it requires an additional procedure, which a woman must engage if she so wishes when her husband leaves her or refuses to accept the paternity of a child issued from the marriage. It is the functional equivalent of common law marriage. To be valid as a religious marriage, it requires the presence of the bride, her father or legal guardian, two witnesses, and a symbolic dowry.[67] The practice is a source of serious troubles. A middle-aged woman entrepreneur contracted *fatiha* marriage but her husband refused to recognize their son. At the hospital where she gave birth, a nurse urged her to sign a consent form to put her son up for adoption. She refused. She introduced her son to me as "my *fatiha* son, Walid," and addressing him "you have my name and all is well, right?"[68]

Islam between Algeria and Morocco

The comparison between Algeria's and France's approaches to an Islam on command is incomplete without a comparison with Morocco. Indeed, all three countries are engaged in a similar task: how to promote an Islam impervious to "radicalization." However, Morocco has been more radical in its religious domestic policy than Algeria and more in tune with France's hard line approach. Morocco's policy of deradicalization has specifically enlisted some women as active allies while targeting others as victims. Consequently, a comparison with Algeria would shed light on the process through which women's path to change is either co-opted or diverted.

Unlike Algeria which experienced a ten-year civil war pitting Islamists and state, Morocco has had episodic brushes with political Islam. Its own faith-based opposition had operated underground and had been severely repressed throughout the reign of King Hassan II, before some of its leaders were allowed to enter the political field after the death of the monarch in 1999. However, Morocco's socio-political stability has been secured through a combination of geopolitical maneuvers, including alignment with powerful Western countries (such as the United States and France), and its role as a player in a United States Middle Eastern policy resting on support for conservative governments.[69] On May 16, 2003, twelve suicide bombers belonging to a Salafi Jihadist group named Groupe Islamique Combatant Marocain (GICM), born out of Moroccan recruits fighting in Afghanistan in the 1990s, killed upward of 45 people in the city of Casablanca. Other attacks followed in 2006, 2007, and 2008.[70] In 2016, the government foiled an attack planned by ten women members of ISIL (Islamic State in the Levant), four of whom were teenagers.[71] Immediately after the 2003 bombings, the Moroccan government devised an aggressive anti-terrorist strategy combining social measures (poverty alleviation and job creation), a determined security policy, and an ambitious religion reeducation program. This program is the centerpiece of an ideological warfare whose long-term outcome has yet to be assessed. Its scope is as vast as its targets are far flung; it trains not only Moroccan citizens, but also Muslims anywhere in the world. In an echo of France's war strategy in Algeria in 1954–1962, which featured behavior modification through colonial propaganda specifically focusing on women, the program prominently features women among its target population. It is this (much publicized) female audience that gives the program its significance in the global "war on terror," just as it highlights the appropriation of feminist discourses and ideals for the benefit of the state.

Briefly, the Moroccan religion education and reeducation "training" program began with women. In 2006, three years after the Casablanca bombings, the government started to train a contingent of fifty *murshidat*[72] (Algeria, it will be recalled, had started in 1991) in its effort to reach a population that had been ignored—a new and more liberal family code had already been adopted in 2004. In addition, in 2006 the Moroccan government appointed 36 *'alimat*, or women theologians to sit on *'Ulema* councils.[73] In 2008, the League of Ulema, now renamed the Mohammadia League (*Al-Rabita al-Mohammadiyya*) sponsored a "women in Islam" group presided by noted Islamic feminist, Asma Lamrabet,[74] officially making the study of women a royal affair. However, it was not until 2015 that the Mohammed VI Institute for Training Imams, *Murshidin* and *Murshidat* was inaugurated. However, just like in Algeria, Moroccan *murshidat* cannot become *imams*. Unlike Algeria, Moroccan *murshidat* operate among Moroccan Muslims abroad.[75] The king clearly identified their strategic role in Moroccan *wasatiya* Islam as "making possible the emergence of a new management of religious assets (*les biens*), capable of re-reading the facts of revelation in light of historical Reason."[76] In disseminating its normative Islam, the Institute passed agreements to train *imams* in seven African countries including neighboring Tunisia, as well as Europe. The Institute, which in 2015 hosted 447 students from Africa and 23 from France is built as a self-sufficient campus sprawled over seven square acres, with the capacity "to train up to 1,000 students at a time."[77] An extension covering 10,000 square meters and featuring, among others things, an 1,100-seat auditorium was added in 2017 ostensibly to accommodate growing demand.[78] The goal of the Institute is to "instill the values of Morocco's open, moderate form of Islam, based on the Maliki rite and Sunni Sufism, in the next generation of Muslim religious leaders (imams) and preachers (morchidines and morchidates) from across the region and the world." Ultimately the Institute aims for a "counter-radicalization."[79] Hence, the strategy of the Institute is at once pre-emptive as well as corrective. It is political (its purpose is inscribed in national and global politics), ideological (since the Institute functions as the ideological arm of the "war on terror"), as well as psychological (as it engages in an educational program tailored to shape a docile individual Muslim trained to be different from the Muslims defined as extremists).

Within this context, the (inevitable) inclusion of women, much publicized in the local and foreign media, supported by conferences on the merit of "Islamic feminism," disseminated in academic studies, with local and foreign NGO funding establishes *wasatiya* Islam as a new knowledge in the process of becoming normalized. In explaining the inclusion of women in the state's anti-terrorism strategy, a member of the Moroccan parliament, Loubna Amhair, reviewed the various reasons why women were attracted to "extremism" as suicide bombers, and concluded: "the feelings resulting from marginalization, discrimination, and gender inequality are often used by terrorist groups who push women to extremism as a form of empowerment."[80] However, another and possibly more compelling reason motivating women suicide bombers is "revenge for a family member against those perceived to be the administrator [the state]." The parliamentarian notes that women can be empowered in a different way, by being involved "in the decision-making process, particularly in terms of development policies and strategies that deal with extremism and anti-terrorism initiatives." The question is whether a woman who lost a relative to the aggressive state anti-terror policy can feel empowered by the Institute's religious training, which attributes her anger and behavior to her purportedly erroneous religious beliefs. More important, what kind of training, short of brainwashing, would empower her to adopt the ideas promoted by the Institute? This question goes to the heart of this book: how are women socialized into acceptance of the cultural turn? In Morocco women appear as targets of religious re-education as well as its agents. Their training is meant to woe them from those who "empowered" them to stake their lives for real or imaginary change, by entrusting them with positions of "executive leadership." Can these women be re-empowered by adopting a different perspective on themselves and their religion? By the same token, the Institute wishes women to become active agents in the constitution of new believing bodies holding the place assigned them in the global understanding of the relationship between Islam and peace. In the end, compared to Morocco, Algeria's effort at promoting a "Maghrebin Islam" pales before the scope and ambitions of the Moroccan experience. However, both seize upon women as the linchpin in their cultural strategy: Algeria favors customs over rights, including those inscribed in religious texts; Morocco squarely enrolls women in a religious ideology touted as egalitarian.[81]

Algeria and Morocco are not the only countries enlisting women to disseminate a "moderate" Islam. Egypt started its own *murshidat* program in 2006. It too does not allow them to be *imams*. In a test of its moderation, the state-sponsored Islam ran into difficulty with the Islam it sought to suppress when *murshidat* in *niqab* presented it with a conundrum: allowing women to live by their Muslim conviction. In a move reminiscent of France's interpretation of *niqab* as a sign of proselytizing, the Egyptian state, backed by al-Azhar University, which considers the niqab a custom not a religious requirement, reassigned the *murshidat* to administrative tasks, thus preventing them from preaching.[82]

This chapter pointed to the evolution of the Algerian state's orientation toward religion as a source of continuity in cultural values. The creation of a relatively autonomous sphere in which the constitutional right to a gender-neutral citizenship could be suspended in order for family law, which spells out gender inequality in marriage, divorce, child custody and inheritance, be implemented. Since the Civil War, the state has enlarged this sphere through an active multi-pronged policy, *wasatiya* Islam, that clearly defines what Islam is in Algeria, establishes an institutional setting for it, and trains its personnel. By the same token, in light of the salience of women's rights in international machineries as well as the rise of Islamic feminism, the state selects features of Islamic law (such as *khul'* divorce) to enforce while restricting their use. In the end, the state prefers to abide by a literal reading of religious texts. However, the Algerian state's cooperation with France's policy of control and (incipient) reform of Islam in order to ward off the "radicalization" of young French Muslims reveals in all its starkness the purely ideological use of culture in justifying the maintenance of gender inequality in family matters. The state's active religious policy is focused on politics, political stability, resistance to oppositional demands for change, and cooperation with France in fighting "extremism." In the convention signed with France women are not mentioned albeit at home the Algerian state creates a special corps of *murshidat* designated especially for them. Where religious literacy is taught, it is meant to reconcile women to their status. Sensitizing women to their "rights" in Islam (the *murshidat*'s stated goal) is a compensatory gesture for the state's sponsored violation of their civil rights in family law as well as the constitution. By

the same token, the participation of women in the religious domain independently of the state cultural policy is in itself an opportunity for women to be
actively engaged in a field generally perceived as the monopoly of men.

Notes

1 *Waqf* or *habus* in Islamic law refers to property (usually real estate) donated by an
   individual to a mosque or other religious institution. Such property cannot be sold
   or bought. An individual may also bequeath part or all of his property to a third
   party to enjoy but is prohibited to sell it.
2 It is true that the Civil War brought together young people holding different views
   and interpretations of Islam. Some of them had started their engagement as
   volunteers fighting alongside the Taliban against the Soviet support for the Afghan
   government in the 1980s. Among the various factions fighting in the Civil War,
   some young men also adopted *shi'i* practices such as *mut'a* (temporary) marriage
   that were barely known in Algeria, in order to legitimate forced sexual unions with
   (frequently kidnapped) women. However, the Civil War transcended such occur-
   rences as it pitted state forces, some of which have been accused of committing acts
   of violence targeting women, against those of their faith-based opponents.
3 Liamine Zeroual was president of Algeria in 1995–1999 (during the Civil War); he
   resigned in April 27, 1999.
4 As a matter of precision, the President of the Haut Conseil Islamique, Bouabdallah Ghoulamallah, indicates that he approached President Zeroual's adviser to
   draw his attention to the 1997 decree which had yet to be implemented. Zeroual
   asked Ghoulamallah to propose names of persons who might lead the new structure. Ghoulamallah proposed three names to choose from. Interview with Bouabdallah Ghoulamallah, Algiers, July 10, 2018.
5 Ibid. Through *khul'*, a wife is permitted to obtain a divorce in exchange for a
   compensation paid to her husband.
6 Ibid.
7 Interview with Noureddine Mohammedi, Director of Islamic Orientation and
   Quranic Education, Ministry of Religious Affairs and Waqfs, Algiers, July 12,
   2018.
8 Interview with Bouabdallah Ghoulamallah, Algiers, July 10, 2018. The universities
   in question focus on Islamic learning.
9 Amazigh language denotes a stock language bringing together regional spoken
   variations; it was declared an official language in Algeria in 2011.
10 Interview with Noureddine Mohammedi, Algiers, July 12, 2018.
11 In this regard, a man of 36 I interviewed on June 29, 2019 in Algiers mentioned
   that his mother learned the Quran at one of these instruction sessions and started
   teaching it to other women in the city of Bouira.
12 *Fatwas* are usually issued by a 15-member council of learned men at the HCI.
13 Interview with Noureddine Mohammedi, Algiers, July 12, 2018.
14 Ibid. Mr. Mohammedi points out that the concept of *murshida* was developed in
   Algeria, before it was borrowed by Morocco.
15 Ibid.
16 Interview with a *murshida ra'isiya*, Islamic Orientation and Quranic Education,
   Ministry of Religious Affairs and Waqfs, Algiers, July 12, 2018.
17 Ibid.
18 Ibid. Article 48 of the official legal registry (*al jarida al ra'isiya lil Jamahiriya al
   jaza'iriya*, no. 73, December 8, 2018), details the functions of the *murshida diniya*
   as follows: "Teach women the principles of Islamic sciences as well as the holy
   Quran in mosques and Quranic schools; participate in mosque-sponsored social

activities; the eradication of illiteracy among women; religious action (*i'ada*) in the [principles of] education (*tarbiya*) of women and the family; the preservation of the religious unity and cohesiveness of the community; instruction for the preparation for the ritual of pilgrimage as well as the '*omra*; and assistance in the protection of the mother and child."

19 In her "*Al murshida ad-diniya*" (document in Arabic provided to the author), Mrs. K. (name withheld at the respondent's request) at the Ministry of Religious Affairs and Waqfs, dates this after 1995, during the Civil War.

20 The official decree published in the official legal registry (*al jarida al ra'isiya lil jamhouriya al jaza'iriya*, no. 73, December 8, 2018), details the functions of both the *murshida diniya* and *murshida diniya ra'isiya*.

21 Ibid, article 49.

22 One of the demands of unionized imams, who staged sit-ins on and off since 2018 before the Ministry of Religious Affairs, as well as the General Union of Algerian Workers (UGTA) was, in addition to status upgrade and salary increase, to "decriminalize" their profession. See *Le Quotidien d'Oran*, July 28, 2019.

23 Figure provided by a *murshida ra'isiya* at the Ministry of Religious Affairs and Waqfs, Algiers, June 19, 2019.

24 Interview with three *murshidat ra'isiyat*, Ministry of Religious Affairs and Waqfs, Algiers, June 19, 2019.

25 Ibid.

26 For an explanation this (*qiwama*) *sura* see, among others, Azizah Al Hibri, "Islamic Herstory or How Did We Ever Get into This Mess?" *Women's Studies International Forum* 5, no. 2 (1982): 207–219.

27 Interview with a *murshida ra'isiya*, Ministry of Religious Affairs and Waqfs, Algiers, July 12, 2018.

28 Interview with three *murshidat ra'isiyat*, Ministry of Religious Affairs and Waqfs, Algiers, June 19, 2019.

29 Ibid.

30 Interview with two *murshidat*, Ministry of Religious Affairs and Waqf, Algiers, July 1, 2019. Literally "*wasatiya*" means "of the middle," the Islam of the mean, not the extremes. Abdelhamid Ibn Badis (1889–1940) was one of the leading religious figures in nineteenth-century Algeria who advocated a rejuvenation of Islam (freed of superstitious and fossilized customs) as the foundation of a national and linguistic identity.

31 Interview with A. and K., *murshidat ra'isiyat*, Ministry of Religious Affairs and Waqfs, Algiers, July 1, 2019.

32 Ibid.

33 Ibid.

34 Discussion with F.T., Algiers July 11, 2018.

35 Interview with F.L., Algiers, June 29, 2018.

36 Interview with M.T. and S., Mostaganem, June 28, 2018.

37 "La France et l'Algérie s'accordent pour former les imams à la laïcité," *Le Figaro*, December 19, 2014, www.lefigaro.fr, accessed April 24, 2019.

38 Ibid.

39 Anne-Bénédicte Hoffner, "Les imams algériens en France y poursuivront leur formation," *Urbi et Orbi, La documentation catholique*, December 23, 2014, www.la-croix.com/Religion/Actualite/Les-imams-algeriens-envoyes-en-France-y-poursuivront-leur-formation-2014-12-23-1257940, accessed April 25, 2019.

40 Ibid.

41 Ibid. The Algerian daily, *Le Quotidien d'Oran*, reported on April 21, 2019 that the Grande Mosquée of Paris had welcomed 49 *imams* assigned for a period of four years who would be trained after taking a test of their fluency in French. The article indicates that there are twenty-five universities involved in the training of *imams*, which include the University of Paris 1 Sorbonne-Panthéon. The University Diploma is called in French "Diplôme d'Université République et

Religions (DU)." It was designed by the Office of Religions (*Cultes*) of the Ministry of the Interior and co-sponsored by the European Institute of the Sciences of Religion (IESR) of the Ecole Pratique des Hautes Etudes (EPHE). It is part of a broader "civic and civil" education and training program required of chaplains in the military, hospitals, and prisons. One of its objectives is to train personnel in the role of laïcité in the exercise of the rights that guarantee freedom of religion, and of conscience. See "DU République et Religions-Faculté Jean Monet," accessed April 26, 2019, www.jm.u-psud.fr/du-republique-religion. In Paris, the degree is offered at the Jean Monet Faculty–Paris Sud, as well as the University of Paris Sorbonne-Panthéon, among others. Versions of this diploma concentrate on Islam specifically as is the case in the French colony of Mayotte. See www. univ-mayotte.fr/fr/formation/formation-continue/diplomes-universitaires/du-va leurs-de-la-republique-et-religions.html.

42 Hoffner, "*les imams algériens.*"
43 Ibid.
44 Ibid. According to this researcher, the new Islamic universities have graduated a number of Salafi imams.
45 Ibid.
46 Interview with three *murshidat*, Ministry of Religious Affairs and Waqfs, Algiers, June 19, 2019.
47 Created by former Minister of the Interior, Bernard Cazeneuve, one year after the November 13, 2015 attacks attributed to ISIS on a number of sites, including the Bataclan concert hall in Paris, The *Fondation de l'Islam de France* in Paris, "was born principally out of the will to combat, through knowledge and culture, the reductive and Manichean Salafi ideology which fosters jihadist terrorism." See https:// fondationdelislamdefrance.fr, accessed April 26, 2019.
48 The Algerian press reports that for Algerian *imams*, to be sent in France is a sought-after opportunity not only because their salary, paid in euro, is higher (depending on their education) than at home, but also, they value practicing in France. Some manage to obtain a permanent contract and do not return home; others go underground and live off fellow Muslims' generosity. There are cases of independent imams who make the trip to France on their own, and seek employment with the Mosquée de Paris. One *imam* purportedly indicated that "I live my religion better in France than in Algeria." *TSA* (Tout sur l'Algérie), "Le business ramadhanesque des imams en France," accessed May 16, 2019, www.tsa-algerie.com/societe.
49 AFP, "Les imams algériens envoyés en France devront 'dépoussiérer' l'Islam," *Le Point*, January 18, 2015, www.lepoint.fr/societe/les-imams-envoyes-en-france-devront-depoussierer.l.islam-18-01-2015-189753923.php, accessed April 28, 2019.
50 See my *Torture and the Twilight of Empire, From Algiers to Baghdad* (Princeton, NJ: Princeton University Press, 2017), ch. 8.
51 Sénat, Travaux Parlementaires. Mission d'Information. "Comptes Rendus de la MI Organisation, Place et Financement de l'Islam en France," Audition de S.E ambassadeur d'Algérie en France, Tuesday, May 31, 2016, (Hearing of His Excellency Amar Bendjama, Ambassador of Algeria to France), www.senat.fr, accessed April 21, 2019. "MI" refers to Mission.
52 Ibid.
53 The ambassador revealed that financial support went to the maintenance of the mosques to bring them up to the local French standards, and seed money for associations. The total amount was less than 4 million euros allocated five years earlier to about 50 associations.
54 Daech is another name for ISIS.
55 Ibid.
56 Anne-Bénédicte Hoffner, "Emmanuel Macron face au défi de l'"Islam de France"" *La Croix*, November 2, 2018, www.la-croix.com/rpint/articl/1200912947, accessed 3 May 2019.

57 Macron notes that the personnel teaching about Islam, be they *imams* or educators, not only "lacks mastery of the French language, French history, and law, but also theology." Ibid. France's program to create a French Islam finds strong support in the banker, consultant, and on occasion writer, Hakim El Karoui, a son of a Tunisian father and a French mother, who was purportedly brought up in both Islam and the protestant religions.

58 Frank Frégosi suggests in this respect that Islam is a challenge to French identity which is stated as based on "primarily Christian civilization and republican values." *L'Islam dans la laïcité* (Paris: Arthème Fayard, 2012), II.

59 Adlène Meddi, "Laïcité en France: les vrais défis de Macron," *Middle East Eye*, January 15, 2018, www.middleeasteye.net, accessed May 3, 2019.

60 Hoffner, "Emmanuel Macron face au défi de l' 'Islam de France'."

61 L'Obs, "300 Personnalités signent un manifeste contre le 'nouvel anti-sémitisme' en France," *Le Nouvel Observateur*, April 22, 2019, http://nouvelobs.com, accessed May 17, 2019.

62 The colonial government had continuously fought to bring Islam under control in colonial Algeria. It used a multi-pronged technique, which included the seizure of mosques' property as a means to deprive them of financial autonomy; militarily subdued heads of Sufi orders who fought against its occupation as it did with the Emir Abd-El-Kader; watched over and actively contributed to the decline of Sufi orders deemed unfriendly; closely monitored imams' Friday lectures; turned imams into lower level salaried functionaries; and even sought to replace a consecrated formula usually recited in mosques to praise the Caliph with a homage to France as the legitimate leader of a Muslim country. The colonial linguistic policy of replacing Arabic with French as the official language of Algeria as well as the language of instruction in schools; and the disenfranchisement of Algerians unless they relinquished their "personal status," a euphemism for religion, framed the control apparatus. The colonial religious policy was also elaborated in the name of a form of *laïcité* that predated the 1905 law.

63 See www.aps.dz/algerie/72989-l-algerie-expose-son-eperience-a-des-imams-america ins-en-matiere-de-deradicalisation, accessed October 1, 2020; www.aps.dz/algerie/ 72989-l-algerie-expose-son-experience-a-des-imams-americains-en-matiere-de-dera dicalisation, accessed July 28, 2019.

64 See "Algeria, Italy Willing to Sign Agreement on Imam-Training," July 10, 2017, https://algerianembassy.org, accessed July 29, 2019; "Morocco Will Train Italian Muslims in Tuscany, December 14, 2017, www.oasiscenter.eu/en/morocco-will-train-italian-imams; and "Italian Minister Calls for Extension of Imam Training Partnership With Fes; Al Qarawiyyn Univeristy," www.moroccoworldnews.com/2018/02/ 240901/italian-minister-calls-extension-imam-training-partnership-fes-al-qarawiyyin-university

65 "Vidéo. Algérie. Une jeune femme algérienne agressée pour footing en plein Ramadan," *Le360,* June 5, 2018, https://fr.le360.ma/monde/video-algerie-une-jeune-femme-agressee-pour-footing-en-plein-ramadan-167216. The woman, Rym, said "I would like to know if it is a sin (*haram*) to exercise before the break of the fast." See also "Algérie: L'agression d'une joggeuse en plein Ramadan secoue le pays," *Le Point, Afrique,* 12 June 2018, http://www.lepoint.fr/afrique/afrique-l-agression-d-une-joggeuse-en-plein-ramadan-secoue-le-pays-12-06-2018-2226445_3826.php; "Agression d'une joggeuse: 300 algériennes ont couru à Alger pour leur liberté," *Franceinfo: Afrique,* June 11, 2018.

66 Interview with Nadia Zai, Algiers, July 4, 2018.

67 Under *fatiha* marriage, a father can recognize his child. But if he does not and contests the marriage, the child will not bear his name.

68 Interview with Nacéra, Algiers, July 11, 2018.

69 The Rationale for a US–Morocco Strategic Partnership includes economic, trade and military relations, as well as Middle Eastern foreign policy alignment. It also

stresses the "shared values" between the two countries and Morocco's cooperation in fighting terrorism and maintaining "intelligence relationships with the FBI and the CIA." See www.morrocoonthemove.com/wpcontent/uploads/2013/07/FINAL_StratDialRationale091012.pdf, accessed June 20,2020. See also Moroccan American Center of Policy, "Towards a New Moroccan-US Strategic Partnership," Nov. 2012. Appended to this document is a publication by the Center for Contemporary Arab Studies on "Moroccan Islam authored by Kenneth Honerkamp and Fr. Michael Calabria," www.moroccononthemove.com/wp-content/uploads/2013/11/Briefing-Papers-Towards-a-New-Morocco-US-Strategic-Partnership.pdf, accessed 20 June 2020.

70 UNHCR, *Country Report on Terrorism 2007—Morocco*, April 30, 2008, refworld.org, accessed July 29, 2019.
71 James Rothwell, "Morocco Arrests Ten Female ISIL Suicide Bombers Who Planned to Strike on Election Day," *The Telegraph*, Oct. 5, 2016, www.telegraph.co.uk/news/2016/10/05/morocco-arrests-ten-female-isil-suicide-bombers-who-planned-to-s2/?WT.mc_id=tmg_share_em, accessed July 29, 2019.
72 Some evidence suggests that at least initially the educational level of some of the Moroccan *murshidat* may have been lower than that of their Algerian counterparts. See Fatima Sadiqi, *Moroccan Feminist Discourses* (New York: Palgrave Macmillan, 2014), 146.
73 Souad Eddouada and Renata Pepicelli, "Morocco: Towards an 'Islamist State Feminism'," *Critique internationale* 46, no. 1 (2010): 7–11, www.cairn-int.info/revue-critique-internationale-2010-1page-87.htm, accessed June 16, 2020 (pages are numbered differently on Cairn).
74 Ibid., 7.
75 Sonia Sarah Lipsyc and Belkacem Benzenine, "L'accès des femmes aux fonctions religieuses publiques dans le judaïsme et l'Islam: de l'exclusion à 'l'intégration'", in Lisa Anteby-Yemini, eds., *Juives et musulmannes de la Méditerranée* (Paris: Editions Karthala/MMSH, 2014), 114 and 116.
76 Quoted in ibid., 114.
77 Moroccan American Center for Policy, "King Mohammed VI Inaugurates International Imam Training Center in Rabat in Push to Promote Moderate Islam," March 27, 2015, www.https://globenewswire.com, accessed July 29, 2019.
78 "Imam Training, Key Instrument of Morocco's Religious Diplomacy," *The North African Post*, October 21, 2017, https://northafricapost.com, accessed July 29, 2019.
79 Ibid. "*Morchidines*" and "*morchidates*" are French spellings of "*murshidin*" and "*murshidat*." Adding an s is redundant since the Arabic term is already in the plural.
80 Loubna Amhair, "How to Prevent the Radicalization of Women: The Moroccan Model," *Morocco World News*, February 23, 2016, www.moroccoworldnews.com/2016/02/180479/how-to-prevent-the-radicalization-of-women-the-moroccan-model, accessed July 29, 2019.
81 In the wake of the passage of the 2003 Family Code, Moroccan women theologians and legal scholars invited by the king to lecture on women at Ramadan religious seminars in 2003–2006 stressed equity, and complementarity between women and men against the notion of equality dismissed as feminist. See Eddouada and Pepicelli, "Morocco: Towards an 'Islamic State Feminism'," 7–11. Fatima Sadiqi distinguishes between strands of Islamic feminism, some affiliated with faith-based parties, others unaffiliated. *Moroccan Feminist Discourses*, 144–146.
82 Lipsyc and Benzenine, "L'accès," 119–120. The incident delayed the recruitment of the promotion of *murshidat* for the following year.

3

MAGHREBIN ISLAM AND ITS GENDERED FUNCTIONS

The state's intervention strategy in the religious field to redefine an Algerian-qua-Maghrebin Islam rests on two pillars: (1) a trained staff (imams and *murshidat*) required to instill in women and men a *wasatiya* Islam as discussed in the previous chapter; (2) the revival and development of old popular Sufi orders acting (or implicitly encouraged to act) as intermediaries between the public and its elected representatives. If the first strategy targets women specifically, the second is ostensibly gender-blind. Nevertheless, it plays a multifaceted role in women's orientation towards change, which needs to be ascertained.

This chapter focuses on the largely unrecognized ways in which the revival of popular Sufi orders—located in *zawiyat* (pl. of *zawiya* in colloquial Arabic), characteristic of Maghrebin societies—affect women's turn to culture. These include the fostering of a cultural climate, which due to its pervasiveness, contributes to a culture of quiescence, sustained by a rekindled tradition of deference to (spiritual) authority, and oriented towards the symbolic legitimation of political power; a willed blurring of the boundaries between the personal, the religious, and the political; a re-ordering of priorities resulting in damping the urgency of reforms addressing gender inequality. These gendered consequences of the revival of popular Sufi orders on women are inextricably tied to the history of the relationship between political power and popular Sufism[1](which the state has since the 1990s strenuously reinterpreted and channeled to fit its view of religion as an instrument of governance). Hence, a brief examination of this history is needed before addressing the effects of the revival of popular Sufism on women.

Sufism

In the context of the "war on terror," Sufism has become synonymous with "moderate Islam," and at times even a separate Islam altogether somehow inimical to political interpretation or use. That Maghrebin governments or individual Muslims occasionally share this view hardly makes it more credible. Such a conception ignores the simple fact that, as an orientation to faith, Sufism is part and parcel of Islam and cannot be understood outside of the foundational principles of Islam. Although the esoteric component of Sufism has been spurned by Sunni (also referred to as "orthodox") Muslim theologians, as well as puritanical sects such as the Wahabi, the spirituality at the core of Sufism or its acceptance of the pillars of Islam do not make it any more authentic or purer than what is termed "radical" Islam.[2] Hence the view according to which Sufism is fundamentally "moderate" (e.g. opposed to a political understanding of the world) forces a dubious divide within Islam, between "political Islam" (assumed to breed "extremism" or "radicalism" purportedly through misinterpretation of the sacred texts) and Sufism understood (implicitly) as an authentic Islam, if not a religion in its own right, impervious to "radicalization," and in need of revival, restoration, and dissemination as an antidote to "extremism" and "terrorism."

Maghrebin-qua-Algerian Sufism

The mystical practices which developed in the Maghreb since the advent of Islam followed two distinct, albeit at times overlapping paths, one identified as Sufi, the other centered on the cultivation of saints. Prior to the fifteenth century, Sufism was an individual and ascetic search for union with the divine through a process of initiation that included esoteric practices. It typically emerged among individuals steeped in philosophical, theological and literary knowledge. Individual Sufi men who distinguished themselves by their ability to reach a state of quasi-transcendent spiritual knowledge were also considered saintly. Although some Sufi practitioners would seclude themselves from the local community to devote themselves to reaching union with the divine, others lived in centers of initiation called *zawiyat* (or *zwiy*; sing. *zawiya*), some of which doubled up as thriving crucibles of learning.[3] The charisma of a Sufi master (referred as "Sidi" in the Maghreb)[4] derived primarily from his spiritual attainments, including his capacity to "see" beyond the phenomenal world, his *ma'rifa*. Unlike Sufism, the mystical movement of *Marabutism* (in French transcription, *Maraboutisme*), arose out of a primarily rural tradition of holy men whose white or green mausoleums dot the Maghrebin countryside. A *murabit*, colloquially m'rabit (sing. of *murabitun*)[5] rendered among French orientalists as *Marabout,* was a man who, through piety, good deeds, and charisma was revered by the community and acquired the status of *wali* (saint) or *waliya* (fem.) as a number of women (although less than men) were also recognized as such.[6] His charisma resided in his powers of healing, social mediation, and intercession with God through prayer on behalf of individuals in need. The *murabit*'s charisma expressed in his *baraka,* or grace, enhanced the substance as well as symbolic value of everything he touched or said. Typically, notable masters would found or be claimed as founders of a *tariqa* (pl. *turuq*),[7] a brotherhood of sorts usually translated as "order," although its literal meaning is "a way" or "path." Initially saints came from all walks of life, some of whom were illiterate men who achieved union with the divine. With the expansion of the mystical movement, especially in the aftermath of the demise of Islam in the Iberian peninsula, which brought highly cultured mystics displaced from Andalusia to Algeria by way of Morocco, a new category of saints emerged, the shurfa (sing, *sharif*), who claimed their ascendency from Prophet Muhammad.[8] Subsequently, sainthood became hereditary as noble lineage formed the Maghrebin mystical movement's social legitimacy.[9] Although having different origins and practices, and for a while different audiences, Sufism and *Maraboutism* slowly converged into one large mystical movement.[10] In time, the melding of the two meant a loss of knowledge beyond that of the sacred text or language; it also meant a relative impoverishment of Sufism as a form of enlightenment in favor of a more folk-oriented, ritualistic, and less cosmic attitude towards worship. At any rate, it is this convergence, this melding between the two strands of worship that gives Maghebin mysticism its own cachet (imperfectly) captured by the expression, "popular Sufism." The concept "popular" refers in this context to the shift in Maghrebin Sufism, from a privatized, and intellectualized mystical practice based on an elaborate initiation process to a more simplified practice accessible to the common person.[11] This did not mean that Sufism in its more intellectualized form ceased to exist. With the development of Sufi orders (the *khwan*) in the seventeenth century, Maghrebin mysticism took on its enduring characteristic form. Nevertheless the vocabulary used is still inadequate. If the label "*Maraboutism*" obscures the Sufi component (no matter its degree of elaboration) of the Maghrebin "mystique,"[12] "popular Sufism" obscures the mystical core of Sufism, which transcends the popular-intellectual divide. In this chapter, for convenience, the terms "mystical movement" and "popular Sufism" will be used interchangeably to refer to institutionalized practices occurring in and around *zawiyat*, usually lumped together in the political discourse as "Sufism."

This brief synopsis must be replaced in its national and geopolitical context. Maghrebin mysticism was not merely a spiritual or other-worldly, individual or collective endeavor. Its history was intertwined with geopolitical events just as it was with local socio-political events. Mystical movements were frequently involved in the defense of the faith against invaders, or found themselves in opposition to established governments. The proximity with Europe had repercussions on the movement. For example, during the Reconquista in the Iberian Peninsula, ushered in by the fall of Muslim Granada in 1492, the expulsion of Muslims (many of whom found refuge in Algeria, Morocco and Tunisia) was followed by Spanish incursions into Algerian territory and attacks on Algerian vessels on the high seas.[13] It is to ward off such attacks, that Algerians, feeling besieged by a resurgent (Christian) Spain, appealed to the Sublime Porte for help. After Ottomans established their own rule over Algeria, they frequently met with opposition from a number of mystical centers eager to fight against abuse of power and to bring about social justice, or to secure their own social power. Similarly the French invasion and the consolidation of colonial rule had to contend with the armed opposition of the head of the powerful Sufi order of the Qadiriya, Emir Abdelkader, in 1830. After his defeat in 1846, and until 1871, several orders pursued the fight against the new (who also happened to be Christian) rulers. Whether in Algeria, Morocco or Libya, the story of Sufi orders' struggle to defend their faith, entwined with the notion of land, is well known and need not be repeated here in any detail. However what needs pointing out is the dual role of mystical movements as spiritual *and* political depending on the conjuncture. Yet, it is this political dimension that the current Algerian and French policy of promotion of Sufism, or a variant of it, as an antidote to "extremism" which at once obviates and diverts the political impulse of popular Sufism. In the past, the political propensity of the mystical movement stemmed from the movement's tribal social foundation. Although in contact with the centers of power in cities, *zawiyat* were also relatively autonomous rural institutions, and thus attuned to the sentiments of the population.[14] Animated by a strong spirit of belonging to a Muslim community, Sufi orders were traditionally eager to preserve the autonomy and integrity of their adherents. For instance, notable Sufi leaders often made predictions about the political future of their country—a sign of awareness not only of the global religious politics of the time, but also the need to preserve the socio-cultural integrity of the local population.[15] Popular Sufism's frequent role as mediator between state and society in times of crises provides another example of its political ability. Nevertheless, popular Sufism is a heterogeneous institution and counts among its leaders men who privileged their narrowly-defined interests over those of the Muslim community writ large.[16] However, the mobilizing capacity of the popular Sufi movement, as well as the role it frequently played in resisting imperial incursions, a task normally carried out by the state, overshadows its socio-political heterogeneity to win it the status of a forerunner of nationalism.[17]

Popular Sufism and the state

The Ottoman state, the French colonial state, and the postcolonial government of Houari Boumediène, all were leery of the mystical movement's potential or actual power, and attempted to control it. The Ottoman state, as a Muslim state, used several strategies devised to secure its legitimacy, especially in the remote Eastern areas which chafed under its rule:[18] it rewarded cooperative orders with material benefits, and punished recalcitrant ones by weakening their economic power;[19] or attempted to undermine their popularity and diminish their cultural role by undertaking, among other things, a number of reforms.[20] Similarly and perhaps on a much larger scale, the French colonial state, fearful of the religious zeal of the mystical movement, engaged in a policy of repression combining military action, seizure and control of material assets belonging to rebellious tribes or to the *zawiyat* with which they were affiliated. By the end of the nineteenth century, the relentless policy of subjugation of tribes and *zawiyat*, which made room for European settlements on land seized from both, resulted in a general quiescence of *zawiyat* and their leaders, a weakening of their political will, and an impoverishment of their literacy. Their reduced mobility across borders with neighboring countries, as well as with the Middle East, contributed to their relative isolation, and diminished scope of their knowledge.[21]

At the beginning of the twentieth century, the *'Ulema* movement, based in urban centers, emerged as the challenger of popular Sufism perceived, often with good reason, as a force of retrogression spreading superstitious beliefs, and obscurantism. The *'Ulema* called for a rejuvenation of Islam, free of superstitions and practices verging on paganism, the education of women, and greater rights within the colonial system. They thus appeared as a modernist and reformist force. The antagonism between the two movements would persist with various degrees of intensity into the present, as the two competed for the soul of the country as much as for power and influence.[22]

Typically, the wartime FLN wrote off popular Sufism as an ally of the colonial regime making room for some members of the *'Ulema* movement in its ranks. Following this approach, Boumedième, the second president of Algeria (1965–1978), pursued a pre-emptive policy of repression towards *zawiyat,* especially those endowed with an autonomous organizational as well as educational capacity—they had their own Quranic schools—that might enable them to re-emerge as a counter-power. This was the case of the *zawiya al 'Alawiya,* in the city of Mostaganem in Western Algeria, well regarded by the colonial authorities.[23] It offered extensive socio-cultural services and had its own press as well as journal (*Al balagh al djaza'iri*), which helped to spread its syncretic and internally contradictory vision of Islam.[24] It also organizes an annual congress that gathers together large numbers of its disciples from around the world. After the independence of Algeria, it continued to hold its congresses, and even built a new mosque—a sign that could only be interpreted as an assertion of autonomy, just as it revealed its convening power, usually an attribute of the postcolonial state. Sheikh Mehdi Bentounes, the successor to Ben 'Alioua, the founder of the order, was accused of tampering with the February 1967 municipal elections by allegedly burning ballots printed by the press of the *zawiya* that had been cast for a candidate the *zawiya*[25] had not endorsed. Added to the lingering charge of collusion with the colonial regime, and the dubiousness of the Sheikh's religious views, the accusation of electoral tampering acquired even more seriousness, as it demonstrated that the order was meddling in politics and acted as "a state within the state."[26] The charge resulted in the arrest and jailing of the Sheikh for a period of six months on 22 January 1970, a restriction on and surveillance of the *zawiya's* activities, and a seizure of assets.

What is noteworthy in this case is not so much that the state moved in on the order, but the main reason for which it did: political interference. The *zawiya* printed ballots on its press,[27] an indication that it was interested in the politics of the city (Mostaganem) in which it is located. Over the years it had also opposed, among other things, the socialist state agrarian reforms, which entailed the nationalization of large tracts of land previously owned by colonial settlers or native landlords. It had also objected to the educational policy of the state (largely secular at the time). In addition, it created the Association of 'Alawiya Islamic Youth, thus appearing to provide an alternative to the state-sponsored Front of National Liberation Youth Association.[28] The point is not whether the state was right or wrong in its intervention, but that orders, such as that of the *'Alawia,* were not alien to politics even after independence, and that their political potential exists. Playing on this propensity, the General Direction of National Security purportedly proposed to Sheikh Mehdi Bentounes to become one of its agents.[29] The order was not the only institution that felt threatened by the socialist orientation of the newly independent state, even though the 1966 constitution elaborated under Boumediène stipulated, as have all subsequent constitutions, that Islam is the religion of the state.[30] And Boumediène was not off the mark when he dubbed his economic orientation "Islamic socialism" to convey his opposition to secular socialism, which he associated with communism. Besides, Boumediène's hostility to the left was part of the motivation that prompted him to stage a coup d'état on June 5, 1965 against his predecessor, Ahmed Ben Bella, whose closest associates, such as Mohammed Harbi,[31] were on the left.

The fortunes of popular Sufi orders turned when president Chadli Bendjedid ascended to power upon Boumediène's death. Married to a woman whose grandfather was the Sheikh of Bourokba *zawiya* in the town of Mazouna (western Algeria, near Mostaganem),[32] and being uncommitted to the socialist orientation of his predecessor, Bendjedid started the process of political rehabilitation of popular Sufi orders, which developed further under the government that succeeded his.[33] Under his tenure, the October 5, 1988 rebellion broke out, which many *zawiyat* condemned as a *fitna*[34] (disorder), as did non-affiliated mosques. The message emphasized order, obedience to the government, and vigilance against "Satan," the cause of disorder.[35] The government could only be satisfied with a message that remained silent on the excessive violence, including the use of torture, with which security and military forces repressed the riots, as it did twelve years hence during the Civil War. Perhaps not unexpectedly, members of what will become a year later the Front of Islamic Salvation, who were operating mostly as a network of community services provided to the disenfranchised, emerged as mediators—a traditional function of religious leaders—between demonstrators and the government.

The government's support for popular Sufism reached its peak under Bouteflika's tenure (1999–2019) as old orders reconstituted themselves and expanded, others such as the *Tidjaniya*, notable for its collaboration with colonial France, were rehabilitated, and new ones were formed. By political calculation, personal inclination,[36] or expedience, Bouteflika gradually turned orders into power brokers in four ways by: (a) creating a hospitable environment free of oversight or accountability which enabled orders to operate without fearing closure, and consolidate their material wealth; (b) making highly publicized visits to *zawiyat* (and encouraging his Cabinet members to do the same), hence raising their profile and enhancing their symbolic significance in society; (c) tacitly encouraging (by example) local elected officials to openly court Sheikhs for support during electoral campaigns, and oftentimes for delivering votes; and (d) introducing and normalizing the language of popular Sufism in political discourse. The linguistic strategy is particularly important as it consumes the melding of popular Sufism with politics. For example, a minister of education, Baba Ahmed, reportedly declared at a gathering during the presidential electoral campaign for a fourth term in 2014: "it is Bouteflika's *baraka* that's bringing the country rain and oil."[37] That the minister did not believe what he was saying is less important than what his statement revealed about his low opinion of the Algerian people, assumed to be gullible and simple enough to believe Bouteflika to be saintly. The slippage from seeking the *baraka* of a Sheikh to considering the patron of Sheikhs, the president, a Sheikh in his own right, endowed with the holy gift of *baraka,* that special charisma that is divinely imparted to Sheikhs, represents the culmination of a process of embedding the religious-qua-mystical in the political-civil domain. In this process, the traditional functions of Sheikhs, healing, intercession with the divine, mediation, are re-symbolized as the *zawiya* becomes a political site where decisions involving the leadership of the affairs of the state are arranged. In the words of the president of the Association des Zaouias et la Culture Soufie (Associaton of Zawiyat and Sufi Culture), Noureddine Mechouet, "*zawiat* are the first political institution in the country." He stressed that the political engagement of the *zawiyat* is self-evident since "we cannot be on the sidelines, we are full-fledged Algerians. We must support one or the other [presidential candidates]; we support he who in the end gives us recognition."[38] As a way of securing recognition, *zawyiat* provide information and guidance to members about who to vote for. Unabashedly, Mechouet asserted that "the *zawiya* is not only a religious institution, it is also a government where there is everything: ministries of agriculture, since we promote agriculture; justice since we intervene in the resolution of conflicts; culture since we deal with all questions of patrimony; and tourism since we have included spiritual tourism among the objectives of our association. *Zawiyat* can play a big role [in politics], we can be where the Power [the state] cannot be." Mechouet's description of the political functions of his institutions fits the "state within a state" characterization of the charge leveled at *zawiyat* by president Boumediène before he cracked down on them. Mechouet reveals that *zawiyat* are "especially encouraged" to act as mediators in situations of national crisis such as, for example, during the Civil War or social unrest in the Kabylie.[39]

In the interview, Mechouet provides an insight into the *zawiyat's* self-understanding as institutions eager to rekindle the spirit of political engagement characteristic of nineteenth century orders, and are now acting in "the interest" of the country. Furthermore, he reveals his awareness of the government's instrumental use of the *zawiyat*: "in the 1980s positions of responsibility were achieved through the *zawiyat* thanks to the intervention of one sheikh or another. In this respect, men in high places have done amazing things."[40] Nevertheless, the Association does not condemn the practice, which it finds acceptable, but wishes to see it benefit deserving political candidates. Ironically, the use of a politically dubious, if not corrupting practice of anointing candidates to elected office, or facilitating appointments to high office is seen as a possible path to ending the equally corrupt practice of appointing incompetent individuals to positions of power. However, from Mechouet's perspective, there is a difference between being a "son of a *zawiya* [an affiliate] in a position of power" and having the "spirit of *zawiya*," the spirit of tolerance and consultation. This barely veiled critique of the instrumentalization of a *zawiya*'s power of legitimation connotes a degree of frustration as well as an implicit recognition that things must be set right so that the *zawiya* can "do better." Implied in the statement about sheikhs' anointment of those aspiring to high office, is the notion that all *zawiyat* are not the same. Indeed, new *zawiyat* have sprouted, whose commitment to popular Sufism seems dubious, and old ones devote themselves to a whole array of practices, some of which illegal.[41] Some specialize in feats with animals, such as snake-charming, others in healing specific parts of the body, still others devote themselves to Quranic learning.[42] Although most of them claim they are not political, they do benefit from the state's policy of de-radicalization, if not material aid.[43]

Political popular Sufism: power and autonomy

How far a *zawyia* can go in seeking influence, or being used for influence, appears to be at the discretion of the *zawyia*. Just as it can act as a prized mediator in political crises, a *zawiya* can be critical of the state's abuse of its socio-cultural power. For instance, Mechouet objected to a tour of *zawyiat* (implicitly organized with the state's help) arranged to rehabilitate, Chekib Khelil, a former minister of energy and mines, a close associate of former president Bouteflika, accused of taking bribes from foreign businesses for which he was once under investigation by the Italian government, as well as the object of an international arrest warrant. Mechouet's opposition to the rehabilitation of a man whose alleged corruption was initially revealed in

Italy was urged by the *zawyia* Cheurfa 'N Behloul in the town of Azazga, Grande Kabylie, which the former minister planned to visit. Mechouet explained that the idea of touring *zawiyat* for political absolution was part of a "Wahabi design aimed at compromising [the *zawyiat* socio-cultural structures]."[44] The *Wahabi* movement (which has adepts in Algeria) is opposed to popular Sufism.

For *zawiyat*, at least the old rehabilitated ones, obliging state officials or those aspiring to political power, does not mean blind agreement with state policies. Mechouet was not afraid of stating to the press that his association disagrees with the religious policy of de-radicalization. This is a crucial point since the state stakes its religion policy on the retrieval and encouragement of popular Sufism, which it equates with an authentic, Algerian Islam. Bluntly, Mechouet notes, "our politicians know that *zawiyat* cannot accept everything [from them]." Hence, "we do not agree with the Ministry of Religious Affairs at present. It has called for a caravan to sensitize people to [the danger of] extremism in France. We do not consider this to be our problem. Let's work on Algeria first. Besides, we cannot forget the role played by that country in the 1990s. François Mitterrand had called for [an embargo] on the sale of weapons to Algeria."[45] Striking a nationalistic tone, he reminds the government of history: "we have expelled France in our *qashabia* and *haïk* not in a beard and a *gandura*."[46] Exhibiting concern for the security of the country, he evokes threats at the borders (sites of previous attacks on oil installations),[47] and suggests that citizens need to be mobilized at these vulnerable spots, not in France. Reiterating his association's opposition to Wahabism and "terrorism," he stresses the need to "return Islam to its middle ground (in French, *juste milieu*)"[48]—a goal also shared by the state.

Popular Sufism and women

Popular Sufism has traditionally been open to women. They are found among members of *zawiyat*, although they are not usually part of the *dikr* sessions attended by men, generally ending in a trance-like experience.[49] They have their own *dikr*. On occasion a woman has led an order.[50] Since one of the tenets of classical Sufism is to shed one's corporeal self to achieve union with the divine, the female body is hardly an impediment to achieving transcendence. Popular Sufism appears to be indifferent to the gender of its affiliates, although it generally abides by the gendered division of tasks in its rituals. Women's access to rituals of initiation in their quest for spirituality, or their recognition as Sufi leading figures does not mean that gender norms in the profane world have been transformed. The revival of popular Sufism—a state political imperative—has equally political implications for women. Given that women's advancement is predicated on juridico-economic change, which depends on political will, what occurs in the cultural-qua-religious domains affects women's chances of improving their status. Hence, the importance of analyzing the cultural as well as symbolic effects (some evident, others subtle) which the re-emergence of popular Sufism has had in society:

First, the enhanced visibility of *zawiyat*'s symbolic role in culture has to a large extent overshadowed the need for cultural development, the kind identified in the Tripoli Program as outlined in Chapter 1, which intended to fight against superstitions and ignorance. The emphasis on a Sheikh's *baraka* as a gauge of the worth of individuals aspiring to high office shifts political accountability from constituents, including women, to the *zawiyat*'s cultural power. Consequently, state officials may not seek to court women's vote, or protect it when it is jeopardized. Nor do they concern themselves with the urgency of addressing women's needs. By the same token, in publicly supporting *zawiyat*'s anointment of candidates for office, the state implicitly ignores the issue of its agents' professional loyalty. The question rises whether a member of government is loyal to his order in the discharge of his functions, or to the state as the protector of citizens, women and men?

Second, those among the *zawyiat*, which claim to heal individuals for a variety of ailments, some of which requiring medical or psychiatric attention, frequently engage in dubious practices that abuse women. The treatment of individuals, many of whom women, for possession is a case in point. In its original form, the practice, called *roqia shar'iya* (accepted by Islamic legal scholars) was performed sparingly by a notable Sheikh, and consisted in praying and reading relevant passages from the Quran for the person suspected of possession. However, in the context of the proliferation of unreflective customs, *roqia* is often carried out by self-styled sheikhs with methods that resemble those of satanic cults, which include the ingestion of various dubious potions. The sheikhs performing a *roqia* must also have physical contact with the individual seeking help. At any rate, *roqia* as it occurs combines pagan and polytheistic methods—all of which contravene the spirit and the letter of Islam.[51] The practice is also used for a whole range of conditions, such as anxiety before an exam or after a failure to pass one, inability to secure a job or get married, sterility, and serious mental illness. The popularity of *roqia* is such that it is frequently broadcast on television.[52] Indirectly justifying *roqia*, *imams*—religious functionaries of the state—have attempted to banalize exorcism of demons[53] by assimilating the practice to the alleviation of fear and stress. At any rate, practitioners have attempted to create clinics or centers of *roqia* as a sort of alternative medicine in Algeria just as they attempt to offer their services to Muslim communities in Western and African countries.[54] As the most vulnerable members of society in situations of economic and political crises, women, even the highly educated among them, figure prominently among the clients of *roqia* practitioners. The press reports multiple cases of young women beaten to death, raped, or molested by the sheikh performing a *roqia*. Furthermore, women (just like men) are charged excessive fees for quasimagical practices aimed at solving a variety of personal problems they experience in daily life.[55] The widespread use of *roqia* and similar customs aimed at substituting dubious remedies, presented as sanctioned by Islam, for expert medical care prompted the Ministry of Religious Affairs to ban the practice from mosques as well as Quranic schools.[56] The Ministry also declared (in response to a parliamentarian, affiliated with a faith-based party, seeking to give *roqia* medical status) that possession cannot be recognized as an illness.[57] Hence its treatment lacks scientific validity.

What stands out in the spread of the practice of *roqia* and related customs is not simply that superstitions, some resulting in death and shattered lives, have been thriving. Indeed, anxiety, a heightened sense of vulnerability, or a suspension of disbelief are not uncommon in times of economic scarcity, unemployment, diminished resources, political stagnation, and social instability. Rather, the significance of the use of *roqia*, which requires investment of time, energy, and money, lies in its obscuring the concrete causes of the problems for which women and men seek relief, in favor of a cultural placebo. In other words, questions of structural change are reduced to dubious religious practices. It means, especially for women, a form of disengagement from the active search for change in their legal, political and economic circumstances. Debates over the validity, effects, and results of *roqia* overshadow or distract from discussions of pressing gender issues.

Third, the salience of *zawiyat*, apart from promoting or abetting all sorts of practices as substitutes for medical and psychiatric care, fosters a socio-cultural climate which blurs the distinction between the sacred and the customary best captured by the concept of "profane" to such an extent that old customs (including *roqia*) are justified as prescribed by religious texts, or having a religious status. The conflation of customs and religion fosters a mental attitude that submits to the undisputed authority of the sheikh—an essential tenet in Sufi practice. Popular Sufism rests on respect for the sheikh whose guidance is sought, and his *baraka* highly prized.[58] While this may make sense in the journey of the seeker of union with the divine, it is meaningless in the world of everyday life where individuals are confronted with mundane problems. Unquestioned respect for the sheikh's authority (no matter his aptitude for dealing with the complexity of everyday life), as well as the blurring of the sacred and the profane impede discernment. An imam could commit gross mistakes or make statements that stretch credulity to the limit without challenge.[59] Parenthetically, perhaps Algerians' credulity has not yet been pushed to the limit as it did in the 1960s in Egypt when citizens from all over the country sent letters seeking help with their everyday life problems to the Cairo grave of Imam Shaf'i, dead since 820, but whose grace was invoked as if he were still alive.[60] For women, especially those with limited education, screening the multiplicity of messages they are exposed to offers a formidable challenge, compounded by the diversity of *zawiyat*, or the traditionally shifting socio-political postures of their leaders.[61]

Fourth, theoretically, women can, just like men, seek the blessings of sheikhs in the pursuit of high office. However, in practice, and in spite of the widely held notion that Sufism is gender-neutral, women holding public office have not been anointed as men have. In fact, evidence indicates that the purportedly "progressive" *zawiya al 'Alawiya*, which organized a traveling picture exhibition throughout Europe, Canada, and New York in 2015 to demystify veiling as a sole attribute of Islam, has not advocated for gender equality in family law. An all-women conference it organized in 2014 stressed, among others, the positive roles that women have traditionally played in the family and the community.[62] The cultural prominence of the *zawiyat*, their willed political visibility, and the revival of dated customs flourishing in their wake weigh heavily on women's consciousness in steering an independent path towards change. If anything, the layering of the religious discourse over customs such as *roqia*, when combined with the stifling of critical analysis, acts as an obstacle to women's rising above a weighty cultural environment or deciphering the political meanings of the discourses that support it. More important is the state's deliberate use of *zawiyat* as an intermediary between it and the people. This is a double-edged sword as *zawiyat* have the potential of becoming a power unto their own, another force of gender conservation. In this context, the question raised in the previous chapter whether Islamic feminism is a progressive force given how saturated society had become with religious and quasi-religious discourses and practices acquires greater acuteness since the *murshidat* corps does not appear to address the excesses of popular Sufism.

Fifth, *zawiyat* also play an educational role, which reinforces existing representations of women as unequal to men. *Zawiyat* sponsor Quranic schools, and as noted above, at least one, the *zawiya al 'Alawiya* sponsors boy and girl scouts. Besides, some have close ties to universities whose faculty members may be affiliates. Admittedly, a faculty member's spiritual life or affiliation with an order belongs to his/her private life and does not, or should not, affect the discharge of her/his professional duties. The *zawiya al 'Alawiya* has an agreement with the University Abdelhamid Ibn Badis, in the city of Mostaganem, for cooperation in research and other activities. Close ties between a public university—a place of scientific learning—and a *zawiya*, as a private religious institution with its own objectives some of which support the state policy of "deradicalization"[63] raises questions of professional conflicts of interests in teaching. Relatedly such ties further erode faculty members' commitment to a universalistic public education that is not beholden to private religious interests such as they are. The danger resides in the classroom becoming a site for imparting the ideology of de-radicalization through a narrow popular Sufi perspective. Given the flourishing of superstitious customs, the cooperation between *zawiya* and university appears to thwart the nurturing of a scientific modern culture, the aim of the Tripoli Program analyzed in Chapter 1. Among faculty members, the fear of Salafism is an overriding concern, which causes them to embrace popular Sufism in one form or another. As a professor of social science who cooperates with a *zawyia* put it, "they [the leadership of *zawiya Al 'Alawiya*] are fighting Salafism, and I will help them."[64] The interests of students did not figure in his response. Another faculty member, more circumspect, expressed satisfaction with the association of her university with the *zawiya* because it enabled her to participate in colloquia and conferences organized by the *zawiya*, which the university rarely does. Hence, in this case, a *zawyia* drains faculty from the university and enlists them in its own socio-political projects. The blurring of the boundaries between public and privatized education, non-religious and religious, occurs for political reasons. The *zawiya* in this case plays the role of a substitute for the university because it has the means and international network to do so. At times, the lure of popular Sufism as an antidote to "extremism" is remarkably powerful. For instance, a historian wholeheartedly supported the *zawiya al 'Alawyia's* university objectives, refusing to acknowledge their political significance in the broader state policy of "deradicalization."[65] The message of "vivre ensemble" (living together) disseminated by the *zawiya* resonates with a number of academics as well as the press, in spite of its obscuring the material and political conditions that are necessary for its realization. These include the reproduction of gender inequality.

Finally, widespread corruption in politics, state administration as well as business affects women more than men as they generally have more limited resources than men with which to bargain. Furthermore, their own sexuality is a target of corrupt practices from individuals in positions of power. Hence, the return to customs thriving under the aegis of popular Sufism increases women's vulnerability. Individuals may even turn to such customs as a sort of refuge from the excesses of corruption.

In sum, this chapter has outlined the socio-cultural conditions under which women's turn to culture needs to be understood. The state's deliberate *wasatiya* Islam policy of promoting a Maghrebin-qua-Algerian Islam as an antidote to "radical Islam," has meant a revival of popular Sufism that had either lost its relevance, or fallen in disrepute in the first sixteen years after independence, as the country engaged in the path of development for a better life. However, such a revival represents a great deal more than state tolerance for *zawiyat's* cultural activities; or protection of some old cultural identity ostensibly denied by the first two developmentalist governments. The view according to which "orders as well as the cult of saints constitute Maghrebin people's memory and are mobilized as identity resources each time that their integrity is threatened,"[66] assumes a static "memory" unaffected by the demographic and material changes that have occurred in the postcolonial era. It also gives short shrift to the ideological use of "identity" for a political purpose as has been the case since the 1990s. To focus, as the state has done, on the spiritual side such as it is of popular Sufism only means to reduce its complexity and distinctiveness. Conversely, by reducing popular Sufism (at its best) to its inward-looking, individual search for union with the divine, the state wishes to sever the movement from its ever-present resistive political propensity as well as consciousness. The state seeks to re-orient the political impulse of the mystical moment to secure support for its own policies—a double-edged weapon—as Mechouet's comments above made clear.

The analysis offered in this chapter in no way detracts from the social as well psychological role played by popular Sufism during the colonial era. Nor does it dismiss the social functions of rituals or women's and men's need for a spiritual life then and now.[67] However, it questions the functionalist view that hails women's participation in *zawiyat,* in the context of the state's war against "radicalization," as positively reshaping women's roles in Islam.[68] Revival of customs presented as religious norms is different from a revival, which has not taken place, of the philosophical-theological debates of classical Sufism concerning a whole range of issues, including the meaning of mystical experience, or the legitimacy and transmission of charisma-qua-*baraka.*[69] Instead, it is practices of a folkloric nature presented as religious, and the sanctification of quasi-feudal values (such as the anointment of politicians) that have been revived and mobilized to pursue a national and global imperative: how to retrieve or foster a popular Islam impervious to political use. Ironically, in so doing the state re-politicizes popular Sufism.

Popular Sufism, in its old or revived form, is a social practice that takes place in a socio-economic and political milieu. As such, it is an adaptive response to existing conditions, which it attempts to remedy symbolically. The revival of popular Sufism, as a state strategy ostensibly for preventing the recurrence of the Civil War (1992–2002), disregards the concrete reasons that led to the war in the first place. To reiterate, the civil war pitting a faith-based movement against the state in the 1990s was not caused by "radical Islam." It was a response to economic, political and social inequality. That the view imputing unrest to "radical Islam" is short-sighted has been demonstrated in a most dramatic way since February 22, 2019, the start of a non-violent popular movement seeking an end to the old regime. The movement, called the *hirak,* has already compelled former president A. Bouteflika to resign after giving up his claim to a fifth term in office in spite of the support he received from *zawyiat.* It has also prevented a new and hastily arranged presidential election from taking place on July 9, 2019. Equally important, the movement has led to the arrest of cabinet members, high-level politicians, and businessmen for corruption. The movement was still holding out for a complete break with the old political system when the corona virus pandemic caused it to suspend its activities in March 2020. At this time, *zawiyat* have been silent about the *hirak.* The *zawyia 'Alawiya,* also quiet, continues its activities in France. The protest movement, which by its national scope and size has been termed a second Revolution, is also fueled by large numbers of women from all walks of life and age groups. Importantly, it has not been led nor does it claim affiliation with any faith-based party. It also manifests a latent need among young people to look beyond the past to bring about change. An engineering student I interviewed less than a year before the advent of the *hirak* felt that Algeria was not in a transition to modernity, but in state of "modern *jahiliya*"[70] by which he meant a state marked by a transposition of customs and practices that belong in the age of ignorance into the present, side by side with evolved life styles. A linguistics male graduate student suggested that what was needed was a "revolution in knowledge," a "cultural revolution."[71] They both objected to the government's use of the memory of the Civil War as a deterrent to changing the status quo. The *hirak* signaled a will to change no matter what. In its weekly demonstrations it availed itself of a longer past, that of the war of decolonization whose ideals of social justice, freedom, and equality as could be read on the signs carried in its weekly gatherings.

Notes

1 I am borrowing the expression from Fazlur Rahman, who describes the manner in which Sufism was absorbed by popular beliefs and practices in *Islam* (Chicago, IL: University of Chicago Press, 1979) second edition, ch. 9.

2 Gilles Veinstein states with good reason that "The mystical dimension expressed in Sufism is an integral part of Islam and is founded on the Quran as well as the exemplary behavior of the Prophet." Veinstein further notes that Sufism shares with other religions a "universal quest for the divine," which might explain Maghrebin as well as Western countries bias in favor of Sufism. Alexandre Popovic and Gilles Veinstein, *Les voies d'Allah: les ordres mystiques dans le monde musulman des origines à aujourd'hui* (Paris: Arthème Fayard, 1996), 10.

3 Kamel Filali, *L'Algérie mystique: des Marabouts fondateurs aux Khwân insurgés, XV/XIX siècles* (Paris: Publisud, 2002), 35. According to the author, the intellectual flourishing of Sufism in the Maghreb occurred between the XIII and XIV centuries. For a brief historical description of *zawiyat,* see 104–109. For the specificity of Maghrebin mysticial orders, see also Sossie Andezian, "L'Algérie, le Maroc, la Tunisie," in Popovic and Veinstein, *Les voies d'Allah,* 389–408.

4 "Sidi" literally means "my lord." In colloquial Arabic it is used to refer to a mystic who achieved notoriety through a life of devotion and good deeds combined with charisma, usually the capacity to "see" or heal.

5 Andezian, "L'Algérie," 389–390, traces the evolution of the French use of the concept "marabout": initially the term referred to the dynasty of the *Mourabitoun* (Almoravid), established in Marrakesh, Morocco, in 1062. These were men who although warriors, also practiced mysticism in fortress-like structures called *ribat.* After the fall of the dynasty and its successor, the *Muwahidoun* (Almohad), the term continued to be used to mean "a wide range of figures considered saints, including political chiefs, founders and heads of orders, eponymous ancestors, tribal chiefs, pious men, hermits, thaumaturges as well as ancient divinities, caves, springs, and sacred trees."

6 The most notable was Rabi'a al 'Adawiya (713/718–801) of Basrah, Iraq. For books about her, see Margaret Smith, *Muslim Women Mystics: The Life and Work of Rabi'a and Other Women Mystics in Islam* (Oxford: Oneworld, 1994, 2001); Rkia Elaroui, *Rabi'a From Narrative to Myth: The Many Facets of Islam's Most Famous Woman Saint Rabi'a al 'Adawiyya* (Oxford: Oneworld, 2019).

7 The same *tariqa* may have branches in more than one country, claims the same master/saint, and conducts its rituals according to its own distinctive style.

8 Ibid., 393. Andezian points out that the savant Sufis, many of whom from Andalusia, gathered at the notable center of learning of Seguia El Hamra, in Southern Morocco, from which they contributed to the "re-islamization of the rural populations" at a time of economic and political crises. Tribes would select some of

these pious men as their eponyms and confer nobility lineages onto them, 393. By "re-islamization" the author may mean renewed or regained piety. Andezian refers to the emergence of hereditary sainthood mediated by noble lineage as the "maraboutic revolution."

9 Andezian, ibid.; and Filali, *L'Algérie mystique*, 15.

10 Filali, ibid., 16. The junction between the two would have occurred gradually, reaching its consummation at the beginning of the sixteenth century. Andezian, "L'Algérie," 393, dates the junction, which she terms "synthesis" from the seventeenth century.

11 The thesis of the convergence of the two strands of mysticism as formulated by Filali is attractive as it captures the larger ritualistic character of Sufism among swaths of the rural population in Algeria at the end of the nineteenth century and the first half of the twentieth. It does not obviate the existence of a more literate, for lack of a better word, Sufi practice. For example, the head of the Qadiriya order, Emir Abdelkader, who battled French invading forces in Algeria, was a Sufi in the old tradition: he was a literary Sufi scholar. The thesis was also formulated in a different way by Andezian, "L'Algérie," 393, who argues that "In the seventeenth century, a synthesis of savant mysticism and ecstatic practices occurred."

12 Term used by Filali, *L'Algérie mystique*, 3. Noteworthy is the author's intent to capture from within the specificity and complexity of Maghrebin Sufism and from a historical perspective.

13 Spain occupied Mers-El-Kebir and Oran (Wahran) in Western Algeria in 1505 and 1509 respectively.

14 Referring to mysticism in its transnational context, Veinstein, *Les voies*, 10, captures the depth of the dissemination and spread of "the Muslim mystique" as a "phenomenon of 'socialization' and even 'massification,' without any equivalent in Christianity."

15 Filali, *L'Algérie mystique*, 43, cites a mystic, Sidi Ahmad Ben Youcef, who, as legend had it, predicted that the "Turks" as well as the French would rule Algeria.

16 The history of the difficulties Emir Abdelkader encountered with the Tijaniya order in the South which fought him on the side of colonial France or the Rahmaniya order in Kabylie which refused to make common cause are but two examples of how Sufi orders were not always moved by the higher good of the community of Muslims. They also clearly reveal how popular Sufi leaders, in some contexts, can act as unscrupulous, corruptible political men rather than saintly characters with supra-natural foresight.

17 Filali, *L'Algérie mystique*, 111. The author suggests that the Maraboutic movement contributed to the "eclipse" of the Ottomans in Algeria.

18 Filali, ibid., 91–93, recounts an international incident opposing the state to France over the affair of Melle de Bourg, the 14 year old daughter of the ambassador to Spain at the Swedish court, on her way to her father's, whose ship capsized on the Eastern Algerian shore between Bejaia and Jijel, and was rescued by Algerian sailors who refused to turn her over to the Bey of Constantine. She and her retinue were not released until the *Marabout* of Oued Zahrour, contacted by the French consul in Algiers and by the Dey of Algiers, intervened. This incident underscores not only the nature of the challenge that the population presented to Ottoman rule but also the power that popular Sufi leaders could play in situation of crises.

19 An indication of the size of the property owned by one *zawiya*, the *Ouled Sidi-al-Cheikh*, in the South is provided in Filali, *L'Algérie mystique*, 135–137.

20 The eighteenth century Ottoman state attempted to woe and cultivate the *'Ulema* (Islamic scholars) against *zawiyat* in support of a state vision of religion resting on a teaching strategy demonizing popular Sufism that bears similarities with the "deradicalization" policy adopted by contemporary Algeria, Morocco, and France. See Filali, ibid., 159–168. The author uses "re-islamization" to capture the Ottoman state's view of combating popular Sufism which challenged its power, 160.

21 Peregrination, the ability of a mystic to move across countries in quest for Sufi masters' knowledge and initiation became more limited under colonial rule as the movement of people outside the country fell under close scrutiny, and was subjected to administrative authorizations.

22 At the inception of their movement, the *'Ulema* formed the Association of Muslim *'Ulema* on May 5, 1931, in response to which popular sufi groups set up their own, the Association of Sunni *'Ulema* of Algeria. See Ahmed Guessoum, "Le rôle social et politique des zaouias: evolution et pratiques: l'exemple de l'ouest algérien." Doctoral dissertation, University of Paris VIII, Ecole Doctorale Sciences Sociales, July 2017, 208, 74. However, the antagonism between *'Ulema* and popular Sufism should not be overstated. There were heads of zawiyat who agreed with the *'Ulema* movement's goals, and even became members of the Association of *'Ulema*. See Andezian, "L'Algérie," 398.

23 A colonial writer and administrator, Augustin Berque (1884–1946) wrote about the founder of the order, Sheikh Ben 'Alioua, whom he had known, in "Un mystique moderniste, le cheikh Ben 'Alioua," *Revue Africaine*, 79 (1936): 691–776. Perhaps summarizing the popularity of Ben 'Alioua's teaching, he noted: "He [Ben Alioua] had a mass of ignorant affiliates as well as highly cultured European disciples," 692. Ben Alioua's order continues to have European affiliates.

24 Augustin Berque, ibid., provides a lucid analysis of the sources and evolution of the founder of the *zawiya al 'Alawiya*'s vision and message. The colonial tolerance, if not support, of this order is a controversial matter among Algerians. However, one of the statements made by Ben 'Alioua, balancing out the ills of colonial domination with its benefits resonates with the French justification of its occupation: "The only way in my view to erase the past that shocks is to show the natives as well as foreign nations that France came to Algeria to civilize not to dispossess the natives." Cited in Foad Khatir, "Le changement politique algérien, de la persécution à la réhabilitation des confréries religieuses musulmanes: le cas particulier de la confrérie 'Alawiyya 1909–2009," doctoral dissertation, University of Toulouse-Jean Jaurès, June 26, 2016. The quotation was from a publication celebrating the centenary of the colonization of Algeria, *Les Annales coloniales, "le centenaire de l'Algérie*," July 30, 1929. Khatir is a member of the *'Alawi* order.

25 Khatir, "Le changement politique," 223.

26 Ibid., 227. The state-controlled press published an investigative report on July 20 and 23, 1968, intended to reveal the inner workings of the order, its reach within and outside of Algeria, as well as its political ambitions.

27 Foad Khatir, ibid., writing as a sympathetic member of the order, does not dispute this fact.

28 Ibid., 226.

29 Ibid., 229.

30 At a symbolic level, it is noteworthy, as Guessoum, "Le rôle social," 208, points out, that the very name of the president, a wartime pseudonym, was that of a notable saint, Sidi Boumediène, guardian of the city of Tlemcen.

31 Harbi, a historian, was a member of the wartime Front of National Liberation (FLN) and one of the people who drafted the 1963 Charter of Algiers.

32 See, Khatir, "Le changement politique," 254, and Guessoum, "Le rôle social," 210. Guessoum also reports that during his fieldwork members of different orders expressed their gratitude for Chadli Bendjedid's support, 210.

33 President Chadli Bendjedid declared in an interview that he made sure that charges were dropped against Bouteflika, who was about to be imprisoned for embezzlement of government funds during his tenure as Minister of Foreign Affairs (under Boumediène), thanks to the intervention of his father-in-law, Mohammed Bourokba. *Le Matin d'Algérie*, October 17, 2012, www.lematindz.net/9919-3-sans-m oi-bouteflika-aurait-ete-jete-ete-en-prison.html, accessed September 6, 2019.

34 *Fitna* is a loaded term in Arabic; it connotes rebellion, temptation to cause disorder, distress, and social strife.
35 Guessoum, "Le rôle social," 214, analyzed lectures given by Sheikhs of *zawiyat* in Western Algeria.
36 Anecdotal evidence indicates that the president was a frequent visitor of *zawiyat*, especially the *qadiriya*, his support base. Ibid., 136.
37 Ibid., 18. The minister's statement was made in the city of Maghnia, in the wilaya of Tlemcen, on March 30, 2014. See one of the online papers which reported the Minister's comment at www.algerie-focus.com, accessed August 14, 2019.
38 Mechouet in Abla Chérif, "Entretien avec M. Mechouet, président de l'association des zaouias 'Les zaouias sont la première institution politique du pays'," *Le Soir d'Algérie*, March 21, 2016, www.lesoirdalgerie.com/articles/2016/03/21/article.php? sid=193508&cid=2, accessed September 7, 2019.
39 Ibid. Mechouet had in mind political positions.
40 Ibid. The 1980s were the years of president Chadli Bendjedid's tenure.
41 Information relayed by a former mid-level state functionary who visited one such *zawiya* in Western Algeria, Algiers, June 18, 2019, which was used as a cover for an illegitimate business.
42 Discussion with D.G., a researcher on Sufism and *zawiyat*, Oran, June 25, 2018.
43 A leitmotif in interviews and in texts written about the rehabilitation of *zawiyat* since the 1990s is that *zawiyat* receive covert aid from the state, either in building new branches of a given *zawiya* such as that of the *belqaidiya* in Algiers (which was inaugurated by former president Boutleflika on May 15, 2018, at Tixeraïne, in Bir Khadem, a suburb of Algiers), or to convene international conferences as is the case with the *zawiya al 'Alawiya* of Mostaganem, ibid. This is not to say that *zawiyat* do not command sizable wealth from which to draw. However, the question is whether they would spend it freely on events that enhance the state's deradicalization policy.
44 "Mobilisation pour empêcher la visite de la zaouia de Cheurfa," *El Watan*, 2 May 2016, www.elwatan.com/edition/actualite/mobilisation-pour-empecher-la-visite-de-la-zaouia-de-cheurfa-02-05-2016, accessed 8 September 2019. The Minister, Chakib Khelil, also presided over of SONATRACH, a state-owned oil and gas company in 2001–2003.
45 Mechouet in Abla Chérif, "Entretien avec M. Mechouet." François Mitterrand was president of France in 1981–1995. The Civil War in Algeria had been raging for already three years (out of ten) before he left office.
46 Ibid. The *qashabia* (*qashabiya*) is men's traditional, one-piece hooded overcoat, worn by combatants during the Algerian Revolution (1954–1962), the *haïk* is Algerian women's traditional white veil; the *gandura* is the long, white dress usually worn by Islamic militants along with a beard. This piece of clothing was imported from the Middle East. The metaphor flaunts the national character of the war of decolonization.
47 The most notable was the attack against the base camp at a natural gas field at Tingentourine in Southern Algeria on January 16, 2013. See, among others, "Infographie Algérie: Attaque du site gazier de Tiguentourine," *L'OBs*, January 17, 2013, www.nouvelobs.com/monde/20130117.OBS5781/infographie-algerie-attaque-du-site-gazier-de-tiguentourine.html, accessed September 18, 2019.
48 Mechouet in Abla Chérif, "Entretien avec M. Mechouet."
49 In December 2011, I watched an all-male *dikr* session from behind a latticed wooden screen that separated men from women, which allowed women to see without being seen, at the *zawiya al 'Alawiya* in Mostaganem, considered the most "progressive" in Algeria. Gilles Veinstein, *Les voies*, 10, reports that "a few orders, such as the Naqchbandiyya [originating in central Asia], or a more recent order in the Middle East, the Yachrutiyya, admit women as full-fledged affiliates."

50 In Algeria, Lalla Zineb, headed the zawiya El Hamel Errahmaniya in the Southern city of Boussaada in 1897–1904. Guessoum, "Le rôle social," 187. However, Lalla Zineb was the daughter of the Sheilkh of the *zawiya*, who left a will making her his successor as his only child. A number of mausoleums were also erected in honor of women Sufi saints.

51 According to Guessoum, *Le rôle social*, hadiths attributed to the Prophet Muhammad to justify *roqia* do not condone the practice in its current form, 157.

52 Guessoum, *Le rôle social*, 151. The author reports that the private TV chain Ennahar purportedly boosted its audience by broadcasting exorcism session performed by its preacher, Chamseddine. A *roqia* center was created by a sheikh Belahmar, a frequent figure on television once arrested for charlatanism, in the city of Relizane in Western Algeria. See "Le sheikh Belahmar, le patron de la 'clinique' de la 'ruqia' appartenait à un groupe terroriste. December 27, 2016, www.lema tindz.net/news/22786-cheikh-belahmar, accessed September 20, 2019. Regardless of its veracity, the accusation against the exorcist points to the connection established between the civil war trauma and the flourishing of dated practices.

53 Guessoum, *Le rôle social*, 152.

54 Ibid.

55 See, "Roqia, entre violence, sexe, et charlatanisme," *Liberté*, April 5, 2015, www. liberte-algerie.com/actualite/roqia-entre-violence-sexe-et-charlatanisme-223267#. XYdnZyHjiFs.email=0A=0A—=0A. This article reveals that three sisters as well as a young boy were raped in two different parts of the country. See also "Voyantes (chouaffette) des temps modernes," El Watan, July 22, 2012, reprinted at www.dja zaïress.com/fr/elwatan/379206#.XXUF/vr35Lg.twitter, accessed 21 September 2019. A "voyante or in Arabic "shuwafa," (pl. shuwafat) is a female clairvoyant. The term is badly transcribed in the article. Another case of *roqia* was reported during the COVID19 pandemic in which a 10-year girl died after a séance in the presence of her parents in the city of Guelma. Doctors found burns and other traces of physical abuse on her body. *Algérie360*, "Guelma: Une fillette meurt lors d'une séance de 'roqya' dans l'hôpital Abdelhakim Okbi, 29 May 2020, www. algerie360.com/20200529-une-fillette-de-10-ans-meurt-lors-dun-exorcisme, accessed June 15, 2020. Parenthetically, *roqia* is also practiced in neighboring countries and results in similar abuse of women as in Algeria. See for example a case that occurred in Morocco, "Un raki viole une handicapée à El Hajeb," *Le360*, June 1, 2019, http://fr.le360.ma/societe/un-raqui-viole-une-handicapee-a-el-hajeb-181792#. XYYbqLduPds.email, accessed September 21, 2019.

56 See "Les Imams interdits de pratiquer la Roqia dans les mosquées et écoles coraniques," *Huffpost Maghreb*, May 20, 2016, www.huffpostmaghreb.com/2016/05/ 20/roqia-interdite-mosquees_n_10061756.html?ncid=other_email_o63gt2jcad4& utm_campaign=share_email, accessed September 21,2019.

57 "Un député islamiste veut faire reconnaître la roqia," *Huffington Post Maghreb*, May 10, 2016, www.huffpostmaghreb.com/2016/05/10/religion-djinn-sorcelleri_n_ 9888314.html?ncid=other_email_o63gt2jcad4&utm_campaign=share_email, accessed September 21, 2019.

58 Referring to the immense power a sheikh traditionally wields on account of his hereditary status as well as his social power, Gilles Veinstein, *Les voies*, 18, writes: "There is no limit to his [power on individuals] except in the authority of the state in so far as there is a state capable of exercising some authority."

59 Guessoum, "Le rôle social, 227," reports that an imam ended his Friday lecture with a prayer imploring God's protection from the Tatars and the Mongols, an anachronistic reference to a XIIIth invasion of the Middle East. Whether this incident actually occurred is less important than the fact that it became a story at all. The author too worries about the uncritical frame of mind that set in in the wake of the revival of popular Sufism.

60 Alerted by the volume of the mail, the Cairo post office decided to investigate. The story was researched in 1965 by Sayyid Uways at the Centre d'études et de documentation économiques, juridiques et sociales. Cited in Pierre-Jean Luizard, "Le soufisme égyptien contemporain,"*Egypte/Monde arabe,* Première série, 2/1990, http://journals.openaccess.org/ema/218.

61 Addressing the ambiguity of mystical movements, Veinstein, *Les voies,* 22, notes an important factor that has special resonance for women: "In general it can be said of mystical orders ... that they more or less stand for one thing as well as its opposite; they are, depending on the situation, orthodox and unorthodox, purist and laxist, spiritual and materialist, ascetic and opulent, intellectual and superstitious, elitist and populist, learned and ignorant, conservative and revolutionary, reactionary and liberal, clerical and secular, militant and pacifist, opportunist and principled etc."

62 Still, it came under attack for historicizing the veil as well as gender in Islam. Interview with D.G., Oran, June 25, 2018. This researcher recounted that the *moqaddam* (who acts as the spiritual manager) of a branch of the very *zawiya al 'Alawiya,* reputed for its "modernism," was critical of the Sheikh's view expressed at a social gathering that the unequal treatment of women is not supported by the Quran.

63 As a zawiya which had been subjected to president Boumediène's repressive policy in the 1970s, the *zawiya al 'Alawiya* makes no bones about supporting the policy of subsequent governments that allowed its comeback. Its leader is avowedly anti-Islamist. Private communication, New York, September 29, 2016.

64 Discussion with professor N.N., Mostaganem, June 27, 2018.

65 Interview with D.G., Oran, June 16, 2019.

66 Andezian, "L'Algérie," 399.

67 Marnia Lazreg, *The Eloquence of Silence: Algerian Women in Question* (New York: Routledge, 1996, 2018), emphasized such needs and cautioned against dismissing them.

68 See Meriem el Haitami, "Women and Sufism: Religious Expression and the Political Sphere in Contemporary Morocco," *Mediterranean Studies,* 22, no. 2 (2014): 190–212.

69 Andezian, "L'Algérie," 392.

70 Interview with S.M., Mostaganem, June 28, 2018. *Jahiliyia* refers to the pre-Islamic period.

71 Interview with J.H., Mostaganem, June 28, 2018.

4

THE MANAGEMENT OF SALAFISM AND WOMEN

The state policy of fostering an authentic Algerian Islam does not rest on supporting popular Sufism alone. It has also, and less ostentatiously, relies on a strand of Salafism it perceives as apolitical. Known as "quietist Salafism," this strand is seen as an antidote to more contentious Salafi strands. However, "quietist Salafism" is more detrimental to women's emancipatory goals than Sufism, albeit both play a role in the reproduction of gender inequality. This chapter analyzes the state's contradictory policy with regards to Salafism to identify its effects on women's turn to culture.

Salafism

In its origin, this is less a sect than an attitude towards worship. Defining the term with accuracy is fraught with problems as the existing literature on the subject matter is discrepant due to the multiplicity of strands of Salafism, each providing its own account of what it stands for, and makes claims to its own history. The varying definitions used by Salafists prompted a historian to argue that "given our current state of knowledge, even the most cautious definitions of Salafism cannot resolve the deep-seated confusion surrounding the meaning and historical origins for this concept."[1] This definitional difficulty sheds light on the ambiguity of the Algerian state's policy of picking and choosing which Salafi strand to support or combat. Part of the state's ambiguity also stems from the history of Algeria, especially the reformist period, fueled by the 'Ulema at the turn of the twentieth century, and led by Sheikh Ibn Badis. The reformist movement was also labeled Salafi.

The concept Salafism (more properly *Salafiyya*) is derived from the Arabic root *salaf*, which means "predecessor." Initially, Muslim scholars such as Ibn Hanbal (780–855) used it to refer to the first three generations of Muslims as mentioned in the *hadith* according to which "The best generation are those of my generation, then those who follow them and then those who follow."[2] The Salaf were the companions of the Prophet as well as their followers who, by their proximity to the Prophet and the modeling of their behavior on his, represented the ideal of conduct for Muslims. However, beginning in the nineteenth century, the term Salafism was used by social scientists to refer to specific groups, even if they did not claim the label, who upheld two major orientations towards adapting to a changing world while adhering to and maintaining a Muslim identity in the face of imperial encroachments on Muslim lands:[3] a "modernist" Salafist orientation is attributed to nineteenth-century reformists, such as Jamal al-Din Al-Afghani, Rashid Rida, or Muhammad Abduh, because these scholars sought to reconcile modernity (equated with science and technology), with a reformed Islam purified of superstitions and customs inimical to knowledge and cultural development. Theirs was an attempt to rediscover a truer Islam, compatible with scientific reason, that had been ignored or misrepresented due to ignorance or lack of political will. They steered a middle path to bring about a rejuvenated Islam.

A second orientation focusing on a "purist" conception of Islam deemed an authentic Islam, embodied in the Salaf, is represented by the pious Muslims who belong to the first three generations. From this perspective, "Salafism is nothing more than Islam as it was first revealed, unsullied by innovation (*bid'a*), deviation (*inhiraf*), or accretion (*ziyada*), [and] uncontaminated by exogenous influences."[4] A pure Islam in this context means one that prohibits: speculative theology; the interpretation of foundational texts such as the Quran according to one's purpose; the dismissal or relativizing of passages from the Quran because they do not accord with one's taste; submitting blindly to any of the four schools of law (ostensibly because they did not exist at the time of the Prophet); engaging in Sufism because of its reliance on esoteric knowledge and the attendant cult of saints.[5] Accepting all or some of these prohibited acts or beliefs may lead to the charge of *bid'a* (innovation) or, worse, heresy (*kufr*).[6] These two orientations have a common core in so far as both insist on the preservation of an originary Islam untrammelled by practices that have either distorted its progressive message or departed from its literal meaning. However, since the beginning of the twentieth century, analysts have identified various groups according to whether they adhere to the purist orientation only and focus solely on their worship, or intend to spread their purist beliefs in the larger society with various methods, including violence. Hence, "Jihadi Salafism" (*al Salafiyya al-jihadiyya*) refers to groups who reject their government ostensibly because it has deviated from the application of Islamic principles as embodied in the *Salaf*, and intend to change the political system with the use of violence. Whereas "quietist Salafism" (*Salafiyya al-'ilmiyya*) applies to groups who do not use violence preferring to confine themselves to living according to their beliefs, which they will seek to share with others; they may engage in political change through accepted means, such as running for elected office.[7] In between these two poles (Jihadi and quietist Salafism) there is a range of overlapping orientations at times bearing the name of a leading Sheikh who founded a Salafi group or is its leading theorizer.[8] Noteworthy are the intellectual sources of Salafism, which include the classic thinkers, Ibn Taymiyya (1263–1328), Ibn Qayyim al-Jawziyya (1298–1350), and Ibn Khatir (1301–1373) to whom are added the writings of more contemporary theologians such as Syed Qutb (1906–1956), and Sheikhs who rose to prominence as a result of their interpretations of key concepts in the context of local or regional politics.[9]

In any one country there are several groups claiming to practice one type of Salafism or another. For example, Upper Egypt and Lower Egypt evolved two distinct types of Salafism as a result, among others, of their differing conceptions of the principle of *hisba*, the Quranic injunction "to command right and forbid wrong" as expressed in sura 3:104, as well as the use of violence to bring about political change.[10] Parenthetically, the invocation of *hisba* inevitably raises the issue of political legitimacy. Indeed, who has the authority to command and forbid? Can a Muslim obey a ruler who strays from the path of God? Should a Muslim obey a ruler as long as he is a Muslim regardless of his commitment to doing right? In answering such questions, some Salafi groups, such as the quietists, throw their support to the state no matter its policies as long as its leader is a Muslim, and may even justify acquiescence to an unjust political system.[11] Groups vary in their assessment of what constitutes legitimate and illegitimate rule. This is so because it is difficult to determine when a ruler is no longer legitimate as the determination has consequences for the method used in fighting political illegitimacy. The line separating quietism and Jihadism is "fine and subjectively determined." It "explains why most Salafis have been dogmatically politically quietist while a minority of Salafists, including the Wahabi movement, has turned to armed struggle."[12]

The indeterminacy as well as ambiguity of Salafis' positions on a number of issues is further compounded by the fluidity of their memberships. Members may migrate from one group to another, or the same group may change its tactics and adopt an entirely different outlook from the one it started out with, depending on the historico-political conjuncture.[13] This has consequences for a state's religious policy. A government that intends to support one Salafi group may find itself outmaneuvered by the group it does not support, or may discover that there are unsuspected limits to the usefulness of the group it promotes. Indeed, the state can never be sure of the fealty of a Salafi group it defines either as friendly towards its religious policy,[14] or as a pawn in its own struggle against political groups. At any rate, regardless of their labels, claimed or attributed, Salafis generally engage, some more than others, in an in-depth educational and socialization process through study groups or summer camps for youth, which helps spread their message.[15] However, the core message is one of a pristine Islam and an ethical conduct modeled after the Prophet's companions, relatively independent of the political objectives of the group. As such, the Salafi message has a cultural impact that is greater than realized, especially with respect to women as will be discussed below.

Algerian Salafism and the state's religion policy

During the colonial era, analysts labeled the movement initiated by a group of religious scholars at the turn of the twentieth century "reformist." More recently, since the rise of faith-based groups intent upon ascending power in the 1970s, this movement has been identified as modernist Salafi. As indicated above, it was in the tradition of the nineteenth-century reformist movement of Al Afghani and Abduh in so far as it called for a better knowledge of Islam (better still a rediscovery of Islam), the expansion of literacy as well as education in the Arabic language to combat ignorance and superstitions (understood as having denatured the progressive character of Islam), and cultural development. Structural change of the kind Al Afghani called for was not part of Ibn Badis's program of action as it would have meant agitating for an end to colonial rule, which he could not afford to call for at the time. Women in this view would benefit by being educated in order to raise enlightened children and keep the family together. Education would ensure that women would be active participants in the task of regenerating Islamic culture, starting in the family.[16]

In the years preceding the Civil War (1992–2002), a number of faith-based groups emerged or resurfaced due to the political liberalization initiated in the aftermath of the October 1988 riots. Alongside the party of the Front Islamic Salvation (which included individuals with diverse religious orientations) were groups that were essentially offshoots of the old *'Ulema* movement of the 1920s. At the onset of the war of decolonization, leading members of the *'Ulema* reformist group joined the Front of National Liberation (FLN) while others preferred to devote themselves to piety and preaching (*da'wa*) according to the Salaf (companions of the Prophet Muhammad).[17] Dubbed "quietist Salafists," they rose to prominence in the post-Civil War years. However, reports indicate that they were already active during the Civil War as intermediaries between the military and the armed protagonists to bring about a negotiated end to the conflict.[18] This meant that quietist Salafis were an asset to the state in securing support for its 1999 reconciliation policy, which had at first met with some reticence, especially among those who had lost kin and property during the Civil War. The state reached out to Salafis as a force that ostensibly shuns the pursuit of political power, enjoys symbolic power among its followers, and appears to act as a benign moralizing agent in society. Furthermore, the "Arab Spring" added another incentive to the state's strategy of courting quietist Salafis for their predilection for order and rejection of chaos and revolution (*fitna*). As it happened, the best-known quietist Salafi figures, Abdelmalek Ramdani and Ali Ferkous, exhorted the Algerian people not to join in the "Arab Spring" protests, which they attributed to the hidden interference of foreign powers bent upon sowing discord among Muslims. Abdelmalek Ramdani issued a *fatwa* (religious opinion) against protests aimed at overthrowing the political system in which he argued (according to an interpretation of the classic texts on political legitimacy) that as long as a ruler is a Muslim, "you must obey and listen to him." Should a ruler fail to govern according to Islamic principles, he still commanded obedience. Ramdani advised that "prayer and patience" not protest would then be advisable.[19] However, benefiting from the state benevolence, quietist Salafis have been able to expand their reach and build a base of social support that has consequences not only for continued state support but also for the prospect of the sustainability of their quietism. In the absence of a national survey of religious affiliation, it is unclear how many people in Algeria are members of a Salafi group.

Saudi Arabia looms large in the etiology of the *Salafiyya* in Algeria. One of the pioneers of the *'Ulema* movement, Tayeb al 'Oqbi, had spent time in Saudi Arabia. In the 1980s, the Algerian government chose Saudi universities, especially that of Medina, for training Algerian students intending to become *imams* in Islamic sciences.[20] Notable figures of contemporary quietist Salafis such as Ali Ferkous, Azzedine Ramdani, or Al Eid Cherifi were trained in Saudi Arabia. The Saudi influence is not limited to education and training. It is also evident in the close relationship established between Saudi theologians and the Algerian Salafi leadership. For example, a prominent Saudi Salafi sheikh, Rabi'e al-Madkhali, appointed Abdelmadjid Djem'a and Lazhar Snigra as the Algerian representatives of (his brand of) Salafism.[21] Reports indicate that a highly popular Saudi Salafi scholar, Muhammad Al Arefe, "boasts a larger following in Algeria than in the kingdom itself."[22] The Saudi ties to quietist Salafis are a matter of concern for Algerians unaffiliated with Salafis, especially women, as they fear the restrictions Salafis place on individual behavior in daily life.

Quietist Salafism's growing influence

The alarmist articles published about the Algerian state's tolerance and active support of quietist Salafis may overstate the extent to which this group poses a threat to the political system. They do, however, reflect unease about the state policy of fostering a custom-made Islam for Algeria as much as it sheds light on the contested nature of what constitutes faith. Can religious faith be mandated by the state? Can it be nationalized? What happens when faith becomes a commodity to be promoted for its salability regardless of its intrinsic meaning to the individual? At any rate, quietist Salafis have used the media, Internet and satellite TV to disseminate their message and reach young women and men seeking meaning and a sense of belonging in a society that has yet to mend its frayed social fabric or overcome the crisis of confidence it has experienced in the aftermath of the Civil War.

It is tempting to attribute the rise of religious groups and networks to a number of the state's shortcomings, including its ineptitude in stemming poverty; its immiseration of the population; its aloofness from the people's needs and aspirations; or widespread corruption. Indeed, all these factors add up to explain why faith-based groups might find an audience. However, they do not explain satisfactorily the state's unimaginative, albeit commonly used, recourse to religion as the arena in which to recoup legitimacy. It is no surprise that quietist Salafis would concentrate their efforts in the very area, education, which the state had dominated but failed to energize. They have quietly disseminated their social views and religious orientation by securing zones of influence in universities, especially in students' extra-curricular activities, cafeterias, as well as dormitories where adherents agitate for a "purist" Salafi lifestyle. They have also opened their own schools and mosques often flanked by bookstores stocked with Salafi literature as would be expected.[23] Furthermore, they have made inroads in business. Many have become entrepreneurs doing business with the Gulf States, or have managed to control neighborhood shops as well as the ever expanding informal sector.[24] Purportedly, a number of individuals who benefited from the amnesty that put an end to the Civil War found a channel of reinsertion into society in the informal sector, which largely escapes state control.[25] Quietist Salafis' influence extends to individuals' decision-making in a number of areas, such as whether to bank or secure loans from a bank,[26] or how to handle domestic issues concerning marriage and the family.

From the perspective of this book, it is the in-depth work of re-socialization of young women and men, which the network of Salafis has undertaken, that matters as much as, if not more than, their political influence. Salafi re-socialization at the community level reshapes cultural institutions, just as it inflects individual women's and men's attitudes towards self and others. That a similar re-socialization has also been underway at the hands of state-sponsored popular Sufism does not make the battle over the soul of women and men at the heart of the state's *wasatiya* Islam policy any less momentous or socially risky for those who are unaffiliated. In the end, although aware of the risk of being too close to the state, quietist Salafis have taken advantage of the state religious political strategy of propping them up as an alternative to "extremism" to carve out for themselves a cultural domain whose autonomy they seek to preserve. As quietist Salafi Sheikh Abdelfattah Zeraoui put it "Our objective is not to achieve political ends but rather to transform society, which has been negatively influenced by Western values, into a genuine Muslim society."[27]

What specific actions do quietist Salafis undertake to re-socialize individuals in a "genuine" Islam? They publicly denounce behavior or writing deemed un-Islamic and take action against it. Typically, such behavior

includes drinking or selling alcohol, practicing Sufism, engaging in prostitution or in the occult. Quietist Salafis have also carried out acts of cultural
policing reminiscent of the early 1990s. In July 2018, they prevented *rai* con-
certs from taking place in the southern cities of Ouargla and Bechar as well as
Saida and Tiaret where similar events had taken place.[28] Quietist Salafis have
also challenged the preaching of traditional (state-sponsored) *imams*. On
occasion, they have been able to influence state decision-making. For example, they successfully opposed the state administration from requiring that
women appear without a *hijab* on their passport photos.[29] They have also
"held increasing unseen sway over religious policy"[30] as the state cracked
down on the Shi'i Ahmadi sect, which Salafis abhor. In spite of their active
investment in the socio-cultural life of women and men, quietist Salafis have
been relatively more popular among youth than the old faith-based parties at
least until the massive protests initiated in 2019, which have drawn large
numbers of youth, among whom students.

In the absence of reliable surveys or monographs, it is difficult to ascertain
the degree of popularity of Salafis, quietist or otherwise, among young women
and men. At any rate, although not focused on Salafism, a limited, gender-
blind survey carried out in 2011 indicates that young people identify themselves as Muslims, and are keenly aware of the state sponsorship of Sufism as
an antidote to Salafism.[31] Admittedly, such awareness could favorably inflect
youth's attitude towards quietist Salafism. From the state's perspective, the
expanding role of quietist Salafis poses little political risk. Furthermore, it
may even prove rewarding if quietist Salafis' proximity to the state becomes a
bone of contention among other Salafis, or faith-based groups eager to enter
the political fray. Sure enough, the socio-cultural gains, which quietist Salafis
have made thanks to the state's abetment, have started to be challenged by
other Salafis. For instance, Abdel Fattah Hamadache, an outspoken Salafi,
took issue with the quietist Salafi leader Ali Ferkous's critique of *hizbiya*, or
partisanship. He cast doubt on Ferkous' authority to speak about issues such
as politics. Hamadache decided to do exactly what Ferkous condemned: to
form a party, The Islamic Sahwa Front, which the state has not recognized.[32]
Similarly, Madani Mezrag who fought as an "emir" (or regional chief),
against the state in the Civil War, also formed a party, unrecognized by the
state, "The Algerian Front for Reconciliation and Salvation."[33] However, lack
of state recognition, difficult to secure given the constitutional prohibition of
parties formed on the basis of religion, is not synonymous with the state's
dismissal of the importance or usefulness of a (virtual party) leader.[34]

In spite of the nebulous character of where quietist Salafism ends, and
Jihadi Salafism begins, government officials have on occasion publicly defined
Salafism (used generically) as part and parcel of a national Islam. In the
words of Ahmed Ouyahia, who was prime minister in 2017: "we love Salaf-
ism, it is our religion. Let's be Salafists in our nationalism."[35] The Prime
Minister's exhortation left no doubt about the religious identity the

government was eager to promote, one that is pietistic and concerned with managing every detail of everyday life according to moral principles narrowly defined as pure, or purified. The promotion of this mode of being Muslim compounds the state's support for Sufism, as the two religious trends stress an inward-looking Islam, purportedly unconcerned with politics. Nevertheless, the state's religious policy is hardly coherent: on the one hand, the state supports quietist Salafis and makes concessions to them. On the other hand, it also seeks to hedge its bets by becoming actively engaged in the campaign of "deradicalization" of Islam by actively cooperating in the French policy of laicization of the Algerian imams officiating in France.

The 2012 state's upgrading of *imams* to the status of civil servants enabled them to form unions. A study of the unionization of imams indicates that non-Salafi *imams*, feeling the competition from their Salafi counterparts seek to exclude them from their unions.[36] Whether intended or not, the state's upgrading of its imams' status functions as a mechanism for bringing Salafi-affiliated *imams*, who enjoy more autonomy in preaching in their mosques than state-sponsored *imams*, into the fold. Indeed, both categories of *imams* struggle for better working conditions as they also enter into conflict with each other.

Women and Salafism

What is remarkable about the state's religion calculus is the absence of women. Whether throwing its support to Sufism, Salafism, or upgrading *imams*' training, the state religious policy is silent on the effects of its policy on women. To reiterate, the creation of a corps of *murshidat* hardly addresses women except as religious subjects. However, quietist Salafism, as a socializing institution, has appealed to women, just as it has appealed to young men alienated by the state's advancement of Sufism or the uninspiring lectures of state-sponsored *imams*.[37] Women emerge as members of a population assumed to be in need of religious re-socialization by various faith-based groups, which include Salafis as well as the parties that reconstituted themselves out of the ruins of the Front of Islamic Salvation in the aftermath of the Civil War. Each faith-based party has its women constituency, and each engages in a socialization of its youth. For instance, the MSP (Mouvement de la Société pour la Paix), Movement of the Society for Peace, just like the *Alawiya* Sufi order, sponsors its own scouts. Faith-based parties also put forth women candidates to Parliamentary seats in fulfillment of the state-mandated 31 percent women quota. Thus, just like the state, the gender question enters the political calculations of faith-based parties often make for burnishing their "modernist" image as they compete with one another, seek to expand their audience, or adjust their methods of operation to changing times.[38]

Invisible in the state religious policy or in articles concerned with the cultural inroads made by quietist Salafism, women are nevertheless active in

Salafism just as some are active in Sufism. Salafi women are recognizable in streets by their full-length black dress, black niqab, black gloves as well as the socks worn on their sandaled feet. There is a dearth of information about Salafi women in Algeria. A research carried out in the Western city of "N"[39] by a Ph.D. candidate in Algiers over a four-year period of time with a group of twenty women aged 18 to 45 reveals the similarity of the socio-economic circumstances of the women. All the women lived in poor neighborhoods where the GIA (Groupe Islamique Armé), a group that fought the state during the Civil War, operated. They had four or five years of schooling, and none of them worked outside their homes, although they made handicrafts, which they sold in their mosque. In general, the women were introduced to Salafism by a father, although some named a husband or a friend. For some, knowledge of Salafism triggered a reflection on their personal behavior with men, which led them to search for "repentance." A respondent indicated that with the help of her husband, she looked for a path to her salvation. They all wanted "recognition" of their faith as Salafis. It is noteworthy that the women read books on Salafism printed in Saudi Arabia, and were familiar with the ideas of authors such as the Saudi Salafi Ibn al-Baz, as well as the medieval theorists Ibn Taymiyya and Ibn Qayyim al-Jawziyya. They typically shunned the writings of authors associated with the Muslim Brotherhood. Interestingly, once women have accepted Salafi ideas, they act as socializing agents for other women at social events, such as wedding ceremonies. They also act as guardians of the faith. Thus, at meetings in a mosque, an older and charismatic leader made sure that the groups she led understood the tenets of Salafism, and at times did not hesitate to expel a member who appeared to her to have deviated from the core Salafi beliefs. Given the various strands of Salafism, each group seeks to maintain its boundaries and enforce its core beliefs. The author of the research stressed that the women she observed did not question what they learned. Notably, the researcher herself was nudged by some of the Salafi women at the mosque to dress like them in their Saudi-inspired *jilbab*.[40]

Parenthetically, the interview I held with this researcher yielded a significant insight in the potentially transformative effect of research on the researcher. This researcher had started her fieldwork with the question "Why does a woman become Salafi, given that Salafism has no roots in Algeria?"[41] In the discussion of Salafi women's dress, the researcher spoke of her own *hijab*. She revealed that she had not worn it when she entered the University. In her second year, she wore a *khimar* (head dress that also covers the neck). About this time, she started to attend a mosque "to listen to Sheikhs." It is in the mosque that she met other sociology students. At that point, wearing the *hijab* became for her a "*haja thaqafiya*" (a cultural thing). She continued to wear it even though her father preferred that she did not. Soon she became "used to it." However, she wondered "why is the *hijab* said to protect women from *fitna*, when women who wear it in a sexy manner already engage in *fitna.*[42] She had doubts about the Quran, the behavior of the Prophet ("why did he have 13 wives"), and even the existence of God. Although she still accomplished her prayers, she found it unbearable to hold such doubts while continuing to fast and pray during Ramadan. The cognitive dissonance she experienced between the ritualistic performance of her religious duties and her personal beliefs made her feel "uneasy," and caused her to stop attending the additional prayer of *Tawarih,* which occurs after the break of the fast during Ramadan. The researcher was sure she would not wear the *hijab* if she were in France. She further pointed out by association of ideas that a Danish female *imam* and sociologist, Jihan Khanqan [Sherin Khankan], who established the "first all-women mosque, without men," did not wear a *hijab.*[43]

I take these doubts and questions as being precipitated by the participant observation the researcher carried out with Salafi women who reportedly embraced their beliefs wholeheartedly. Although it would be foolhardy to assume that the research caused the researcher to doubt her own religious beliefs, it is not possible either to discount the multiple and subtle ways in which research on an issue that is related to the researcher's own feminine condition could affect her behavior. This case reveals, even if tangentially, the meaning of Salafism for women who are not Salafi, but are Muslim. It may arouse in a non-affiliated woman feelings of estrangement from her own faith. Indeed, Salafism, as practiced in its "purist" form, is a mode of being Muslim that is predicated on the erasure of the female body as well as her total adherence to its core beliefs. Hence, a woman initially wearing a common *hijab*, and doing participant observation of a community of Salafi women, may not remain unaffected by her experience. It goes without saying that the research experience could also have gone another way: becoming sympathetic to Salafism or even joining the movement.

To return to Salafi women, a brief discussion I had with a 37-year-old unmarried high school science teacher in Algiers revealed her commitment to the purist approach to Salafism as part and parcel of Islam, which she strongly defended. She wore the long black garment that is the hallmark of Salafi women's dress but did not wear a face veil.[44] Unlike the women studied by the researcher discussed above, my interlocutor did not display a docile attitude.[45] Rather, she was combative and spoke out of conviction. At any rate, Salafi sheikhs issue *fatwas* about women as they do about men. The respondent's attitude denotes the importance of education in the degree to which a woman affiliated with quietist Salafism identifies with, and feels empowered to defend, the Salafi doctrine. The process of identification with Salafism is enhanced by Satellite television, which disseminates messages to women in their own homes from local as well as Saudi preachers. Television reinforces the socialization process that takes place in mosques, Salafi-sponsored schools, universities, and child-care services. Discussions with researchers in the city of Oran, reveal that child-care services are frequently offered by faith-based groups, including Salafis.

Just like Satellite Television, the Internet is proving to be an avenue for Salafi women to build a presence as well as a following as *da'iyat*, or preachers. A study of forty women preachers on a Salafi website indicates that the women seek to have their views publicized to achieve prominence. Not only are they active agents contributing to the site, they also use their identity as women to speak authoritatively about their Salafi beliefs. They avail themselves of their gender to use the imagery of motherhood, family, and care for others in promoting the Salafi worldview. Their "identity authority" especially when it is publicized through the Internet helps them to build knowledge as well as charisma.[46] It is noteworthy that the website is popular among users from Saudi Arabia, Egypt, Sudan, Morocco, and Algeria.[47] The study confirms the participant observations made by the Algerian researcher quoted above, that women preachers have charisma—a necessary quality for being authoritative—and are active guardians of the integrity of their belief system as Salafis. In other words, the effectiveness of these women is greatly aided by their using their gender as a source of validation of their beliefs to forestall two major types of criticism: feminist as well as "secular." The issue is not whether these women have agency or not.[48] Of course they do. The issue is that they speak from the standpoint of believers who happen to be women and use their experience as women to advance their religious cause. The feminine identity they draw upon (as expressed in motherhood, family and the like) distinguishes their style of preaching from that of men, a style that gives their message authenticity. Unlike men, they tend to avoid references to the *hadith*, and focus more on issues concerning education writ large, the family, as well as the protection of Muslim culture from "Westernization."[49] For all these reasons, Salafi groups welcome women among their ranks and promote their participation. Through them, they reach a wider audience and remain relevant in the lives of their members. Conversely, acceding to the role of preacher and achieving notoriety is a source of empowerment for women. They acquire the recognition which women in the Algerian researcher's study longed for. The implication of the recognition that Algerian Salafi women preachers seek is different from one that a feminist might claim. It is for the sake of having a voice in the dissemination of the faith. In the end, faith trumps the promotion of an emancipatory goal for women where emancipation is equated with freedom from a gendered religious discourse of the quietist Salafi kind.

The question the Algerian researcher asked, "why would women turn to Salafism," is not trivial. Although the context is different, a study carried out among Salafi women in a London mosque provides insights into the benefit, so to speak, that these women derive from Salafism.[50] The clarity and specificity of the Salafi core beliefs, including those pertaining to gender, helps women to know where they stand as well as provide them with guidelines, many of which written, about how to regulate their behavior. The value-confusion reigning in highly industrial and liberal London, or oligarchic and socially restive Algiers, affects women's definition of their situation and sense of purpose. What a Salafi woman in London called the "grey zone areas," which cause confusion and uncertainty, dissipated when she became Salafi. Adepts know what is correct and what is incorrect, right and wrong, and experience as a result a sense of "inner peace."[51] Equally important, Salafi women in Algeria (like most of the women in the London study) were already Muslims. These women's adoption of Salafism appears to be a sort of awakening, a discovery that their behavior as Muslims was amiss and needed to be adjusted through a process of re-learning what it means to be a Muslim.[52] Finally, Salafi women enjoy the added advantage of becoming part of a supportive network of like-minded women through knowledge circles, mosque attendance, and Internet exchange.

In sum, the state religious policy of alternately tolerating and supporting quietist Salafism is strategically silent on women. It is equally silent about the social restrictions Salafi beliefs place on women either directly or indirectly. Indeed, the inroads quietist Salafis made in the domain of culture have a direct bearing on women's freedom of movement, their participation in festive social events, or their choice of occupation. Arguably, women's agency cannot be dismissed in analyzing their involvement in Salafism. However, the exercise of agency is framed by a cultural climate in which Islam is a site of struggle between state and various religious groups, each vying for control over what it means and how it should be practiced. Ironically, the invisibility of women in the state *wasatiya* Islam policy is at the same time a condition of possibility of the policy itself. Absent in the state public discourse of support of quietist Salafism, women are understood to be the guarantor of its viability. Quietist Salafis would not support the state if it challenged their ability to define women's roles and socialize them in their belief system. By the same token, enjoying a relative cultural autonomy, Salafis promote women preachers to expand their reach not only among women but also men skeptical about their social agenda. In so doing, they cause the state to cede a cultural domain, which it avowedly seeks to gain back from "extremists." Consequently, the state's definition of a "national culture," or "national Islam" is predicated upon groups, Sufis and Salafis, whose quiescence is necessary to the task. In other words, the state religious policy results in a (at times barely) managed cultural chaos, which it seeks to rationalize, in which women are at once central and absent. Could women protect their rights as citizens through faith-based groups, such as the Salafis, in the managed cultural chaos so created? Are such groups' activism among women a harbinger of an Algerian version of Islamic feminism? In the end, the worldview of Salafi women is not fundamentally different from that of the Islamic feminists who advocate a re-valuation of institutions such as the family as an organic unit to strengthen faith as a bulwark against "secular" feminism. Salafis are convinced that they are preserving their faith in a pure form, the Islamic feminists want to preserve it by expanding its positive features as a defense against a perceived threat to its socially unifying message.[53]

Notes

1 Henri Lauzière, *The Making of Salafism: Islamic Reform in the Twentieth Century* (New York: Columbia University Press, 2016), 2. In the Algerian context, the concept is at times used as a generic term for all faith-based groups. Consequently it is difficult to distinguish groups from one another except according to whether they use violence or not. Salafism becomes synonymous with religious activism. See Amel Boubekeur, "Salafism and Radical Politics in Post-Conflict Algeria," Carnegie Papers, *Carnegie Endowment For International Peace*, September 2008.
2 Hadith reported by Al-Bukhari, as well as Meslem, both of whom are considered reliable. Cited in Tariq Abdelhaleem, *The Counterfeit Salafis: Deviation from the Methodology of Ahl Al Sunnah Wal Jama'a*. Book one of the Stray Sects Series (Scarborough, Canada: Al Attique Publishers, 2004), 10, fn. 10, 11.
3 For heuristic reasons, Henri Lauzière reduces the complexity of the Salafi movement to two "paradigms": Modernist and Purists. *The Making of Salafism*, 5. However, seeking to preserve the complexity of Salafi groups, their geographic location, as well as their assessment of whether *jihad* is necessary or not, Tariq Abdelhaleem lists eight groups, one of whom (group 3) he names "Academic Salafis," which is focused on Salafi thought; ibid., 15–21.
4 Ibid., 6. It must be noted that *bid'a* in this context means departure from the text so as to make it new.
5 Ibid., 8. The rejection of the four schools of law is motivated by purists' view that the schools violate *tawhid*, the unicity of God, by opening the door to *shirk*, understood as polytheism due to the multiplicity of legal opinions.
6 Ibid.
7 Tariq Abdelhaleem, *The Counterfeit Salafis*, 16.
8 For example, the Madkhali Group bears the name of one of its founder Rabee' al-Madkhali (1931); it operates in Kuwait and Libya among other countries.
9 More recent Sheikhs include 'Umar Abd al-Rahman (Egypt), Nasr al Din al-Albani (Syria; Jordan), Issam Al-Bashir (Sudan), or Abd al-Aziz Ibn Baz (Saudi Arabia). See Tariq Abdelhaleem, *The Counterfeit Salafis*, 15–21.
10 Roel Meijer, *Global Salafism: Islam New Religious Movement* (New York: Columbia University Press, 2009), 196. Salafis in Upper Egypt were considered more quietist than their counterparts in Lower Egypt, although they too have on occasion used violent tactics.
11 This is the case of Ibn Baz group, which supports the Saudi government, or of the Salafis who condemned the Tahrir Square protests in Egypt in 2011 before the state cracked down on them. Traditionally, the Salafis' attitude towards legitimacy has been (at least until the eighteenth and nineteenth centuries) in accordance with "the classical Sunni Islam embodied in the ninth-and tenth-century religious texts," which favored political quietism no matter the depth of the ruler's commitment to his religious duties. However, should the ruler cease to be a Muslim, the texts allow for resistance to his rule by violent means. See Jonathan Brown, "Salafis and Sufis in Egypt," *The Carnegie Papers, Middle East, Carnegie Endowment for International Peace*, December 2011, 3.
12 Ibid. The Wahabi movement was born in the Arabian Peninsula and was instrumental in bringing the House of Saud to power in the eighteenth century.
13 According to Meijer, *Global Salafism*, 204, one quietist Salafi group "can snap and tip over into an activist, even revolutionary movement at the critical point when subservience [to God] is transformed into revolt."

14 Jonathan Brown notes in this respect: "Political acquiescence, however, does not mean that Salafis approve of the modern secular state." See "Salafis and Sufis in Egypt." 4.
15 Roel Meijer, *Global Salafism*, 192.
16 For the role of women in the Algerian reformist movement see Lazreg, *The Eloquence of Silence*, ch. 5. For studies of the reformist movement in Algeria see, among others, Ali Merad, *Le réformisme musulman en Algérie de 1925 à 1940: essai d'histoire religieuse et sociale*, second edition (Algiers: Les Editions El Hikma, 1999); and the more impressionistic study of James McDougall, *History and the Culture of Nationalism in Algeria* (Cambridge: Cambridge University Press, 2006), esp. ch. 3.
17 Amel Boubekeur, "Salafism and Radical Politics," 15.
18 Lamine Chikhi, "Hard-line Islam Steps out of The Shadows in Algeria," Reuters, August 10, 2010, 2, www.reuters.com/article/us-algeria-religion-salafism-idUS TRE6791TQ20100810, accessed October 29, 2019. See also Vish Sakthivel, "Political Islam in Post-Conflict Algeria," Hudson Institute, November 2, 2017, www. hudson.org/research/13934-political-islam-in-post-conflict-algeria, accessed December 1, 2019.
19 Anouar Boukhars, "My Enemy's Enemy," Carnegie Middle East Center, April 18, 2018, 2, https://carnegie-mec.org/diwan76098, accessed October 27, 2019.
20 Amel Boubekeur, "Salafism and Radical Politics," 13. See also Anouar Boukhars, "'Quietist' and 'Firebrand' Salafism in Algeria," Carnegie Endowment for International Peace, November 24, 2015, 2, carnegieendowment.org/2015/11/24/quietists-and-firebrand-salafism-in-algeria-pub-62075.
21 Anouar Boukhars, "My Enemy's Enemy," 3.
22 Cited in James M. Dorsey, "Algerian Controversy Over Salafism Puts Government Control of Religion on the Spot," *Modern Diplomacy*, April 25, 2018, accessed December 9, 2019. https://moderndiplomacy.eu.
23 Lamine Chikhi, "Hard Line Islam," 6, reports that one bookstore in a mosque in the Rouiba suburb of Algiers, displayed a 500-page book on "how to maintain your beard."
24 Anouar Boukhars, "My Enemy's Enemy," 2.
25 Ibid.
26 Chikhi, "Hard Line Islam," 7.
27 Ibid., 6.
28 Lamine Ghanmi, "Salafists' Rise Triggers Concern in Algeria over Cultural Freedom," *The Arab Weekly*, December 8, 2018, https://thearabweekly.com/salafists-rise-triggers-concern-algerians-over-cultural-freedom, accessed December 14, 2019.
29 Ibid., 8.
30 Sakthivel, "Political Islam," 20.
31 Hamid Khemissi, Ricardo René Larémont and Taybi Taj Eddine, "Sufism, Salafism, and State Policy," *The Journal of North African Studies*, 17, 3 (June 2012): 547–558. hhtps://doi.org/10.1080/13629387.2012.675703.
32 Boukhars, "My Enemy," 2. *Hizbiya* also means the creation of a party as a strategy.
33 Boukhars, "Quietist," 3.
34 Ibid. Boukhars mentions that in 2014 Ahmed Ouyahia, then Minister of State and Chief of Staff, consulted a former Front of Islamic Salvation leader who had been active in the Civil War, Madani Mezrag, about the revision of the Constitution. This is an example of the government's instrumental as well as transactional attitude towards faith-based groups in a bid to ensure the perpetuity of the political system.
35 Ibid.,3.
36 Interview with F.M., Oran, June 27, 2018.
37 Visha Sakthivel ("Political Islam," 17) reports that some youth also see Sufism the way Salafis do, as *bid'a*.

38 For the transformative effects on faith-based groups of their failed attempts at seizing or keeping power, see Asef Bayat's *Post-Islamism: The Changing Face of Political Islam* (Oxford: Oxford University Press, 2013), esp. ch. 1.

39 To protect the identity of the researcher, because she revealed personal information, I use the letter N to refer to the city where she carried out her fieldwork.

40 Interview with T.R.A., Algiers, June 14, 2018.

41 The view (commonly held in public discourse) that Salafism is a foreign import conflates Salafism with Wahabism. It is at odds with the view, held by a number of researchers, according to which all faith-based groups (except Sufis) and parties are Salafis. See fn 1, above.

42 *Fitna* means disorder such as that caused by revolution. In this case it means disturbance (of the normative order of modesty) caused by sexual temptation and desire.

43 Interview with T.R.A., Algiers, June 14, 2018. Sherin Khankan, a Danish Muslim born to a Syrian father and a Finnish mother, announced in 2016 the opening of a mosque, the Mariam Mosque, staffed by female imams who would minister to women as well as men except during Friday prayers, which would be reserved for women only. See "Women-Led Mosque Opens in Denmark," *The Guardian*, February 12, 2016, https://theguardian.com/world/2016/feb12/women-led-mosque-opens-denmark, accessed December 17, 2019.

44 Discussion with Fatima (last name cannot be revealed) in her home in Algiers, June 14, 2017.

45 T.R.A. used the consecrated expression, "*sama'na wa ta'na*" (we heard and we obeyed), to indicate that the women accepted what they were told about Salafism blindly. It is difficult to draw any conclusion from the researcher's comment, as it may also reveal something about the researcher's own attitude towards the women. Only when more research has been carried out on Salafi women can such comments be ascertained.

46 Richard A. Nielsen, "Women's Authority in Patriarchal Social Movements: The Case of Female Salafi Preachers," *American Journal of Political Science* 64, no. 1 (January 2020): 52–66. The quoted phrase is on p. 5. This lucid article sees Salafi women as acting out of their beliefs rather than an assumed lack of awareness of women's issues. In fact, one of them saw herself as a writer on "women's issues" instead of *da'iya* (preacher), the title the website, said.net, conferred on her.

47 Ibid., 7.

48 Richard A. Nielsen's otherwise informative article is still concerned with demonstrating that the women in his study have "agency." Ibid., 2.

49 Ibid., figure on p. 9.

50 Anabel Inge, *The Making of Salafi Women* (Oxford: Oxford University Press, 2017).

51 Cited in ibid., 94.

52 Inge uses the term "converts" to women, born Muslim, who adopted Salafism as if it were a new faith acquired after a process of reflection. She also uses the term to capture some Muslim women's attempts to explore various strands of Islam in an immigrant setting before settling on Salafism. It is noteworthy that Inge's respondents refer to themselves as converts or "reverts"—women who have gone back to their Muslim roots through Salafism. Ibid., ch. 3, especially p. 63.

53 See, for example, Ellen Anne McLarney, "Heba Rauf Ezzat's Politics of the Islamic Family," in *Women in Egypt's Islamic Awakening* (Princeton, NJ: Princeton University Press, 2015).

5

ISLAMIC FEMINISM IN THE SHADOW OF DERADICALIZATION

This chapter explores "Islamic feminism," a heterogeneous trend of thought which plays an important part in Morocco's "moderate" Islam policy, but presents a challenge to women who prefer to advocate for change outside the religion framework. It describes the various currents which comprise the trend, especially Quranic attributor contextualism and enquires into its function in local and global policies of combating "radical Islam." The state's *wasatiya* conception of Islam as a means to forestall a political radicalization of Islam re-inscribes women as passive agents in a normative system in which gendered interpretations of the sacred texts are beyond questioning. On occasion, the policy adopts from classical *shari'a* a women-friendly option, such as that of *khul'* (which allows a woman to request a divorce) but leaves in place the inequities of the existing Family Code in matters of divorce, child custody, polygamy, and inheritance.

The Algerian state has not, or not yet, prominently sponsored a more expansive view of Islam as gender egalitarian as neighboring Morocco has at least rhetorically. This does not mean that Algeria is more socially conservative than Morocco; it means that it has not at this time sought to pre-empt or appropriate the feminist vocabulary as well as agenda for political ideological purposes. Conversations with the leadership of the Haut Conseil Islamique reveal acceptance of women's advancement as a gradual process driven by women's own efforts. Religion did not figure prominently in this view. To recall, both countries, Algeria and Morocco, are actively involved in a "deradicalization" campaign alongside France, other European countries as well as the United Sates. Furthermore, as indicated, the idea of creating a corps of *murshidat* to provide education, guidance, and counseling to women in socio-religious matters was initiated by the Algerian state before it was adopted and expanded in Morocco. The Moroccan state's sponsorship of a corps of *murshidat* actively involved in promoting a view of Islam, ostensibly similar to that of feminists seeking reforms within the bounds of Islam, clearly aims for the containment rather than the promotion of genuine and lasting reforms, some political, others juridical, on behalf of women as citizens.

The focus of this chapter is to understand the objectives and consequences of "Islamic feminism," a significant instance of the cultural turn with which this book is concerned. This modality of the cultural turn among women seeking change needs to be unraveled carefully as it has obscured calls for socio-political change outside of the religious realm. In fact, it is frequently presented as a breakthrough for women in the region, and an alternative to what has been defined as "secular" feminism. As such, it has benefited from a benevolent reception by the state in several Middle Eastern countries,[1] garnered support from a number of Western feminists, and has been applauded as a culturally appropriate method of bringing about change.[2] Yet, the label "Islamic feminism" obscures the significance of the scholarship initiated by women whose objective is to explore the formative period of Islam as well as theological issues from a critical perspective to make visible the contribution of women, shed light on zones of shadows in Islamic thought, and broaden debates. Women in Algeria have not turned to Islamic feminism in the manner that Moroccan or Egyptian women have. The differences between the two countries raise an important question: does the Algerian *wasatiya* policy leave a space within which women can envisage change outside the framework of religion? The question is all the more important that since February 22, 2019 a movement of mass protest has emerged as a de facto counterpower, raising hopes of women and men for reforms to fulfill citizenship rights.

The limits of *wasatiya* Islam

Whether encouraging the development of popular Sufism, supporting quietist Salafism, or upgrading and professionalizing the function of *imam*, the Algerian state's official policy views women as a group who must be managed in the immediacy of their status as believers. In its struggle against "radical Islam" the state reinforces women's acceptance of their roles as mothers, wives and daughters who (implicitly) might have to continue to put up with male relatives' abuse of their authority rather than question males' empowerment when it is contrary to the letter and spirit of Islam. The state's strategy is predicated upon a conception of women as somehow more religious than men, and less aware of the religious justifications of inequality. The strategy conflates the socio-economic vulnerability of women with their assumed blind religious belief, if not gullibility, best captured by a Ministry of Religious Affairs director's assertion (reported in Chapter 3) that women, as good Muslims, would never accept a reform of the *shari'a*'s unequal inheritance prescriptions. Admittedly, the director's response may betray his own feeling about inheritance. Nevertheless, he spoke with the assurance of a man who was confident in women's conviction that they cannot challenge texts that cause them harm as Muslims. Hence, women are assumed to be yielding subjects of *wasatiya* Islam.

The state's *wasatiya* policy aims for a sort of pacification of social life through religious and quasi-religious practices. Since, from the state's perspective, revolts, dissidence, mass movements, or organized political opposition are usually led by men (albeit with the participation of women), it would make sense to reinforce the existing gender social order rather than alter it, as it is the order which men generally do not question. In comparison, the *wasatiya* policy which the Moroccan state adopted actively intervenes in the religious domain by rhetorically promoting a liberal interpretation of Islam aimed at incorporating women in religious structures such as the corps of *'Ulema*, giving them a platform as *murshidat* for disseminating among other women a purportedly progressive view of Islam. This policy, when considered alongside the 2004 revision of the Family Code, which allowed women to contract marriage without a guardian, or assume custody of a child, burnished Morocco's sheen as a progressive state.[3] The difference between the two countries may very well be one of style. For instance, Algeria enables a woman to be a de facto *'alima* who engages in the drafting and evaluation of *fatawa* as pointed out in Chapter 2. The prohibition of women from the function of *imam* or the retention of polygamy in both countries reinforces their similarity. However, there are historical differences between Algeria and Morocco which might shed light on the relative opportunity each country has to bring about change in women's status. Algeria is a republic established after a long war of decolonization, and its president's power to manipulate religion, albeit real, is relatively limited. In contrast, in Morocco, the monarch owes his legitimacy to traditional authority (in a Weberian sense) and has greater latitude in the management of religion. Unlike a president, the king, as "commander of the faithful," a traditionally ritualistic function which became codified in 1962, has greater authority over religious matters in the pursuit of political goals.[4] However, just like Algeria, Morocco is actively engaged in a policy aimed at weakening its religious-based opposition. More importantly, since 2003 it has spearheaded a more ambitious deradicalization program than Algeria with the support of Western powers.[5] More than Algeria, Morocco inscribed women as active agents of its program, albeit presenting it to them as an instance of the King's gender-friendly conception of Islam. Women's engagement in the state's *wasatiya* Islam policy means their consent to the state's active participation in the "war on terror," but raises questions about the ethical-political orientation of feminism in Morocco, either liberal or Islamic.[6] Algeria's experience with the Civil War may have loomed large in the Moroccan strategy of weakening religion-based parties by playing them off against "secular" left-leaning parties. However,

Morocco went beyond Algeria in enlisting women as a counter-force. Furthermore, as indicated in Chapter 3, Morocco's deradicalization program targets women as its victims too by enlisting women to fight (literally or symbolically) other women as discussed in Chapter 3. The Moroccan approach too is one of pacification of women through induction into the religious establishment as directed by the monarch. To a greater degree than Algeria, Morocco's policy rests on the control of mosques and their staff, support for popular expressions of Sufism as well as quietist Salafism. The Moroccan state is actively engaged in an apparent policy of tolerance and encouragement of selective public cultural displays of freedom of speech as exemplified in some television programs, or films normally subject to censorship. For instance, the government permitted an adaptation of *The Vagina Monologues* performed under the title *Dialy* ("mine"). It also allowed artist Latifa Ahrar, to remove her clothes one piece at a time and "lay half naked on the stage" in performance of her play, Kafr Naum, in violation of the state law prohibiting nudity in public.[7] Ostensibly a strategy of baiting the conservatism of faith-based parties, the selective tolerance for female nudity, normally punishable by three to six months' imprisonment founders on the treatment of homosexuals.[8] Interestingly, and in a sort of competition for ostentatious openness of mind, a controversial and quirky cleric who supported the government's deradicalization policy, Abd Al Bari Al-Zamzami, issued a fatwa authorizing women to masturbate with a number of objects.[9] Lest this fatwa be interpreted as a positive act of social change, it must be remembered that the fatwa intervenes in, and intrudes on, the intimacy of a woman's body and sexuality.

The Moroccan case is important for comparative purposes. Algeria and Morocco stand at opposite ends of the political instrumentalization of religion. Other countries can be placed in between them with Egypt occupying a mid-position. At this conjuncture, the apparent convergence between the Moroccan state religious policy and "Islamic feminism," poses an important question: does the Moroccan state religious strategy, as compared with Algeria's, create the conditions of possibility for gender equality? Conversely, does the state strategy impede alternative modes of activism among women to achieve change outside of a controlled religious framework? Indeed, it is one thing for a woman to be a *'alima*, it is another for her to be legally and politically empowered to overcome poverty, perform her professional duties without undue obstacles if she works, have equal access to paid employment as men, move about freely, and generally live as she pleases without feeling the pressure to conform to customary images of gender as exist in the collective conscience?

Islamic feminism: concept and etiology

Whether the emergence of "Islamic feminism" as a method of change in Algeria, as compared with Morocco, is inevitable or unlikely requires an exploration of what is meant by this trend of thought; its political implications; and its role in the geopolitical management of Islam. When viewed from a broad historical perspective, "Islamic feminism," in spite of its contested definitions, is the third pole in the constellation of events that characterize the management of religion since the 1970s in the Middle East and North Africa (MENA). Although "Islamic feminism" has not yet taken root in Algeria, it needs to be analyzed as an event with an indirect effect on the state's religious policy. Against the background of the Civil War, the generic term "Islamic feminism" crystallizes Algerian women activists' fears of a recurrence of a time when women's socio-economic roles became restricted and redefined. Admittedly, Algeria's proximity with Morocco where "Islamic feminism" has become an integral part of the state's religion policy would have helped to disseminate ideas espoused by Islamic feminists. Why this has not occurred may be an effect of a long-lasting political enmity between the two countries stemming from conflict over the Western Sahara's movement of independence, which Algeria supports and Morocco combats. It is also due to a historic lack of trust between the two countries stemming from skirmishes over their borders that began immediately after Algeria's independence, or to ideological differences as can emerge between a monarchy and a republic with socialist aspirations (at least until 1978) and a non-aligned foreign policy.[10] For Algerian women to adopt the views of Moroccan Islamic feminists would be politically inappropriate as well as a social faux pas. At any rate, "Islamic feminism's" grounding in religion requires critical scrutiny, without detracting from its significance or doubting the integrity of its proponents. Ultimately, what is at stake is women's emancipatory progress as well as the future direction of change in gender relations in the region as a whole.

The concept

Attempts at tracing the etiology of "Islamic feminism" stumble on the meaning of the term. Indeed, the label conjoins two terms, Islam and feminism. Islam as a religion is the domain of the sacred, of beliefs in a transcendental being, and matters of individual salvation even as it seeks to moralize the social order. Feminism belongs in the domain of the profane because of its critical stance towards the existing socio-cultural order, its demystifying bent, and liberatory impulse. Admittedly, the dichotomy, "sacred" and "profane,"[11] may not capture the complex reality of life, especially if one accepts the prevailing conception of Islam as a faith and a culture. However, in most MENA countries, everyday life, at work or play, unfolds in its own space, according to its own tempo, and is regulated by non-religious norms. It is precisely the management of this space (with its psychological implications) that challenges the accepted wisdom about the purportedly all-encompassing role of Islam in everyday life. The often-contested distinction which Muslims make between *din*, the domain of religion as belief, and *dunia*, life, the domain of mundane activity that may contradict *din*, in reality captures the relationship between two related yet relatively autonomous spheres of life. Furthermore, feminism articulates demands for change on behalf of women, which are assumed to be a matter of political rather than divine will. The conjoining of the two terms, Islam and feminism, presumes that the two orders of reality are translatable into each other—a chancy presumption that needs to be substantiated. Hence, discussions of the validity of the conjoined concepts, Islam and feminism, focuses on two related issues: that Islam is compatible with feminism, and that a woman can be both a Muslim and a feminist. The expression "Islamic feminism" further obviates the intrinsic as well as extrinsic factors that would hamper the conjoining of the two terms just as it ignores the multiple effects of their assumed translatability on women. In other words, the label "Islamic feminism" is constitutive of a referent that is at odds with the reality it is presumed to connote. Hence, it is no surprise that a leading feminist who writes about Islam and women, Azizah al-Hibri, who pioneered this stance in the United States, did not refer to herself as an Islamic feminist when she undertook the task of deconstructing the accepted meanings of problematic *suras* in order to dispel the prevailing notion that Islam "oppresses" women. Interestingly, her iconic piece was entitled "A study of Islamic *herstory*" (emphasis added)—a title that captured her claiming the power to tell her story as a Muslim.[12] This is different from claiming to speak to Islam under the banner of a concept, feminism, which in the public discourse of women has its own history built outside of Islam. But, Asma Barlas who avails herself of the language of feminism also strenuously objects to her work being characterized as Islamic feminist.[13] This is not to say that Islam cannot accommodate feminism, that women committed to their religion cannot be feminist, or that their feminism is necessarily suspect. It simply means that some concepts (in this case "feminism") have, for right or wrong, acquired a history and cultural meanings tied to particular countries from which disentangling one's self is a constant challenge. Hence, acceptance of the concept (of feminism) need not be coupled with religion, precedents established by Christian or Jewish feminisms notwithstanding. Indeed, academic feminist scholarship itself inflects the orientation of the religious critique, if not its very terms. In the words of Hibba Abugideiri, "an interesting irony characterizes the limitations of the Islamic feminist project more broadly: while the academic profession affords Muslim feminists the authority and forum through which we can "unread patriarchy" from Islam's sacred past, it also restricts the feminist engagement to disciplinary modes of inquiry".[14] Admittedly, it is time to rewrite the entire history of Muslim cultures from a fresh woman's perspective.[15] Naturally, however, a project of this kind is qualitatively different from what "Islamic feminism" appears to be. Adding a qualifier such as "Western" or "Islamic" to feminism is meant to take the sting out "feminism," and by the same token give Islam as a religion an attribute that alters, at least semantically, its theological character. That this might be one of the goals of those who pro-mote Islamic feminism as the only method to bring about change is plausible. However, the goal of a few, presented somehow as universal, engages the lives of those who do not share it. I am not only thinking of the women labeled "secular" because they disagree with the political implications of "Islamic feminism," but also of the women who live outside of academia, are uncon-cerned about feminist theory and practice, experience firsthand the self-empowerment of their male relatives over them, and whose daily activities unfold in the profane world.

A widely used historical account presents Islamic feminism as one of two competing "paradigms," the other being "secular." It identifies as "secular" nationalism, Islamic modernism, human rights, humanitarianism, and democracy.[16] The baffling inclusion of Islamic modernism as a feature of the "secular paradigm" is indicative of the expansive use of the term "Islamic." Islam as a concept belongs in the class of concepts that establish a common-ality of meaning between diverse phenomena, assume linkages between them, or infer a unity among them in spite of their dispersal in time. Such concepts have a totalizing function, which obscures the reality they are meant to con-note.[17] Hence "Islamic feminism," just like "modernist Islam," leaves unad-dressed the multiplicity of historical and religious realities, which the concept subsumes, just as it obviates the equally diverse ways of practicing Islam or being Muslim. These realities transcend the signifiers, modern or feminist, as illustrated by the very exclusion of modernist Islam from the definition of "Islamic feminist paradigm." Does this "paradigm" imply that Islamic fem-inism is unrelated to modernism, that it transcends modernism, or that it operates in a pre-modern space? If so, the prospect for social change in the here and now on which Islamic feminism stakes its *raison d'être* would be unfounded.

The academic justification of the concept of "Islamic feminism" rests on two arguments. First, the assertion of the universality of feminism that needs to be protected from conservative Muslim males who oppose reforms in favor of women on the grounds that they represent a "Western" incursion in local culture. Second, and relatedly, the need to support women as challengers of Islam to achieve "gender equality." Islamic feminists are thus seen as doing what Western feminists could not do without being taxed with transgression: remake Islam as only a woman could. If the first argument is well founded and defensible, the second one is more dubious, albeit attractive, and may speak to the historian's vicarious experience of partaking in the act of taking on religion. Both arguments stem from a profound sense of feminist entitle-ment to brandish the flag of liberation for Muslim women who must be defended and protected even from themselves.

By way of digression, and without impugning the integrity or the scholar-ship of non-Muslim feminists, the debate between Asma Barlas and Margot Badran[18] about whether Islamic feminism is "feminist" is indexical of a broader issue which manifests itself in two ways: first, the inability of Muslims to examine their religion unchallenged by others. By comparison, when Christians, among them feminists, have examined their religion from a critical perspective, they have done so within their communities, among other Christians, unhampered by extraneous intervention, free of the need to justify themselves to others. This has allowed them to debate one another to advance their demands for change. On the contrary, for Muslims, to address Islam means to address not only Muslims like themselves who may hold different views, but also non-Muslims who speak as authorities on Islam, its history, the interpretations of its texts, its capacity to change, and challenge Muslims' own views. More important, Muslims often feel compelled to accept the views of their non-Muslim challengers. Admittedly, the plural knowledge context within which discussions of Islam take place can only enrich debates. However, whatever enrichment there is, it does not make up for the loss of self-empowerment which the individual Muslim experiences in writing about her religion: she is constantly reminded that her own belief is a matter of contest or approval by others who act as experts on her own salvation. In essence, the insights that she might have as a Muslim (whether practicing or not) are to a large extent devalued by being ceaselessly contested.[19] That this is an instance of the global unequal distribution of knowledge, particularly of Islam, with the attendant power to determine what voices should be heard, and what perspective should be accepted, goes without saying. This said, Badran was not wrong in her assertion of the feminist impulse behind "Islamic feminism;" Barlas's denegation, even when qualified, mistook form for content.[20] The issue will be further explored in Chapter 7.

In the end, scholars hailing from a Muslim background tend to compensate for the challenge they expect from non-Muslims by disparaging those among their fellow coreligionists who express their critique of their cultural heritage using concepts such as "secularism," which have historically been associated with Western history. In other words, either these critics (perceived as one homogeneous group) acquiesce to Islam-as-feminist discourse or become political dupes, if not cultural traitors.

Situating Islamic feminism

There are several accounts of "Islamic feminism," some formulated by women who identify themselves as "Muslim feminists,"[21] or women whose religion is Islam, but shun the label,[22] others by Muslims critical of Islamic feminism's method,[23] still others by non-Muslim academic feminists, such as Margot Badran, cited above.[24] I will focus on Badran's simply because it is frequently quoted by women addressing "Islamic feminism," attempts a sweeping historico-theoretic account of the issue, and is challenged by the women it characterizes as Islamic feminists. According to her account, Islamic feminism is first and foremost feminism. Hence its etiology is the same as that of feminism. From this perspective, feminism finds its origin in the long history of the nineteenth century, beginning with the reforms initiated in Turkey; the Arab national awakening in Syria and Iraq; the advent of the printing press; and the extension of education to women. This etiology rightly draws attention to the imperial context within which and against which intellectual as well as political movements for recovering national sovereignty emerged, and which in one way or another opened a space for women to articulate their views and interests.[25] The etiology further dates the inception of "Islamic feminism" (the conjoining of the two terms, Islam and feminism) to the 1990s as a result of a combination of events, including the rise of a newly urbanized class, which is more susceptible to the comforting messages of "Islamism" because it finds itself in the throes of social anomie resulting from the challenge of adjusting to city life.[26] This view echoes the prevailing notion in the relevant literature according to which the apparent popularity of faith-based movements in the late 1980s and 1990s (especially in Algeria) is due to a failure of the modernization efforts of post-colonial governments. Debating the merits of this proposition would require more space than is available, suffice it to say that it begs the question whether postcolonial governments were truly modernist, and if they were, how could their modernism be defined and measured before it is declared failed?[27] Nevertheless, this view informs the characterization of "Islamic feminism" as a viable alternative to "secular" feminism which, indebted to "Islamic modernism," had purportedly failed to achieve juridical reforms beneficial to women, bring about a "new ideology, or new tools."[28] By contrast, "Islamic feminism" has the capacity to inspire and mobilize women just as it has the potential to bring about reform. Once feminists have rid it of its patriarchal distortions, the Quran is Islamic feminism's "new edge," which paves the way for *shari'a* reform. In doing so, "Islamic feminism" purportedly radicalizes the Islamic modernist component of "secular" feminism and uses it as a tool for building a "progressive religious discourse," which promotes "the unqualified equality of all human beings."[29] To recall, the definition of the Islamic feminist paradigm outlined above did not include Islamic modernism as one of its sources. Unlike "secular" feminism, which purportedly accepted "gender complementarity" in the family and in society, Islamic feminism aims for gender equality as a precondition for achieving "social justice." Besides, because Islamic feminism exists in a number of Middle Eastern and North African countries, it is on its way to becoming a progressive "social movement." Given that Islamic feminism "takes the Quran as its central text," it is home-grown since it uses the cultural vernacular.[30] Although this analysis of Islamic feminism allows that all feminisms in the Middle East are "home grown" and not mere importations from the West, it clearly upholds Islamic feminism as a genuine, autochthonous feminist event. As such it has a genealogy, which traces the names of the women who since the 1940s engaged religious texts in one way or another.[31] Said in passing autochthony is a contested reality as it can take on a regressive (in the sense of dipping in a recessive past) character.[32]

The agents of Islamic feminism so constructed include disgruntled former female members of "Islamist" parties; women concerned about or fearful of the socially conservative agenda of faith-based parties; and those among women, primarily rural, who were able to study the religious sciences thanks to the democratization of education.[33] In other words, the carriers of the idea of Islamic feminism are "secular" women as well as women who are committed to change within religion alone. The question is what brings these diverse women together to uphold Islamic feminist ideas? How do "secular" women negotiate the two domains, Islam and feminism, where they may be in contradiction with each other, or neutralize each other? For instance, there are problematic theological restrictions—by definition non-negotiable—as opposed to juridical restrictions—which may be unacceptable to "secular" feminists.

There are a number of questions, which this construction of Islamic feminism invites: first, on the one hand, it defines Islamic feminism as paradigmatic in opposition to the equally paradigmatic view of "secular" feminism. On the other hand, it claims that both paradigms find their roots in "Islamic modernism," an undefined term. Presumably, Islamic modernism affected the effectiveness of "secular" feminists. By contrast, Islamic feminists were able to radicalize Islamic modernisms and forge ahead with a more galvanizing agenda, at once more culturally adapted and progressive. Implied is a perception of Islamic modernism as a sort of hybrid, neither truly Muslim nor modern, which "secular" women were unable to manage, causing them to fail to bring about needed reforms. In other words, "secular" feminists were either not entirely "secular" since they operated within the framework of "Islamic" modernism (not modernism tout court), or conversely, were not authentically "Islamic" since they were "secular." Either way, it is unclear what "secular" feminism actually means, or what is "secular" about "secular feminism." Nevertheless, the imprecision of the concept of "secular feminism" is made necessary by the claim that "Islamic feminism" is a new paradigm, ostensibly better suited for Middle Eastern cultures, and endowed with the capacity to become a movement. It is unclear why one "paradigm" should replace another (as if this were a scientific revolution)[34] when the issue at hand is feminist orientations towards, and strategies for, change rather than one normative view of the world. Admittedly, the concept "paradigm," is often used liberally. However, because "Islamic feminism" *is* presented as having displaced a failed "secular" feminist "paradigm," it must be questioned as it presumes that feminism in MENA is an either/or proposition. The multiplicities of ways of being feminist and activating for change are by definition foreclosed, and must be brought in line with Islamic feminism, which is deemed "universal."[35] And it is under the banner of its universalism that the two types of feminism (Islamic and secular) "are recovering holistic Islam in which secular and religious dissolve back into each other. The two feminisms are producing Islam's gender revolution—indeed, Islam's revolution in the

Middle East and beyond."[36] Such an impassioned conclusion contradicts the premise of the uniqueness of Islamic feminism as being a more genuine and adapted "paradigm" of feminism than "secular" feminism. It asserts a synthesis of feminisms, a reconciliation of feminists who find themselves in the newly discovered universalism of a re-invented Islam as promoted by women engaged in a two-pronged struggle of *ijtihad* and *jihad*.[37]

Second, and related to the preceding, the contradiction inherent in this etiology of Islamic feminism conflates three major orientations towards Islam: (a) being a feminist who advocates for change, especially the implementation of citizenship rights, while conducting one's life as a Muslim; (b) being a feminist who is convinced by whatever circumstances (situational or global) and by sheer pragmatism that some change can only occur within the para-meters of Islamic law; (c) being a feminist who is convinced that Islam as a religion allows for change in gender relations if it is wrested away from the patriarchal interpretations that shaped Islamic law. The latter orientation is also characteristic of women who focus on re-interpreting texts in order to pinpoint masculinist interpretations of key *suras* focused on women, and offer a more egalitarian interpretation. These women engage religious texts in a manner made familiar by Christian or Jewish feminists to carve out a space for women not only in worship but also in ministering (for lack of a better word) to worshippers. Hence, they seek to be counted as scholars of religion on a par with men. Even though these women may also seek change in Isla-mic law (since it is partially derived from the Quran), their focus is primarily to contest men's monopoly over interpretation and knowledge, and enrich knowledge of Islam. The conflation of these three feminist orientations towards Islam explains why distinguishing "secular" from "Islamic feminism" without defining "secular" vitiates the distinction. It permits the proponents of Islamic feminism, however, to peremptorily assert the unifying power of their worldview. Hence, by fiat, "secular" feminism (or any other kind of feminism) is deemed to have acquiesced to its own undoing without a struggle since it was already spent and defunct. The totalizing concept of "secular" conceals other forms of feminism such as skeptical feminism—a feminist stance that is unconvinced by these perspectives on change in women's live.

Third, the claim that Islamic feminism is bringing about a revolution in Islam to which all other feminisms have rallied presumes that there is a con-sensus among women in the region about the inevitability of Islamic feminism as well as its viability as the only adequate avenue for structural change ben-eficial to women. This is the most problematic assertion. One may quibble about whether Islamic feminism is revolutionary or not, but the implied con-sensus reveals two unexamined assumptions: religion is the source of women's unequal status as well as its solution, and women have no other aspirations but to retrieve a putatively lost liberatory religious meaning concealed in religious texts. Additionally, it is assumed that texts have lain dormant for centuries, and women are now opening them to bring them to a new

revolutionary light. The history of Islam and women appears as one of felicitous rupture. In other words, there is a seamless thread that is presumed to
span various national and transregional political as well as cultural histories,
before culminating in the phenomenon of Islamic feminism.

Admittedly, the act of empowering one's self to read religious texts directly
and interpret them—an act made possible by the democratization of education—is an expression of the will, and a singular challenge to the inter-
pretative monopoly heretofore held by men. However, such an act, albeit
valuable, concerns the religious domain, not the profane world, which continues to function according to its gendered political, economic, as well as
social inequities. In the world of everyday life, customs generally escape the
grip of religious norms. Customs that have become unquestioned through
time, and inform unreflective practices do not easily lend themselves to re-
interpretation of the kind Islamic feminism proposes for religious texts. More
often than not, they contradict religious norms and values.

The all-encompassing nature of Islamic feminism as constructed is clearly
meant to characterize feminism in the Middle East as an autochthonous
adaptive system of ideas different from Western feminism albeit resonating
with it. There is no doubt that women in the Middle East have acted in the
remote past in ways that reflect a keen awareness of gender inequities which
they questioned, and which we can interpret in hindsight as expressing a
"feminist" consciousness. However, it is undeniable that autochthonic feminist thought overlooks some compelling sociological facts. Significant, yet
omitted, is the role played by the United Nations Decade for the advancement of women. At the risk of belaboring the obvious, these gatherings
brought together women from all parts of the world who heard the status of
women debated in various fora and were provided an opportunity for inter-
acting with one another. Furthermore, before the ten-year interval gatherings,
each country wrote a report describing steps made to advance women's rights
and identify areas of improvement. Although some of these reports were
state-sponsored and possibly not accurate, they compelled women leaders and
intellectuals to take stock of women's situations in their own countries.
Women started thinking of themselves as a separate category of people in
their own right, having needs that had not been met, and compared their lot
to others in an act akin to consciousness-raising. Furthermore, the United
Nations Decade was partially informed by Western feminists' thought as well
as activism, which had made inroads in the United Nations own methods of
carrying out its development projects. The pulling power of the United
Nations Decade cannot be minimized in discussing the dissemination of
feminist (or women-centered) ideas. During the United Nations Decade, there
had been conventions that drew attention to discrimination against women,
such as the 1979 Convention on the Elimination of All Forms of Discrimination Against Women.[38] It goes without saying that this women-sensi-
tive international framework did not affect women in developing countries

only; it also enabled Western countries to catch up with one another.[39] It must be recalled that the idea that gender inequality was an issue to be discussed, debated, and remedied arose in the aftermath of struggles for decolonization as well as the civil rights movement in the United States of America, both of which preceded the United Nations Decade. It was the combination of all these events that constituted women and gender inequality as *issues*, or *questions* worthy of special and immediate attention. To reiterate, the emphatic and inflated character of the etiology of Islamic feminism under consideration ignores and silences the voices of the women who do not agree with the Islamic feminist orientation or may think it does not represent their vision for viable change. Moreover, when highly educated women call for a re-interpretation of texts, or when women become *'alimat,* they are engaged in the momentous act of feminizing access to specialized knowledge. It is doubtful whether their ultimate purpose is to create an autochthonous feminism. They are functioning in a sphere removed from that of the illiterate, poor, or politically disenfranchised women, albeit the hoped-for reform of the *shari'a* would benefit all women, if and when it occurs.

Women's and feminist contextualism

It is clear that the construction of an etiology of Islamic feminism discussed above is a defense and an apologia. How do women (about whom the etiology was constructed) engage religious texts? Some avail themselves of a feminist perspective, others do not, although they all take ownership of their religion, Islam. Generally, theirs is a woman-centered Quranic contextualism[40]. The literature on contextualism as a philosophy (which Islamic feminism has yet to engage) and a method is vast. As a method it has been used in biblical studies to counter literalism—a task that bears strong similarities to that of the women labeled "Islamic feminist." Contextualism captures the relationship between context (in its multiple presentations), meaning, and the interpreter. Contextualists employ hermeneutics for its usefulness in sensitizing the reader to the dependence of meaning not only on the context of a *sura,* for example, but also the context within which *the interpreter* attributes (or re-constructs) the meaning of the *sura.*[41] Typically, a scholar selects a concept that lends itself to several meanings, focuses on an alternative meaning, which she proceeds to justify as the truer or true meaning *in the context* of other Quranic injunctions which convey a broader, less gender-bound, and more universal message. In other words, if the more universal message (which addresses women equally with men) is taken as the *context* of meaning within which to interpret specific *suras,* which at first glance contradict the spirit of the Quran, the true meaning of these *suras* (which had been distorted by masculinist[42] interpretations) is revealed. By the same token, the contradiction dissipates. However, contextualism does not end here. It enlarges the context of analysis and interpretation to embrace history on two analytically distinct levels: the history of a specific injunction, such as for example that of witnessing; and the history of Islam as a religion, its birth, its evolution, its key figures, and its institutionalization. At times, the two levels are conflated. However, the interpreter's own context is seldom reckoned with *as part of* the truth construction.

There are a number of ways women use contextualism. To digress, I have myself, without being a religious scholar, engaged in the exercise of questioning veiling, which women often take to be a religious obligation, using a soft contextualist approach.[43] My transgressive act was contextualist in a narrow sense, as it did not include an historicization of the entire Quran. The subject matter itself, veiling, does not question the validity of gender differences in the Quran. My intervention merely intended to point to the act of veiling (wearing a *khimar* or *thaub*) as contingent (it varied with the status of the women summoned by the *suras*) rather than necessary. Besides, I found support in a little quoted *sura* allowing women who have no hope for marriage or bearing children to dispense with veiling altogether.[44] Hence, to address veiling contextually is to understand and clarify what the relevant *sura*s in the text said rather than explain away the practice of veiling.

A woman scholar may identify her contextualist task as feminist. Such is the case of Amina Wadud who "re-reads" the text from a woman as well as a feminist perspective, and qualifies her advocacy for feminizing the Quran as a *jihad*, or a religious mission.[45] Contextualism can also be motivated by a critical impulse without claiming feminism as its purpose. Rather it seeks to demonstrate the distorting effects of "patriarchal" interpretations of key *suras*. This type of contextualism is not bent upon reforming Islam as a religion. On the contrary, it intends to debunk misconceptions of Islam in order to make a case for its compatibility with institutions routinely perceived as Western and thus modern. For example, Azizah Al Hibri does not address gender issues only; she further intends to demonstrate the relevance of Islamic political thought and institutions to the contemporary world. Hence, her orientation is qualitatively different from that of feminist contextualists. It is, for lack of a better word, "institutionalist." She builds on the heritage of Islamic political and legal philosophy in the manner that nineteenth- and twentieth-century Muslim thinkers did in their search for political change. Therefore, Al Hibri's scholarship is also constructivist and encompasses both women and men. She writes for the retrieval of a different socio-political order adapted to the present. A third contextualist approach characteristic of Asma Barlas[46] overlaps to some degree with Wadud's. It is a woman-centered interpretation of the Quran as well as the *shari'a,* using the language of feminism.

Unlike Wadud, Barlas "unreads" masculinist texts in order to unearth their true (egalitarian) meaning. Her purpose is to argue that the Quran, when deciphered from a woman's perspective, yields a different meaning. This is akin to arguing that there is a hidden subtext or a liminal text, which must be found. As noted, Barlas does not claim to be a feminist, a posture that needs to be taken seriously. Her goal is not to reconstruct the Quran but to reveal its hidden meaning through a grid that enables her to find a meaning beyond, not to "read," the existing text. In other words, Barlas's view is not to reform but bring to life what is already there. However, "unreading," if taken literally, presumes two things: another (possibly non-conventional) method of comprehending a text; and the belief in the existence of another text, which the method may bring to light. This bringing to light is itself a process of infinite regress since "unreading" cannot be stopped without being a reading in its own right. Without characterizing the author's belief, this places Barlas close to the *shi'i* conception of a hidden Quran decipherable with the proper method, which might require esoteric knowledge. *Shi'i* scholars have traditionally claimed the existence of an original Quran kept by Ali, Prophet Muhammad's son-in-law, and willfully distorted by succeeding Caliphs who created an Orthodox version.[47] Barlas's method of "unreading," however, obscures the fact that there are multiple ways of "reading" and that reading is a personal experience that cannot be undone.[48] Nevertheless, the method is meant to reveal an unknown and undistorted, gender egalitarian Islam which makes redundant any other method, especially the purportedly secular method, but yields a culturally authentic solution to women's demands for juridical change. The newly found text is a *re-formed* Islam. I will refer to the women who use contextualism from a stated or unstated feminist perspective as an antidote to "secular" feminism for the purpose of re-forming Islam as "attributor contextualists." This concept, often used synonymously with "epistemic contextualism," draws attention to the interpreter's own context as a factor of interpretation. Without claiming expertise in the philosophy of contextualism, I use this term descriptively to indicate that the normative Islam these scholars advocate depends on their own existential context which includes their positionality towards feminism and their aspiration to cultural autochthony as the only method of change. In this case, the historicization of the Quran becomes not only the context for interpreting problematic *suras* but also the grounds for making the new interpretation normative to justify the interpreter's attribution of meaning.

One form of unbridled contextualism and historicism veers into downright tendentiousness. Using *shi'i* where *sunni* sources fail to support her point of view, Hela Ouardi, takes the death of Prophet Muhammad as a metaphor for a religion purportedly pieced together by unscrupulous Caliphs who imposed their own version of the Quran.[49] Furthermore, and more important, she constructs a portrait of Muhammad as a flawed man and father who implicitly does not deserve the reverence he commands. Whether this is true or false is beside the point. A great deal of what Ouardi cobbled together is not unknown, but her intention and orientation depart from those of the women contextualists mentioned above. She neither re-interprets specific *suras*, nor provides the foundations for a reformist view of Islam. Rather, she presents an incomplete harmatography grounded in multiple sources some less reliable than others, and many still being debated, but which she harnesses as established facts. Admittedly, and according to the prevailing feminist understanding, she is a brave woman who empowered herself to construct *her* view of Islam. However, because she speaks as a woman in our gender-aware era, the reception of her book, if not its credibility, owes as much to her gender as to the subject-matter, Islam. Furthermore, her intention implicates other women whose religion is Islam, including those attempting to bring about change within Islam, and whose task will henceforth become more complicated. This is not to say that the author should not have written her book. Rather, the point is that writing as a woman, or from a woman-centered perspective about other women's (since they are part of the audience too) beliefs entails a degree of care and ethical concern for others. This raises the crucial question of what critique is, and not any critique but that of Islam in a context saturated with critiques carrying varying degrees of convincingness.

How should a critique of Islam be carried out so that it is not imitative or repetitive of existing critiques, but enlightening to those who practice their religion, and productive of ideas for change? The subject of critique is a delicate one in general, and even more so for feminists. It is not that feminists should be subjected to different standards of criticism than men. It means that women's/feminists' critiques are more compelling when they set standards that are better than those of men in their sharpness and in their power to unsettle taken-for-granted gendered notions; they are more compelling when they help to lift women's sights up rather than launch them on a slide of infinite interpretations at the risk of dismissing or undermining their *experience* of their faith.

Selective responses to women's contextualism

The intent of this discussion is not to do a review of the literature but to provide a sense of the attention spurred by the idea of "Islamic feminism"[50] in the aftermath of the "Arab Spring" which, among other things, signaled a containment of faith-based movements—which women's Quranic contextualism intends to counter.[51] As might be expected, responses run the gamut from critical, supportive, to skeptical. The earliest critical responses focused on Iran, which was one of the countries where women, living under an "Islamic republic," sought to bring about change in their status by examining religious texts since these formed the foundation of the state's gender policy.[52] Among more recent critiques, Fatima Seedat's response is instructive.[53] She questions the apparent "convergence" of Islam and feminism implied in the conjoining of the two terms. She sees the conjoining as bringing about a closure of the space between religion and feminism needed to allow the expression of different modalities of working towards gender equality to develop.[54] She attributes the apparent convergence to the tension between "Western feminism," which cannot be ignored in spite of its short-comings, and "postcolonial feminism," which challenges its presuppositions. She also rightly thinks that a groping for modernity lies behind the impulse towards Islamic feminism.[55] Regardless of its modest conclusion, this view has the merit of asking the right questions even as it does not distinguish between strands of "Islamic feminism." Noteworthy is the author's quandary at having her and her associates' work labeled "Islamic feminist."[56] Raja Rhouni, who identifies herself as a "progressive Muslim," questions Islamic feminists' reliance on foundational texts as a source of gender equality. She advocates instead a "post-foundational path" which cannot dispense with the method of the social and human sciences.[57]

That there would be women and feminist advocates of feminist con-textualism goes without saying. What is notable is men's embrace and apology for feminist contextualism originating from scholars of religion as well as social scientists. Taking Morocco as his case study, sociologist Ilyass Bouzghaia gives credence to the notion that "Islamic feminism" is a "third way," a solution to the dichotomous view of his society as balancing like a pendulum from tradition to modernity.[58] He notes that, in Morocco, Islamic feminism emerged in the aftermath of the "Arab Spring," which precipitated the need for a value change, as a method for bridging the gap between mod-ernity and tradition. It heralds for women "a modern understanding of reli-gion to keep loyal to their faith and meanwhile enjoy the rights of equality."[59] The unintended consequence of the author's uncritical view of "Islamic fem-inism" is to burden women with the complex task of reforming religion as well as the political apparatus responsible for maintaining the existing unequal gender order.[60] Grounded in gender studies as well as Islamic studies, Adis Duderija assesses the merits of "Islamic feminism" in order to determine "the viability of the Islamic feminist scriptural hermeneutic project."[61] Invoking contextualism, he finds extant Islamic feminism wanting, as it has yet to realize its potential. He defines "Islamic Feminism" as "a faith-based, global, intellectual, and activist-based movement, [which] seeks to engage systematically and productively not only with the sacred texts of the Islamic weltanschauung, namely the Qur'an, Sunna, but also the accumulated Islamic tradition as a whole, generally known as thurath."[62] However, the goal he sets for women is not different from what women and feminist contextualists have already identified. Grounding his arguments in secondary sources, he defines Islamic feminism's method as an "interpreter-centered hermeneutics," which intersects with literary theory, derives meaning from the texts in a dialogic exercise that teases out the universal value of social justice just as it histor-icizes them. He suggests that there are six methodological approaches to deriving meaning women might consider. Although a useful reminder to women to further develop their perspective, these approaches are not mutually exclusive with the approaches already used by women con-textualists.[63] Other male scholars, supportive of women's contextualism, are motivated by sentiments similar to women's. For instance, Khaled Abou El Fadel, an Islamic law scholar, engaged religious texts for the purpose of questioning the grounding of authoritativeness in writing or speaking about Islam, especially with respect to women.[64]

Questions raised by contextualist interpretations

A woman-centered or feminist contextualist interpretation of the Quran raises a number of questions: first, it must be remembered that *tafsir*, or interpretation of the Quran, exists and has been compiled over time, before the advent of feminism. Authors (generally men) of *tafsir* too availed themselves of context in order to shed light on this and that word or concept that made a *sura* difficult to understand. Hence, a woman-centered re-interpretation has to contend with *tafsir* to develop its own as Asma Barlas had to do. Going beyond existing *tafsir* means that a woman's interpretation must be compelling. It also means that a woman must decide what standard of knowledge of the Quran she is using in order for her to determine whether her proposed interpretation yields a truer knowledge of Islam. The targeted audience, women as well as men, is an important factor in ensuring that a woman-centered (re)-interpretation is heard. It cannot be taken for granted that women, whether versed in religious matters or ordinary, would accept a woman-centered reading of the Quran.

Second, faith and knowledge are not necessarily the same. What if a woman-centered interpretation goes against a woman's experience of Islam who is convinced that the Quran as it is written cannot and should not be re-interpreted? I am reminded in this respect of a young American-Muslim woman who, in the context of a discussion of veiling, exclaimed: "one cannot pick and choose from Islam." She explained that a woman cannot decide to select what to accept and what to reject in Islam according to her whim. What she meant was that attempts at explaining away selective *suras* threatened the integrity of the Quran. Admittedly, the young woman's comment expressed a male-centered conservative attitude, which should be dismissed. Yet, it is a woman's perspective, expressed freely, even if sociologically questionable. I am also reminded of another comment a woman in early middle age made in an Algerian context. She argued that she ignored what she perceived as Quranic prescriptions (which "we" believe as problematic) but hoped that God would forgive her. Hence, women, in their daily lives, have differing attitudes towards God, the Quran, knowledge of religious duties or of what Islam means, which may not square with a woman's Quranic contextualism.

Third, a woman-centered interpretation availing itself of contextualism as well as historicism assumes that meaning shifts depending on context and historical period. Thus—and this is the point the young woman cited above implied—the woman-centered interpretation espouses a relativist point of view. Relativism in this context is at odds with a believer's conviction that her religion is immutable. This is no idle question. It sheds light in retrospect on the difficulty the nineteenth century reformist movement encountered in its attempt to bring about change to the Middle East and North Africa, at a time when the region was falling prey to imperial rule. There are similarities between the reformist project and that of women contextualists. If the reformist movement as articulated by Jamal Ed Din Al-Afghani, and Muhammed Abduh[65] was a response to one-sided Western critiques, women's contextualism is a delayed and adaptive response to the global dissemination of feminism—a critical outlook on constituted knowledge and institutions, which brought with it awareness of local gender inequities as socially construed rather than ordained. It is also empowered by one strand of feminism, postfeminism, as will be discussed in the next chapter. Nevertheless, the positioning of the "reformists" towards Islam bears similarities with that of women contextualists. Al-Afghani focused on political and cultural development, including the spread of education to combat ignorance and superstition (which had negatively affected knowledge of religion as well as religious practices) to empower Muslims heretofore neglected by their governments; Abduh engaged in an avowedly progressive reading of the texts (theological and juridical). Those among the scholars, such as the Egyptian Qasim Amin (1863–1908), or the Tunisian Tahar Haddad (1899–1935) who attempted to address the woman question in their own way also did so within the parameters of religious texts, which they interpreted somewhat liberally. The point is that the geopolitical context of the time framed a critical intellectual reflection on Islam to inflect the direction of change then as it is today. Said in passing, the reformists' attempts cannot be adequately grasped under the generic term "Islamic modernism" just as the various strands of women's contextualism cannot be understood through the totalizing concept of Islamic feminism.

Fourth, and no less important, the various strands of contextualism construct a discourse out of the Quran and related texts presented as an emanation of the truth presumed to be located in the interpreter. Indulging in a devil's advocate point of view, the qualification of the interpreter as the source of (a presumably lost) truth is consequently grounded in biology. Since the presumed concealment of the truth by men is also attributable to biology,[66] on what grounds does the reader decide to accept one truth rather than the other? Could it be also on the basis of biology? Women would believe a woman-centered truth and men a man-grounded religious truth? The idea, worthy as it is, that contextualists wish to retrieve a universalist message that had been lost finds its limit in the very biological grounding of the contextualizer. The epistemological circle thus reaches its closure. This is hardly a new problem; it is encountered by anti-foundationalism as expressed in standpoint knowledge. Feminist work involved in demonstrating the sex bias inherent in the practice of science-as-usual as well as the institution of science itself have explained the merits and downside of standpoint knowledge.[67] The practical implications of this epistemic closure will be explored in Chapter 6.

This chapter attempted to clarify the meaning and operation of Islamic feminism which it identifies as women's (epistemological) Quranic contextualism—a set of ideas and a method aimed at re-interpreting and/or revealing the meaning of key *suras* from the Quran with a view to ultimately bring about gender equality in Islam. Although raising logical questions it did not make a judgment about the validity of women's contextualism, the significance of which is beyond doubt. Before concluding, a final remark is in order: the various strands of contextualism and historicism unfold in a sort of intellectual bubble removed from the practical socio-economic and political concerns of women (and men), even though these concerns are presumed to be the ultimate impetus behind the expressed intention of bringing about reform. The assumption of contextualists rests on a religious view of existing societies in the Middle East and North Africa, presumed to live in a Comtian theological age—an assumption that biases the contextualist enterprise. The next chapter will analyze the theoretical framework that empowered women's Quranic contextualism *qua* Islamic feminism.

Notes

1 In Iran, for example, women advocates of "Islamic feminism" were related to the leadership of the Islamic Republic, and not opposed to it. See Ziba Mir-Hosseini, "Beyond 'Islam' vs 'Feminism,'" *IDS Bulletin* 42, no. 1 (January 2011): 70.
2 Sympathetic academic scholars include, among others, Doris H. Gray, *Beyond Feminism and Islamism: Gender and Inequality in North Africa* (New York: I. B Tauris, 2015), ch. 3.
3 See Katja Žvan Elliott, "Morocco and Its Women's Rights Struggle: A Failure to Live Up to Its Progressive Image," *Journal of Middle Eastern Women's Studies* 10, no. 2 (Spring 2014): 1–30. This is an excellent analysis of the instrumental use of women in the state's religious policy.
4 Annelle Sheline, "Royal Religious Authority: Morocco's 'Commander of the Faithful,'" Rice University's Baker Institute of Public Policy, Center for the Middle East, March 2019, 4–5, www.bakerinstitute.org/media/files/files/02d67a3e/cme-p ub-luce-sheline-030719_hvUZDee.pdf, accessed March 24, 2020.
5 A firsthand account of the United States funding of a play portraying the apparent hypocrisy of an overly religious man in an attempt to discredit members of faith-based parties is provided by Annelle Sheline, ibid., 16.
6 Using a functionalist approach, Zakia Salime argues that feminists in Morocco "subverted the discourse and agenda of the war on terrorism" in their pursuit of reforming family law and expanding the role of women in religion. See her "The War on Terrorism. Appropriation and Subversion by Moroccan Women," *Signs*, 33, no. 1 (Autumn 2007): 20. It is unclear from the text how adherence to a state policy undertaken in the context of geopolitics is a subversion. Nevertheless, the article provides insights into the dynamics of Moroccan feminism as well as into the state's ultimate control of feminism in its active role as a regional relay in the "war on terror."
7 Abdelilah Bouasria, "Bits and Tits: The Dialectics of Bodily Encounters in Moroccan Politics," in Joshen Lobah and Hamza Tayebi, eds., *Trajectories of Change in Post 2011 MENA: Challenges and Prospects* (Rabat, Morocco: Hans Stiftung

Foundation. Takamul Center for Interdisciplinary Studies and Research, Oct. 2017), 183.

8 Ibid. The law against homosexuality is selective too as it varies with the social status of the offender. Bouasria reports that a known gay writer, Abdellah Taia, lectures unscathed. Furthermore, two French members of FEMEN (the Ukrainian feminist activist group which gained notoriety for protesting gender inequality by appearing topless in public), were expelled from Morocco when they staged a protest outside the court in Beni Mellal during the trial of a homosexual in 2016. By the same token, sex offenders such as Daniel Galvan, convicted of the rape of eleven children, were pardoned. Just as Galvan left the country, his pardon was withdrawn as a result of mounting protests. Ibid., 187.

9 Ibid., 184. See also "Moroccan Cleric Abd Al Bari Al Zamzami: Husbands May Have Sex with Dead Wives' Corpses and Women Use carrots as Vibrators," MEMRI (Middle East Media Research Institute) March 24, 2012, www.memri. org/legacy/clip/3426, accessed March 27, 2020. Al Zamzami (1943–2016) had been a member of the faith-based Party of Reform and Virtue, which he once represented in the Moroccan parliament (2007–2011).

10 There are political-historic reasons for why Algeria does not have as close a relationship with the United states as Morocco does. See in this respect, Yahia H. Zoubir, "Algeria and U.S. Interests: Containing Radical Islamism and Promoting Democracy," *Middle East Policy* IX, no. 1 (March 2002): 64–81.

11 For convenience, I am using Émile Durkheim's categories defining religion descriptively not substantively. Said in passing, in spite of his insistence on these binary categories, he evinced awareness of their interconnectedness: "if the profane could in no way enter into relations with the sacred, the latter could be good for nothing." *The Elementary Forms of Religious Life*, trans. Joseph Ward Swain (New York: Dover Publications, 2008), 37; 40. It is noteworthy that an Egyptian broadcaster for a Muslim Brotherhood TV station explained why his station could no longer focus on religious issues alone: "man is not so religious all the time ... Even when he does all his prayers, it's only thirty minutes a day. The rest of the time we eat, we work, we have sex, we have love. Why would we make the station about religion, religion, religion all the time?" interview by Peter Hessler, "Arab Summer: A Reportage at Large," *The New Yorker*, June 18, 2012, cited in Tarek Chamkhi, "Neo-Islamism in the Post-Arab Spring," *Contemporary Politics* 20, no. 4 (2014): 453–468.

12 Azizah al-Hibri, "A Study of Islamic Herstory or How did we Ever Get into this Mess?" *Women's Studies International Forum* 5, no. 2 (1982): 207–219. A similar method is adopted by Zeenath Kausar in her review of Muslim male scholars' interpretations of selective *suras* and women's issues, some positive others negative, "The Battle of Books! Diverse Trends in Muslim Thought on Women's Issues," *Journal of International Women's Studies*15, no. 2 (2014): 165–181, https://vc. bridgew.edu/jiws/vol15/iss2/1, accessed April 14, 2020.

13 Asma Barlas, "Engaging Islamic Feminism: Provincializing Feminism as A Master Narrative," in Anitta Kynsilehto, ed., *Islamic Feminism: Current Perspectives* (Tampere, Finland: Tampere Research Institute, Occasional Paper 96, 2008), esp. 20–23.

14 Hibba Abugideiri, "Revisiting the Islamic Past, Deconstructing Male Authority: The Project of Islamic Feminism," *Religion and Literature* 42, no. 1/2 (Spring–Summer 2010): 137.

15 Asma Asfaruddin, for example, wrote a valuable history of early Islam that debunks highly problematic reconstructions of the history of Islam. Her book integrates women in chapters where appropriate; see Asma Asfaruddin, *The First Muslims: History and Memory* (Oxford: Oneworld, 2007), ch. 5, 11.

16 Margot Badran, "Between Secular and Islamic Feminism/s: Reflections on the Middle East and Beyond," *Journal of Middle Eastern Women's Studies* 1, no. 1

(Winter 2005): 6. See also Badran, *Feminism in Islam: Secular, Religious Convergences* (London: Oneworld, 2009), ch. 10, 242; and "Feminism and a New Mediterranean Culture: A Close-Up in Spain," *Samyukta: a Journal of Gender and Culture* 12, no. 1 (January 2017):145.

17 For a discussion of such concepts, which include mentality, oeuvre, tradition, development, or influence, see Michel Foucault, *L'Archéologie du savoir* (Paris: Gallimard, 1969), 31–38. Foucault suggests that such concepts be problematized, suspended, unearthed and "brought out of the shadows," 32. (English translation, 25). *The Archaeology of Knowledge*, trans. A. M. Sheridan Smith (New York: Vintage Books, 1972), 21–28.

18 See Asma Barlas, "Secular and Feminist Critiques of the Qur'an: Anti-Hermeneutics as Liberation?" *Journal of Feminist Studies in Religion* 32, no. 2 (Fall 2016): 112; Margot Badran, "Letter to the Editors," *Journal of Feminist Studies in Religion* 33, no. 1 (Spring 2017): 5–8; Asma Barlas, "Letter to the Editors," *Journal of Feminist Studies in Religion* 34, no. 1 (Sept. 2018): 5; "Engaging Islamic Feminism: Provincializing Feminism as a Master Narrative," in Anitta Kynsilehto, ed. *Islamic feminism: Current Perspectives* (Tampere: Finland, Tampere Research Institute. Occasional Paper 96, 2008), 14–24.

19 I have discussed the meaning of writing as a woman in the context of existing Western feminism. See Marnia Lazreg, "Feminism and Difference: The Perils of Writing as a Woman on Women in Algeria," *Feminist Studies* 14, no. 1 (1988): 81–107.

20 However, Barlas's resistance may reflect a concern she does not express: the application of a feminist framework to the Qur'an may lead away from the advancement of women proper to a reading that stretches Islam to lengths that make it less recognizable as an integral, holistic faith. For instance, Jerusha Tanner Lamptey reads the Qur'an for the purpose of advancing religious diversity and pluralism. "Toward a Muslim Theology: Theology, Constructive, Comparative Possibilities," *Journal of Feminist Studies in Religion* 33, no. 1 (Spring 2017): 27–44.

21 See in particular legal anthropologist, Ziba Mir-Hosseini who articulates her view not only in her writings but also on a video, "What is Islamic Feminism," https://youtube.com/watch?v=Fzf2D43wcTc viewed April 14, 2020. In her video she eloquently presents Islamic feminism as expressing a reclaiming of the humanity of women, a feminist critical consciousness of inequality and a movement for justice and equality grounding its legitimacy in religion. Among her writings, see "Islam and Gender Justice," in Vincent Cornell and Omid Safi, eds., *Voices of Islam, Voices of Diversity and Change*, vol. 5 (Westport, CT: Greenwood, 2007), 85–113. Raja Rhouni, who is critical of the "foundational" bias in Islamic feminism as expounded by Fatima Mernissi, identifies herself as "a believer trained in the social and human sciences" in her book *Secular and Feminist Critiques in the Works of Fatima Mernissi* (Leiden: Brill, 2010), 13. For an anthology of Islamic feminist views, see Kynsilehto, *Islamic Feminism*.

22 Fatima Seedat, in "Islam, Feminism, and Islamic Feminism: Between Inadequacy and Inevitability," *Journal of Feminist Studies in Religion* 29, no. 2 (Fall 2013): 25, attributes the start of Islamic feminism to Fatima Mernissi's work, among others, *The Veil and the Male Elite: A Feminist Interpretation of Women's Rights in Islam*, translated by Mary Jo Lakeland (New York: Perseus Publishers, 1991); Leila Ahmed, *Women and Gender in Islam: Historical Roots of a Modern Debate* (New Haven, CT: Yale University Press, 1993); and Amina Wadud, *Qur'an and Woman: Re-Reading the Sacred Text* (New York: Oxford University Press, 2007). This attribution implicitly focuses on these authors' critiques of selective aspects of Islam and religious practices not whether they offer solutions within the parameters of religion–a hallmark of contextualists seeking reforms. Among other accounts of Islamic feminism see Mulki Al-Sharmani', "Islamic Feminism: Transnational and National Reflections," *Approaching Religion* 4, no. 2 (December

2014): 83–94. For a review essay of six books on Islam and feminism see Laura Zahra McDonald "Islamic Feminism," *Feminist Theory* 9, no. 3 (2018): 347–354.
23 Among these, Ayesha Hidayatullah, "Muslim Theology in the United States," in Ednan Aslan, Marcia Hermansen and Elif Medeni. eds., *Muslima Theology: The Voices of Women Theologians* (Bern: Switzerland: Peter Lang AG, 2013): 81–99; Kecia Ali, *Sexual Ethics in Islam: Feminist Reflections on Qur'an, Hadith, and Jurisprudence* (Oxford: Oneworld, 2006), esp. Introduction and ch. 9.
24 Among non-Muslim feminists' assessments of Islamic feminism, see a brief and apologetic piece by Rachelle Fawcett, "The Reality and Future of Islamic Feminism: What Constitutes 'Islamic Feminism' and Where it is Headed," *Aljazeera*, 28 March 2013, www.aljazeera.com/indepth/opinion/2013/03/20133271558558, accessed February 18, 2020.
25 Badran, "Between Secular," 7.
26 Ibid., 9.
27 One of the unintended consequences of attributing the rise of faith-based movements to a putative failure of modernization is to support another myth, that Islam is incompatible with modernity.
28 Badran, "Between Secular," 13.
29 Ibid., 13–14.
30 The text allows that all feminisms in the Middle East are "home grown" and not mere importations from the West; ibid., 13.
31 Ibid., 17–23.
32 Fatima Sadiqi, for example, suggests that the feminist movement undergoes a transformation when it is cast in a Berber(ist?) framework. Since the ethnic stock in Morocco is Berber, the author's suggestion verges on essentialism. See Sadiqi, *Moroccan Feminist Discourses*, ch. 1, 5.
33 Badran, "Between Secular," 9. The list includes a variety of feminists such as scholars who reconstructed the history of Islam by selecting key moments seen as having inflected the course of the religion in a manner such that they impacted women negatively as Leila Ahmed did; focused on male-centered representations of women in a manner made familiar by Fatima Mernissi, and/or identified problematic interpretations of women in the Quran for which re-interpretations are offered.
34 It must be remembered that the concept of paradigm was best suited to capture changes in scientific conceptions as exemplified in Thomas Kuhn, *The Structure of Scientific Revolutions* (Chicago, IL: University of Chicago Press, 1962).
35 The author broadens her view of the universal character of Islamic feminism in her "Feminism and a New Mediterranean Culture," 145–164.
36 Badran, "Between Secular," 23.
37 Ibid., 16.
38 Ziba Mir-Hosseini cites CEDAW as a "catalyst" for the emergence of Islamic feminism in Iran, "Beyond Islam," 69.
39 It must be remembered that Swiss women did not receive the right to vote until 1971. This fact is frequently invoked in conferences on gender as a reminder of the anomalous inequities that exist(ed) in Europe.
40 The use of this term in this book does not imply that the interpretation women provide is limited by their sex. It simply means a woman's standpoint. In this and subsequent chapters, I will use women's and at times feminist, contextualism interchangeably to avoid repetition and to indicate that all versions of contextualism use a feminist vocabulary or adopt a critical approach grounded in the legacy of academic feminism.
41 For a discussion of epistemological contextualism see, among others, Rui Silva, "Hermeneutics and Epistemological Contextualism," *Proceedings of the XXIII World Congress of Philosophy*, *Philosophical Hermeneutics*, 30 (2018), 55–59; Sarah Jane Conrad, "Linguistic Meaning and the Minimalism

Contextualism Debate," *Logique et Analyse* 54, no. 216 (2011), especially 453–469. For a discussion of the meanings of contextualism see Keith DeRose, "Contextualism and Knowledge Attribution," *Philosophical and Phenomenological Research* 52, no. 54 (December 1992): 913–929. See also "Epistemic Contextualism," *Stanford University Encyclopedia*, March 29, 2016, https://plato.sta nford.edu/entries/contextualism-epistemology/#Bib, accessed July 3, 2020.

42 To avoid the totalizing concept of "patriarchy," I use the concept of "masculinism," as analytically distinct from "patriarchy." The concept has been used before, but I am inspired in adopting it by Roslyn Bologh, *Love or Greatness: Max Weber's Masculine Thinking—A Feminist Inquiry* (New York: Routledge, 2009), which points to the individual as well as psycho-sexual character of what is routinely referred to as patriarchy. It leaves open the possibility that a man may overcome the grip of the "patriarchal" worldview, normally seen as all-pervasive.

43 It is true that a key sura, often interpreted as determinative of veiling, 24/31 is symmetrical to 24/30 which is addressed to men and uses the same word, *furuj*, or pudenda, which must be safeguarded. The *sura* addressed to women adds other attitudes towards the body that are specific to women, such as the beautification of the body (*zina*), the protection of *juyu*b (bosom) and the clicking of anklets which signal the gender of the person wearing them. Of all these terms *zina* is the most resistant to a stable meaning as it has several referents, which explains why it has sometimes been translated as face (hence the resulting *niqab* which covers the face). It is also used to mean fornication. In conformity with a contextualist approach, I focused on concepts such as *hijab, khimar, thaub, furuj* (pudenda), pointed to their different meanings, identified the social context within which they were used, and indicated to whom the injunctions were addressed at the time that they were issued. The goal was to present veiling as a contingent part of being a Muslim, and intimate that it refers to a relation to the body aimed at making it inconspicuous–a relation that is prescribed to both males and females.

44 See *sura* 24.60.

45 Amina Wadud, *Qur'an and Woman: Re-reading the Sacred Text* (New York: Oxford University Press, 2007), and *Inside the Gender Jihad: Women's Reforms in Islam* (London: Oneworld Publishers, 2008). Her approach is similar to Riff'at Hassan's (a pioneer in Islamic feminism) in "Muslim Women and Post-Patriarchal Islam," in Paula M. Cooey, William R. Eakin, and Jay B. McDaniel eds., *After Patriarchy: Feminist Transformations of the World of Religions* (Maryknoll, NY: Orbis Books, 1991), 39–64.

46 Asma Barlas, "Believing Women," in *Islam: Unreading Patriarchal Interpretations of the Quran* (Austin, TX: Texas, Texas University Press, 2002). For a pointed assessment of her view see Shadaab Rahemtulla, *Qur'an of the Oppressed: Liberation Theology and Gender Justice in Islam* (Oxford: Oxford University Press, 2017). Barlas distinguishes her method from Wadud's in "Secular and Feminist," 112.

47 For a learned discussion of the controversy over an original Quran see Mohammed Ali Amir-Moezzi, *Le Coran parlant et le Coran silencieux: nouvelles perspectives sur les origines de l'Islam* (Paris: Editions CNRS, 2011). Translated by Eric Ormsby as *The Silent Qur'an and the Speaking Qur'an: Scriptural Sources of Islam Between History and Fervor* (New York: Columbia University Press, 2015).

48 For a lucid text on reading critical of contextualism see Paul B. Armstrong, "In Defense of Reading: Or, why Reading Still Matters in a Contextual Age," *New Literary History* 42, no. 1 (Winter 2011): 87–113.

49 Hela Ouardi, *Les derniers jours de Muhammad: Enquête sur la mort du Prophète* (Paris: Albin Michel, 2017). The book is not solely focused on the Prophet's death as its title implies.

50 In this section I will use "Islamic feminism" to be faithful to the literature under discussion.

51 No intimation is intended here of the success or failure of faith-based parties since 2011.
52 Haideh Moghissi, *Feminism and Islamic Fundamentalism: The Limits of Post-Modern Analysis* (London: Zed Books, 1999). Moghissi establishes a relationship between Islamic Feminism and Postmodernism–an important move which calls for greater scrutiny.
53 Fatima Seedat, "Islam, Feminism, and Islamic Feminism: Between inadequacy and Inevitability," *Journal of Feminist Studies and Religion* 29, no. 2 (Fall 2013). See also a critical account from a former Islamic feminist, Esra Özcan, "Turkish Women in Islamism: Gender and the Mirage of 'Islamic Feminism'," *Samuykta*, 182–192.
54 Ibid., 27.
55 Ibid.
56 Ibid. Seedat suggests on p. 36 that "Badran believes that Muslim women may somehow save feminism."
57 Raja Rhouni, *Secular and Feminist Critiques in the Work of Fatima Mernissi* (Leiden: Brill, 2010), 16; 13. The author suggests that foundationalism falls prey to essentialism (ibid., 16).
58 Ilyass Bouzghaia, "Gender Relations and Social Values in Morocco: Prospects of a 'Third Way' Islamic Feminism After the 'Arab Spring'," in Joshen Lobah and Hamza Tayebi, eds., *Trajectories of Change in Post 2011 MENA: Challenges and Prospects* (Rabat: Hans Seidel Foundation, and Takamul Center for Inter-disciplinary Studies and Research, Oct. 2017), 175.
59 Ibid., 177. The author relies on the work of feminist contextualist Asma Lamrabet as well as non-Muslim writers who support feminist contextualism. For Asma Lamrabet, see among others, *Women in the Qur'an: An Emancipatory Reading*, translated by Myriam François-Cerrah (Marketfield: United Kingdom, 2016).
60 The author's view must be contrasted with Abdelila Bouasria's in "Bits and Tits" cited above, which documents the role played by the government in promoting women as agents of its apparent liberal conception of Islam.
61 Adis Duderija, "Towards a Scriptural Hermeneutics of Islamic Feminism, *Journal of Feminist Studies in Religion* 31, no. 2 (Fall 2015): 46.
62 Ibid.
63 Ibid., 57. These include a "thematico-historic approach to textual sources based on an inductive corroboration of textual evidence."
64 See in particular Khaled Abou El Fadel, *Speaking in God's Name: Islamic Law, Authority and Women* (Oxford: Oneworld Press, 2001) and *And God Knows the Soldiers: The Authoritative and Authoritarian in Islamic Discourse* (Lanham, MA: University Press of America. Roman and Littlefied, 2001). A liberation theology advocate, Farid Esack, takes up gender inequality in his work, particularly, *The Quran: A Short Introduction* (Oxford: Oneworld) 2002.
65 For a lucid discussion of Al-Afghani, Abduh, as well as Rash Rida, who interpreted religious texts restrictively, see Albert Hourani, *Arabic Thought in the Liberal Age, 1788–1939* (Cambridge: Cambridge University Press, 2014), ch. 5, 6, 9.
66 Admittedly, it is the social construction of biology, not biology as such that is at stake. Nevertheless, some texts do comfort masculinity to a degree that makes relinquishing them difficult.
67 See, among others, Sandra Harding, ed., *The Feminist Standpoint Theory Reader: Intellectual and Political Controversies* (New York: Routledge, 204), especially Harding's Introduction and Donna Haraway, "Situated Knowledges: The Science Question in Feminism and the Privileged Partial Perspective," ch. 6.

6

FEMINIST ANTECEDENT KNOWLEDGE AND QURANIC ATTRIBUTOR CONTEXTUALISM

This chapter explores the epistemic and theoretical conditions that enabled the emergence of a strand of women's Quranic contextualism to present itself and be received as the only method for bringing about change in gender relations. The previous chapter described a prevailing etiology, which attributes the emergence of women's Quranic attributor contextualism to the failure of "secular" feminism. Linked to "Islamic modernism," women's Quranic attributor contextualism is cast in the *longue durée* of continuity in Middle Eastern and North African women's efforts to bring about change in the history of their societies. However, putative historical continuity elides the unrecognized, or unexamined, knowledge effects of feminist theorizing on women in MENA that took place particularly in the United States of America beginning in the 1960s where a complex and varied academic feminist production of ideas and theories were elaborated. Constructing a seamless feminist history, whether in the West or in the Middle East, is an important part of making visible women's awareness of their suffering (more or less intense depending on their social class) as well as documenting the ways in which women expressed their aspirations. However, this history cannot be blind to the fact that a vocabulary, concepts, and reasoned *theories* were formulated to articulate in a more or less systematic fashion women's experience, defined as universal, in the second half of the twentieth century. That this conceptual apparatus, deemed suited to account for women's experiences globally, was not always adequate goes without saying. Nevertheless, its formulation in the second phase of feminism stressed some ideals and principles, which expressed exigencies and desires that implicate women cross-culturally. From the perspective of this book, the ideal of freedom and the recognition of the universality of gender inequality, no matter the contentiousness of the debates they ignited, cut across cultures, and their theorization cannot be obscured. This chapter contends that the vicissitudes of these two principles as they evolved from second wave feminism to postfeminism shed light on the peculiarity of women's Quranic attributor contextualism. Drawing its legitimation as a culturally adapted method of change from academic postfeminist theory, which guaranteed its positive reception, women's Quranic contextualism often refuses to be identified as feminist, and makes claim to autochthony.

Second wave feminism and postfeminism as antecedent knowledge

The use of "wave" in referring to the evolution of feminist thought in this discussion is more expedient than substantive. I am solely concerned with one shift in theorizing women and gender from a liberatory conception with universalistic aspirations to a more privatized perspective.[1] The shift to a postfeminist theorizing evolved slowly before rising to dominance. The history of American feminist theories need not be repeated here.[2] Suffice it to say that far from being unitary, trends in feminist theorizing are part of a complex configuration of local as well as global socio-political and economic events that shaped their formulations. Moreover, academic postfeminism and its relationship to postmodernism is also plural and complicated. In this book, I focus on the most salient features of postfeminism as a successor to second wave feminism.[3] To recall, while second wave feminist theorizing evolved in the wake of the Civil Rights and decolonization movements, postfeminist theoretical thought emerged in the 1990s as the Cold War was ending and neoliberal theory gained ascendancy across the world. Since its inception in the mid-1960s, second wave academic feminism expressed a whole range of perspectives which ran the gamut from essentialist to socialist.[4] Similarly, postfeminism expresses itself in multiple ways, some heavily reliant on postmodern thought, others more focused on self-centered practical or libertarian actions. How has this global context affected the rise of women's Quranic attributor contextualism as well as its reception? An answer to this question will further help to understand whether the appeal to re-interpretations of the Quran provides a theoretical alternative to either the liberatory feminist theory, or postfeminist thought. Second wave feminism, whether in its academic or activist form, implicitly and explicitly aimed for women's attainment of freedom from insidious as well as patent prejudices, which prevent women from having the same life chances as men in the social, economic and political domains. It further sought freedom from the taken-for-granted perceptions, which perpetuate prejudices against women through language and unreflective practices. It understood that freedom is not achievable at once; rather it is a process that begins with a woman becoming conscious of the myriad of ways in which she internalized perceptions of herself as a socially marked subject because of her biology. Hence consciousness-raising in the mid to late 1960s was a method for questioning one's own active involvement in sustaining a gender system predicated on a socially constructed conception of women as deserving of an institutionalized discrimination that is not recognized as such. Acknowledged was also the notion that across cultures women have traditionally been subjected to gender systems that impeded their freedom. However, second wave academic feminism took women in the Middle East and North Africa as an empirical ground for testing its claim to the universality of its theorizing. In the same breath that it asserted the universality of the woman condition, it also took the experience of Western women as the normative standard against which to gauge the "oppression" of other women from which it all but exempted its own. From this perspective, American (*qua* Western) women were deemed free, or freer, and their societies perfectible, whereas Middle Eastern women were not. Hence Islam was seized upon as the cause of "Muslim" women's problems perceived as total, irremediable, and irredeemable. Consequently, the notion of the universal became synonymous with the assertion of a cultural bias in studying "Muslim" women. In this, second wave feminist thought reproduced the "imperialism of the universal"[5] inherent in anthropology and sociology-as-usual.

A retreat from second wave feminism's ideals, academic postfeminism attempted to resolve the contradiction at the heart of second wave academic feminism in a deceptively latitudinarian manner. Its inaugural act was a sharp critique of its predecessor's contradictory assertion of the universality of women's experience at the level of theory and the denial of it in practice. Assuming a poststructuralist stance, it rejected the universality of women's experience in favor of a culturalist and reified view of women as bounded and constituted by the cultures in which they are born. In essence, postfeminism drew to their logical conclusions the theoretical inconsistencies of its predecessor. By the same token, it crystallized the distinguishing features of feminism in the "global" era.[6] What are these features?[7]

First, a retreat from any form of universalism and the flaunting of particularism seen as the freedom to choose as well as experiment with different identities. Second, a conception of social diversity based on the multiplicity of discrete identities. The celebration of difference within and between women takes precedence over their shared commonalities. Third, a de-emphasis of the structural context, local as well as global, that inflects women's lives. Hence, the sites of activism are moved to the media, technology, or academia depending on the immediate personal needs of a woman. Fourth, and as a corollary of the preceding, an acceptance of a poststructuralist conception of power that vitiates structural change.

Perhaps the most telling characteristic of postfeminism is the rejection of second wave feminism's humanist conception of the female subject whose agency (seen as active consciousness) enables her to transcend the cultural practices that seek to construct her as a "woman." Thus, Judith Butler argues that such a view is based on an implicit Cartesian binary distinction between body and mind, a mind that somehow escapes the power of the cultural norms that target it; a body that is assumed to precede cultural norms just as the mind is situated outside of the normative systems the female subject is mired in. This dualism, she further argues, reveals itself in the structuralist (presumably after Lévi-Strauss's fashion) binary opposition between nature and culture. Furthermore, the body is assumed to be malleable and therefore a passive instrument of culture. Although Butler's ultimate purpose is to question and reveal the assumption of heterosexuality which informs the body so conceived, she unmistakably seeks to do away with consciousness. (Parenthetically, her critique, although plausible and useful, does not take into consideration philosophical critiques of structuralism.) She points out that the body as conceived in second wave feminist thought is already constituted by the prevailing cultural norms, rules and regulations. In reality, the body is constantly constituted and reconstituted through discourse (the language of cultural rules) and its iteration.[8] In a radical act, Butler claims that "gender" identity is an act, a performative act, the "stylized repetitions" of which maintain its tenuous stability. The repetition of the rules constituting gender militates against the assumption of a substantive, or enduring and stable gender identity, and exposes its "phantasmic" character.[9] Simply put, women's agency does not have a stable locus. If it is found anywhere, it is in the multiplicity of discourses. This conceptualization leaves unaddressed what happens to identity when contradictory discourses occur at the same time and or overlap, as for example, the "secular" and faith-based discourses, or the political, the economic and faith-based discourses. By the same token, discursive practices presuppose a social context that makes language understandable. As Nancy Fraser has noted, Butler is unable to theorize not only the "relations of embodied individuals" to one another, but also "intersubjectivity."[10]

Aware that she destroyed (at least semantically) the epistemic foundation of the women's movement, she declares that political action need not assume the existence of a gender identity. To wit: "there need not be a 'doer behind the deed,' but that the 'doer' is variably constructed in and through the deed."[11] or that "to be constituted by discourse [need not mean] to be determined by discourse, where determination forecloses the possibility of agency."[12] This linguistic sleight of hand leaves intact the question of how does the doer decide to do the deed, especially if the deed is itself discursively constructed by other doers. Butler believes that the "predicates" of identity (such as race, ethnicity, and the like) are a "supplement," which second wave feminism did not incorporate in its notion of a pre-discursive "I." Although Butler's critique seems to note an apparent problem in presupposing a pre-discursive "I" that is at the same time "enmired" in culture, the critique ignores that which is posited with the "I," namely consciousness which is both enmired but also able to rise above the mire. Hers is no more and no less than a critique of the philosophy of consciousness, which grounds not only Marx but also Freud's theories. Predictably, she turns the tables on second wave feminism's claim to universality without engaging its alternative uses. As she put it "The critical task for feminism is not to establish a point of view outside of constructed identities; that conceit is the construction of an epistemological model that would disavow its own cultural location and hence, promotes itself as a global subject, a position that deploys precisely the imperialist strategies that feminism ought to criticize."[13] This powerful critique of second wave feminism's theoretical claim of the universality of women's experience, which is (yes) contradicted by its practice of setting itself up as the standard against which to measure Other women's condition, still does not provide a viable alternative, a way out of the epistemic circularity it denounces. Indeed, Butler adds, "the critical task is, rather, to locate strategies of subversive repetition enabled by those constructions, to affirm the *local* (emphasis added) possibilities of intervention through participating precisely in those practices of repetition that constitute identity and, therefore, present the immanent possibility of contesting them."[14] In other words, local discursive practices produce their own subversive possibilities without a consciousness that identities them as subversive.

Butler's removal of the subject "women," and its replacement with discourse still begs the question of the relationship between power, discourse and identity. Furthermore, once agency is presented as a language artifact, not only power but also ideology is either eliminated from the field of culture, or flattened out as mere linguistic significations. Most important from the perspective of this book, the notion of subversion needs specification. It is treated as a given, an inevitable effect of normative discourse. Yet, it presupposes a knowing subject who can distinguish true from false, endowed with memory and is able to understand her best interests. In the case of women in Algeria or the Middle East, how would a woman engage in subversive action if her fiancé insists that she sign a stipulation to her marriage contract engaging her to stop working and to wear the *hijab*? Is her acquiescence a sign of subversion?

The postfeminist discursive dissolution of agency erases women as a universal category of analysis and facilitates the reification of difference as an unmediated condition. Consequently, from this perspective there are multiple cultures that construct different ways of being woman—an anthropological fact; their constructions must be accepted as constructions independent of their effects on women. This apparent unbridled cultural tolerance in reality conceals the same standard, which second wave feminism left in abeyance, which is that "we" (academic feminists in New York or Paris) are in a position to claim that other women are limited by their cultures, a limitation "we" recognize and respect. Conversely, "we" do not have culture-as-problem; we are free of culture but at the same time "we" are the universal standard of culture, since in recognizing the limiting character of other women's cultures, we are using the standard of "our" (non-limiting) culture. What is good for us, including the ideal of freedom, is not good for them. Hence, postfeminist theorizing clearly assumes that women in American society, for example, have already achieved equality with men in areas that matter the most, law, access to employment, and politics. Freed from the burden of gender inequality as experienced by second wave feminists, postfeminist women can now turn their sights to their individual desires and fantasies; they no longer have a political "enemy" in the state or in blatant sexism; they are free to live more or less dangerously for the fun of it if they so wish. They can celebrate difference among women as a means to celebrating their own freedom; they are beyond "feminism."

The legacy of postfeminist academic thought

What does the epistemological shift from second wave to postfeminism have to do with North African and Middle East women's shift to a culturalist form of feminism? As it developed and traveled, postfeminism resonated with Middle Eastern and North African women's own critiques of second wave feminism. Its reception among academic women occurred as the increase in the scholarship on gender in the region provided women with a greater sense of intellectual confidence aided by the publication in 1978 of Edward Said's *Orientalism.* Although not focused on women, this book provided MENA intellectuals with a tool to open a breach into a body of knowledge about MENA societies that had hitherto been presented as authoritative and unquestionable. Beyond its usefulness as a tool of analysis, "orientalism" further helped to endorse the relevance of a Foucauldian approach to the Middle East of which it availed itself. The postmodernist bent of academic postfeminism could only make it more palatable. Admittedly, academic feminism in MENA did not have to be aware of academic postfeminism to adopt a poststructuralist mode of analysis. However, there is a distinction between Foucault's thought and a feminist interpretation of Foucault.[15]

Directly or indirectly, postfeminism created the conditions of possibility for MENA academic feminism to momentarily manage the contradictory forces under which it has traditionally labored since its inception. To recall, MENA feminism as knowledge is derivative in nature; it functions in the median or interstitial space between the political power of the state, which has shown a great deal of ambivalence towards women, the social power wielded by faith-based groups in their prescriptive and disciplinary programs of gender "re-traditionalization" (for lack of a better word); and knowledge (especially theoretical) acquired from the global women's movement since the United Nations Decade for Women. In the wake of the academic postfeminist trend of thought, women were able to avail themselves of their median location to lay claim to the cultural power usually monopolized by faith-based groups, while eschewing the clichéd charge routinely leveled at them of mimicking "Western" feminists. Hence, academic postfeminist thought has a legitimating function for the cultural turn in MENA feminism. This function played itself out on two levels: first, it helped to deterritorialize the origins of academic feminism in MENA (routinely associated with the "West"). By turning to (religious) culture, women could assert the autochthonous nature of their own modality of feminism, as for example "Islamic feminism." By the same token, the philosophico-theoretical legacy of second wave academic feminism's liberatory ideal is obviated. Liberation takes on a different meaning.

Before it became manifest in the unstated legitimation of "Islamic feminism," the legacy of academic postfeminist thought has proceeded incrementally and in a diffuse manner, appearing in thematic studies using post-structuralist theoretical concepts or orientation. It informs four major trends in the academic feminist literature on MENA towards relativism and localism; the elision of power from analyses; a neglect of a changing socio-political context; and a neglect or loss of theory. The trend towards relativism and localism arguably captures the essence of the path that leads to the turn to culturalism. It relies on a functionalist conception of social life, which stresses the positive aspects of local cultural practices, including the revival of customs inimical to women. For instance, veiling is hailed as a new form of modernity or as downright liberation from the Western tyranny of sexualized fashion. Nevertheless, fashion is not abandoned, it is adapted to "modest" dress, and fashion designers for dress and footwear create new lines suitable to the culturalist mood. Or, *'urf* marriage (religious marriage) is viewed as a welcome custom allowing for the satisfaction of sexual desire.[16] Hence, what in reality is a creative adaptation to cultural conservatism appears as revolutionary. This mode of cultural relativism raised to the level of ideological justification of cultural practices regardless of their dysfunctions for categories of people (including women) is different from the anthropological notion of the relativity of cultures. To put one's cultural values in abeyance (to avoid ethnocentrism) while learning how cultures function in a pre-literate society presumed to be an organic unit is different from straining to find positive functions to a custom in a contemporary society. The modality of relativism in academic feminism eschews the negative gendered aspects of the customs it focuses upon, just as it overlooks the differential effects of the custom on women in comparison with men. It results in the normalization of the revival of customs and obscures the subterranean ways in which these customs shape women's consciousness. This relativistic trend mirrors the American academic feminists' adoption of an unbridled form of cultural relativism in a reversal of their erstwhile view of MENA women as "oppressed," bearers of the weight of a religion resistant to change. Instead, the re-activation or revival of customs inimical to women is presented as adequate, even if contrary to women's interests, implicitly on the grounds that such customs cannot be changed, and have an unrecognized positive function for women. Consequently, a critical view of such an attitude appears suspect as it smacks of Western feminism. In other words, local cultural practices maybe dysfunctional, but they are appropriate for local women. This modality of relativism obviates the significance of history in studying gender inequality in favor of a reified conception of culture as a fossilized present. Indeed, as Butler put it, women are "mired" in the present. However, this enmiring is willed.

An outcome of the reification of cultural practices when they become normalized is an individualized conception of power. A woman availing herself of a cultural practice that reinforces her gendered inequality appears as having "agency" and engaging in self-empowerment. Hence, agency is reified. Putative agency/resistance and self-empowerment frequently depict acquiescence to pressure as subversion from within. The idea is that women empower themselves by accepting cultural practices inimical to their interests; accepting such practices also means resisting them.[17] Hence, women's connivance is but a ruse. This conception of "agency" covers over the depth and extent of the social and psychological pressures women may experience in their daily lives. For instance, the power of groups such as *imams* and women preachers, or *murshidat* in redefining existing religious and customary practices for women is elided. The assertion of empowerment without an analysis of the power behind cultural practices inimical to women results in the elision of the power structure sustaining the revival of cultural practices.

Furthermore, and no less important, academic feminist practice tends to shy away from theoretical elaboration or engagement with theory. The use of Foucauldian concepts as full-fledged theories compensates for the formulation of theories amenable to explaining the retreat in cultural practices, and sustains the illusion of radical criticism. Hence neglect of theory also permits a disengagement from the ideal of freedom. The idea of freedom in the MENA context becomes synonymous with and restricted to freedom from religion, and thus to be shunned.

Finally, the cumulative effect of these trends reflects an insufficient appreciation of socio-political changes, affecting the *context* within which cultural practices unfold, and which the turn to culture conceals. For instance, the state role has shifted since the 1990s from governing to ensuring security by proxy—a sort of conveyor belt of the West's "war on terror." Under these circumstances, meaningful reforms lose their urgency as analyzed in Chapter 4, and women's gains can be undone.[18] The changed nature of the state in the region as well as its entanglements with new hegemonic geopolitical interests complicates the analysis of policies that appear to be taken on behalf of women as they pursue objectives dictated by geopolitical strategies rather than women's lasting welfare.

In sum, when women in the Middle East and North Africa turn to culture as a privileged mark of difference to be claimed, and transform its dysfunctions into positivities, they engage in a conceptual narrative that for all intents and purposes shores up, rather than confronts the political, juridical and social structures that sustain, if not reproduce, the cultural taboos, rules and regulations that impinge on women's freedom. Thus, postfeminist theoretical concepts have a dual function when they become a dominant trend in academic feminism, or when they travel across cultures: on the one hand, they help to validate a notion of cultural difference that flaunts its uniqueness; on the other hand, they enable the omission of freedom as an essential component part of women's political demands. The use of cultural specificity as a ground for feminist theorizing in Middle Eastern and North African societies yields a form of cultural identity politics that forsakes questions of political economy and (geo)politics which frame women's lives in favor of a focus on religion perceived as the only framework for change.

Notes

1 A retreat into the sexualized female body as a source of empowerment in a hyper consumer society illustrates this trend. See, for example Angela McRobbie, "Post-feminism and Popular Culture: Bridget Jones and the New Gender Regime," in Y. Tasker and D. Negra, eds., *Interrogating Postfeminism: Gender and the Politics of Popular Culture* (Durham, NC: Duke University Press, 2007), 27–39.
2 For a classic overview of the various trends within second wave feminism see Alison Jaggar and Paula Rothenberg, eds., *Feminist Frameworks: Alternative Theoretical Accounts of the Relations Between Women and Men* (New York: McGraw Hill, 1978). A third revised edition is also available.
3 The stance adopted in this chapter does not deny that for some of its proponents postfeminism may be liberatory.
4 Second wave feminism in this book refers to the academic expression of the women's liberation movement in the United of America, which resulted, among others, in the passage of the Equal Rights Amendment of 1971–1972.
5 I am borrowing the expression from Pierre Bourdieu, *Acts of Resistance: Against the Tyranny of the Market*, translated by Richard Nice (New York: The New Press, 1998), 19.
6 The global is placed between quotation marks to signify its contingent yet dominant character in a world brought physically closer together, but pulled economically and ideologically apart.
7 This discussion draws on the works of Stéphanie Genz and Benjamin A. Brabon, *Postfeminism: Cultural Texts and Theories* (Edinburgh: Edinburgh University Press, 2009).
8 Judith Butler, *Gender Trouble: Feminism and the Subversion of Identity* (New York: Routledge, 1999), 165.
9 Ibid., 179.
10 Nancy Fraser, *Justice Interruptus: Critical Reflections on the "Postsocialist" Condition* (New York: Routledge, 1997), 215.
11 Butler, *Gender Trouble*, 181.
12 Ibid., 182.
13 Ibid., 87.
14 Ibid., 188.
15 Parenthetically, it needs reiterating that although the feminist adaptation or appropriation of selective concepts from Foucault's own research program is insightful, and satisfies the feminist task of demystifying the gendered social system, it sacrifices the liberatory goal of feminism. For lucid works on Foucault and feminism see Irene Diamond and Lee Quimby, *Feminism and Foucault: Reflection on Resistance* (Boston, MA: Northeastern University Press, 1995); Susan Hekman, ed., *Feminist Interpretations of Foucault (Re-reading the Canon)* (Philadelphia, PA: University of Pennsylvania Press, 2007); Margaret McLaren, *Feminism, Foucault, and Embodied Subjectivity* (Buffalo, NY: State University of New York Press, 2002). For the relationship between feminism and postmodernism see Nancy Fraser and Linda Nicholson, "Social Criticism Without Philosophy: An Encounter Between Feminism and Postmodernism," *Social Text* 21 (1980): 83–104; Noretta Koertge, "'New Age' Philosophies of Science: Constructivism,

Feminism, and Postmodernism," *The British Journal of Philosophy* 51 (2000): 667–683.

16 See the otherwise insightful analysis of the psychosocial meaning of *'urf* marriage in Egypt and the United Arab Emirates provided by Frances S. Hasso, *Consuming Desires: Family Crises and State in the Middle East* (Palo Alto, CA: Stanford University Press, 2011).

17 I have discussed this issue in "Poststructuralist Theory and Women in the Middle East: Going in Circles?" *Journal of Contemporary Arab Affairs*, Special Issue, "Feminism in the Arab World: Four Perspectives," 6, no. 1 (January 2013): 71–84.

18 For example, Kuwait granted women suffrage in 1985 but revoked it before reinstating it in 2005.

7

POSTLIBERATION AND QURANIC ATTRIBUTOR CONTEXTUALISM

> The critique of what we are is at one and the same time the historical analysis of the limits imposed on us, and experiment with the possibility of going beyond.
>
> —*Michael Foucault*[1]

The adequacy of the turn to religious texts as a culturally adapted mode of advocacy for change in women's lives hinges on the vision of society it promotes, the goals it pursues, and the audience it targets. Previous chapters have shown that academic feminists' attraction to Quranic contextualism (aka Islamic feminism) is attributable not only to its recognizable (albeit unstated) postfeminist academic background knowledge, but also to its being powered by women as a well as its questioning of existing male-centered interpretations of the texts. To reiterate, this double challenge to theologians and practitioners of Islam, regardless of its outcome, makes women's Quranic contextualism a singular event. However, its significance as a transgressive act of intervention in the field of interpretation of the Quran is frequently conflated with women's aspirations to social, political, and legal reforms. Consequently, the heterogeneity of Quranic contextualism is obscured as are the messages it conveys or the goals it pursues. This chapter assesses one strand of contextualism, Quranic attributor contextualism from a sociological perspective paying attention to its method of operation, orientation, meanings, claims, and functions.

Epistemology of (feminist) Quranic attributor contextualism

The ascendant trend of Quranic contextualism, which I will focus upon, uses a mix of hermeneutics and feminist constructivism. I will briefly examine

Asma Barlas's method of proceeding only because her presuppositions are spelled out and her background sources are ascertainable. Her method further provides an opportunity to gauge the meaning of the deniability of the referent "feminism."[2] The purpose of the author is to answer questions frequently posed outside of Islam, usually by non-Muslims: "is it [Islam] patriarchal and even sexist and misogynistic?"[3] The question is answered negatively from the start. However, there are "authoritarian and patriarchal readings of Islam"[4] which have justified the "oppression of women." Although the author is aware that sexual "oppression" and misogyny are not the monopoly of any one religion, she posits that "no meaningful change can occur in these [Muslim] societies that does not derive its legitimacy from the Qur'an's teachings, a lesson secular Muslims everywhere are having to learn to their own detriment."[5] She further asserts that "even though Muslim women directly experience the consequences of oppressive *misreadings* of religious texts, few question their legitimacy and fewer still have explored the liberatory aspects of the Quran's teachings" (emphasis added). Hence the task is to retrieve a liberating Quran, which would reveal another Islam, and provide the foundation of a theory of gender equality. The tool for achieving this double purpose is critical hermeneutics encapsulated in the concept of *ijtihad*[6] and a "holistic and thematically linked interpretation of [the Quran's] teachings."[7] The point is to determine how "Muslims produce religious meaning" by examining the contents of the Quran, *tafsir* (or old commentaries elucidating the meaning of the Quran, often considered by theologians as a science of interpretation with its own codified rules), as well as the *ahadith* (pl. of *hadith*), compilations of sayings attributed to Prophet Muhammad as well as records of his behavior (*sunnah*) in specifics situations. These too were the object of classification according to their degree of reliability. By shuttling back and forth from these texts, tracing their relation to one another and to their larger juridical and political contexts (e.g. *shari'a* and the state),[8] their true meaning is revealed. The case for "misreading" or distorting the liberatory message of the Quran rests on "Muslims'" use of a method that leads them to "confusing the Qur'an with the secondary religious texts and to marginalizing it in Muslim religious discourse in spite of its unique status in Islam's Scripture."[9] Most detrimental from this point of view is Muslims' "confusion" of the Quran with the *Sunnah* (with a capital S) of the Prophet; the *Sunnah* and *Ahadith*, or utterances attributed to the Prophet (which are embedded in Arab cultural mores); and *Sunnah* and *Ahadith* with customary practices (sunnah with a lower case s) which Muslims consider to be imitative of the Prophet's behavior and utterances.[10] Aided by the Arabic language, which facilitates the polysemic character of various *suras*, the purported "confusions" lead to unwarranted generalizations from specific *suras,* whose subject matter is bounded in time and space, to all matters at all time.

Although the theological validity of these claims (especially with regard to the use of *hadith* and *sunnah* as coterminous and separate, or the religious symbolism of the term "father" transposed from Christianity to Islam) is a matter for experts to determine, the construction of the arguments invites a few comments. The text points to the Arab character of the social milieu in which Islam arose (a frequently mentioned fact in the relevant literature), but does not pursue it at great length except to flag it as a biasing factor in the *hadith*. It leaves hanging the question whether it is culture, or specifically "Arab" culture, that is the problem.[11] If it is the latter, exempting the Arabness of the Prophet from the critique of *sunnah* and *hadith* (seen as "secondary religious texts") requires elucidation. Is it culture or Arab culture that is an issue? This is not simply a devil's advocate question. Nor is it a critique of cultural relativism; it calls out the cultural positionality of the re-reader of religious texts. It goes to the heart of the contextualist method. How does a contextualist disentangle the human (as a being endowed with culture) from the divine in re-reading (un-reading) religious texts? The author proposes to create a zone of autonomy around the divine, and around the vehicle through which "the divine discourse" is communicated, the Prophet. Nevertheless, in spite of being questioned, the *Sunnah* is retained as a conceptual shell to which a new meaning is imparted through reinterpretation.

Focusing on Islam's conception of the divine as un-gendered, the author refutes the notion that Islam is patriarchal, and interprets it instead as an unrecognized critique of patriarchies' "resistance to Divine Truth."[12] However, the prime criterion for reaching the truth is the contextualist method. Ultimately, the hermeneutics of contextualism ascends from the written texts, Quran, sunnah, hadith, tafsir, and shari'a, to the Prophet's "mind," and "Divine discourse."[13] The attribution of a "discourse" to the Divine implies that it has some materiality, which also exists (or is deposited) in the "mind" of the Prophet. It is unclear to the reader how and why the Divine would have a discourse, or how did the Prophet reproduce the Divine's discourse. The notion of a Divine discourse removes the transcendental character of the Divine and liminally inserts the possibility of error in the Prophet's "mind" in its effort to convey (or reproduce) the discourse. Unwittingly, this representation of the Divine undermines the search for a liberatory Quran as it connotes a liberation from the divine-as-discourse through a series of historicizations. Although not its purpose, this rendition of epistemological contextualism opens the door to a questioning of its own contexts, including its academic antecedents as well as its societal project.

If theological questions are held in abeyance, there is little in this critique of problematic perceptions of Islam that one would quibble with. It harnesses the writing of mid-twentieth-century reformists such as Muhammad Taha Mahmood and his follower Abdullahi An-Naim, or secular humanist and Islamicist Mohammed Arkoun, or Farid Esack's theology of liberation[14] to build both a defense of Islam and a feminist critique of it. While rejecting the (Western) feminist liberatory view ostensibly for its equating religion and gender inequality with patriarchy, it also avails itself of the feminist critical methodology and language. The deniability of the feminist impulse of the very critique of Islam as interpreted by conservative men speaks to another, more fundamental issue: how does a liberatory view of Islam affect juridical or political change–the goal of the text? On what grounds is this Quranic attributor contextualism better than any other method of advocacy for change? Why would a woman accept the premise that no change can occur in the Middle East and North Africa unless she accepts the notion that religion is *the* source of freedom from and an answer to existing gender inequality? Before answering these questions, it is worth noting the audience the book targets: non-Muslims, Muslims, and feminists. At times, the multiplicity of audiences affects the convincingness of the arguments made on behalf of a more progressive reading of the Quran. Theoretically the search for a liberating Islam would concern Muslim women first and foremost. Seeking to convince non-Muslims of the validity of the arguments in favor of such a view displaces the centrality of "Muslim women," defined as the objects of "abuse" and "degradation,"[15] to the liberatory project pursued; it further displaces Muslim women and replaces them with an elusive (Western) feminist from whom the writer seeks to distance herself while speaking her language. By the same token, a woman engaging in contextualism must necessarily distinguish her task from that of the male contextualists (even when they appear to espouse women's ideals), or incur the risk of merely agreeing with their view of gender equality, which may or may not articulate the depth and range of women's experience.

It is noteworthy that male contextualists often reproduce at length entire passages from the *tafsir* to compare them to one another. In other words, they allow interpretations to unfold while pointing out how they differ or overlap with one another.[16] The issue is not to elevate men's work over women's work. Rather women readers, if they were the main audience of a work aimed at revealing to them the liberatory potential of their religion, would need to be convinced of the religious truthfulness of this claim, and be given the detailed demonstration of how misrepresentations operate in the very texts being questioned.[17] Barring this, it is legitimate to ask an unsettling question: if past men's attempts at contextualizations of the Quran and related foundational texts did not succeed, what are the chances that women's attempts, which heavily rely on men's work, would? Or what should women do to succeed where men have not? More important, could there be a different critical and innovative path for women to pursue successfully and claim as their own?

To return to attributor contextualism, it rests on a dogmatic, and all too common assertion, that Middle Eastern and North African societies, if not all "Muslim" societies, are so enmired in Islam that no change can occur unless it is framed in and channeled through religion. Undeniably, religion plays an important role in the personal and social life of people, including in "secular" societies. However, to assume that religion is all encompassing in MENA betrays a deterministic view, which flies in the face of historical reality.

The mythic character of this view has political functions; it clearly conflates, as faith-based groups do, religion as experience with religion as politics. It disregards the variations between countries in the centrality accorded religion. Some countries, such as Saudi Arabia, the Islamic Republic of Iran, or Pakistan, use Islamic law and religion in general to "mobilize political life."[18] In such cases, politics suffuses and animates religion, which appears to dominate politics. The strategic turn to Islamic law to suit the moment, as happened in Libya under Qaddafi partakes in the same logic, albeit Islam becomes a tool of political control. In both cases "religion as well as politics are eliminated."[19] However, there are countries, such as Algeria, Tunisia, or Syria (before sinking into civil war), whose laws are primarily "secular" in the sense that they are not implementations of the *shari'a*. For example, Algeria and Tunisia have penal codes modeled after the Napoleonic code and their business practices do not follow Islamic ethical norms. Nevertheless, Algeria (but not Tunisia since February 2011), in violation of its constitution, which proclaims the equality of its citizens before the law regardless of sex, adopted a family law based on a codified form of Islamic law. To reiterate, the exemption of the family, marriage, divorce, child custody, and inheritance from civil law is a political decision– the outcome of a political will, rather than a matter of religious conviction or concern. If the latter were the issue, the entire governments in MENA would need to function according to Islamic principles of justice as spelled out in Islamic political thought. Indeed, codification of family law is a state decision, not a religious imperative.[20] Moreover, returning to an original *shari'a* may not be the best method of dealing with the pressing demands of the present. Consequently, to argue that change in family law can occur only within the parameters of religion (without questioning the legitimacy of states' violation of their constitutions) discounts the factor of political will, which animates the imposition of family codes. By the same token, the argument turns these codes into the product of misguided religious imperatives originating in "patriarchal," or "misogynistic" distortions of true Islam. In other words, the argument implies that such codes would be acceptable if they reflected truer religious principles. Therefore, a non-"patriarchal" Islam would free women (and men) from inegalitarian family law by removing its gendered presuppositions. Yet to achieve this goal requires a dystopian belief that "patriarchy" only manifests itself in the *shari'a* as one of the misinterpretations of the "Divine discourse." Passed under silence is whether women would not be subject to other contingencies within a religious realm free of misinterpretations of gender. Indeed, if some misinterpretations are easy to identify, other may not be. Misrepresentations or "distortions" in the religious domain are value judgments which vary with the positionality of the interpreter. What if misrepresentations in areas other than gender are perceived to be so extensive, that redressing them requires no less than a whole rewriting of religious texts – a dizzying possibility. What then?

The myth of MENA societies as enmired in religion also disregards the changes that have taken place in women's lives in a number of countries, especially those that put an end to colonial rule, in spite of the emergence of faith-based parties, and parallel to restrictive family codes as is the case of Algerian women. It further discounts the significance of the anti-systemic movements that have swept over MENA, which, even if in some countries (such as Syria and Egypt) they have been rolled back or beaten back. Besides, where faith-based parties rode to power in the wake of these movements, they stayed the course by tampering their social messages about women as happened in Tunisia, or were severely repressed. Where the state wished to combat such groups, it did so and continues to do so not to protect women's rights, but secure its power.

The myth plays at least two important functions in the religious policies of individual states. On the one hand, it helps to legitimize a state's religious politics by deflecting its responsibility for protecting women's rights as citizens and focusing instead on religion as the cause of gender inequality. On the other hand, it conflates the concrete struggle for political and economic change with the search for liberation within theology. Given this history, where does a woman's Quranic attributor contextualism fit in the broader (geo-)politics of Islam?

Pacification or liberation?

Were women's Quranic attributor contextualism concerned solely with questions of theology and understanding of Islam's message across time and place, it would improve women's and men's comprehension of the richness of their faith, and reinforce their spirituality. It would, by its focus on religious meaning for a better practice, provide a counterpoint to gendered interpretations. It would, through meticulous and systematic examination of *tafsir* reveal a more spiritual way of approaching one's faith. Admittedly, this is no small task. Where women's Quranic attributor contextualism pursues a political purpose and thinks of itself in political terms as the only path to change, it loses in trust what it gains in popularity. By political I mean delving into the religious domain for non-religious goals and as part of a mundane strategy. Enlightening women about religious meanings is different from attempting to convince them that their beliefs are erroneous, and that for practical purposes they have been led astray. This schematic description highlights the afore-mentioned convergence of strands of women's Quranic contextualism and state's religious deradicalization policies adopted by Morocco and Algeria, among others. Where women Quranic contextualists are actively involved in a state policy of deradicalization, they are acting as political agents of the state. Whatever motivations behind women's support which may range from a genuine concern for feminizing the occupations of *'ulema* and *imams*, to pragmatic considerations, born out of a desire to bring about some change in the *sharia*, to endorse (through silence) the state's deradicalization policy of promoting *"wasatiya"* Islam is tantamount to acknowledging that Women's Quranic contextualism makes theology the handmaid of politics. The case of the Moroccan Quranic contextualist, Asma Lamrabet, illustrates the point. An ardent promoter of contextualism for the purpose of bringing about change, she joined her government's policy of *wasatiya* Islam as it appeared to be open to juridical change on behalf of women. The 2004 revised family code looked like it would usher in a new dawn for women's rights. However, it soon became clear that women were not central to the policy; preventing "radicalization" of youth and disseminating a version of Islam aimed at protecting the interests of the state from a religion-based opposition was the primary goal of the policy. Lamrabet understood the limits of the state religious politics when her advocacy for change in inheritance law met with stiff resistance from the very body of *'Ulema* she was affiliated with. She resigned.[21] Oddly, she explained that she had to tender her resignation because her view about women's equality made at the presentation of book on the subject had become public and created a stir in the media. She felt obligated to assure the public of her commitment to the monarch and to the unity of her country ("les constantes du pays"). She reminded the public that she promoted an "Islam of the third way, peaceful, specific ['contextualisé'], and in keeping with the universal humanist values as well as our cultural values."[22] In other words, she affirmed her full support for the state's national *wasatiya* Islam policy.

Lamrabet's predicament is a reminder of the hollowness of words with a historically specific context when used in a different context. She, like Barlas, refers to her project as one of "liberation."[23] Originating in Latin America (where Lamrabet once lived) and in the Catholic Church during dictatorships in the 1950s and 1960s, liberation theology was a complex movement aimed at alleviating poverty and government neglect of the poor, including indigenous people. It expressed a trend of activism within the Catholic Church, which integrated socialist ideas and analyses into the Church's moral concern for the poor.[24] The idea of a theology of liberation found resonance among Christian feminists seeking to free their religion of its male-centeredness. It is important to note that leading figures in this movement, such as Mary Daly and Rosemary Radford Ruether who carried their critical knowledge to its logical consequences, were trained in religion studies and were steeped in religious scholarship.[25] Mary Daly found herself arguing for a "post-Christian" theology. Rosemary Ruether's critical posture included not only advocacy for the ordination of women but also involvement in African-Americans' civil rights and Palestinians' political rights. Jewish feminists also have availed themselves of liberation theology to feminize their religion.[26] Moreover, in the wake of Mary Daly's advocacy of a post Christian feminism, a number of feminists have at times used an iteration of the "postcolonial" to characterize the psychological violence they experienced as Christian women. They compare their situation to that of colonized peoples who were subjected to psychic domination under colonial rule. From this perspective, feminists seek to free the domain of the sacred from its masculinization (which had "colonized" their lifeworld) and, by the same token, revalue forms of spirituality that do not conform to the masculine Christian norm.[27] This brief incursion into Christian feminism points to the trajectory of feminist critical inquiry once it starts peering into the gendered foundations of religion. At any rate, although it overlaps with feminist Quranic contextualism in securing a notion of the divine as transcending gender, Christian feminists also carry criticism to its logical conclusion in seeking to develop their own conception of divinity and spirituality. Ultimately, because women are at the center of established religions' self-understanding, they are the only ones who can go the farthest in their questioning of dogma, ritual, and law. That monotheistic religions differ from one another on specific treatment of women is evident. Quranic contextualists argue with good reason that Islam is less heavily gendered than Christianity, for example, because the divine in Islam is un-gendered and genderless. As Barlas notes, it is also true that women spoke out as challengers of men from the inception of Islam. Furthermore, Islamic law allows for negotiation between women and men on issues of marriage and divorce, which bespeaks flexibility in the application of the law. However, the overarching purpose of women's Quranic attributor contextualism is to bring about change in the status of women in society through a redefinition of the sacred. Yet, change calls for tangible, immediate social and economic policies. These are not central to questions of theology, the nature of the divine, the search for a genderless spirituality, or the relative religious content of Islamic law, even when states seek to make them so.

Theoretical effects of Quranic attributor contextualism

To recall, the various strands of Quranic contextualism originated mostly among academic women, many of whom teaching or writing in Western countries. Since the conceptualization of Quranic attributor contextualism occurred against the background of academic postfeminism, it is appropriate to determine whether it makes a contribution to, or builds the groundwork for a feminist theoretical framework that would advance knowledge of women in MENA. Before delving into the matter, it is important to note that on the margins of contextualism, feminist advocates have demanded the application of selected provisions of the *shari'a,* which various states failed to integrate in family law–a codification of *shari'a.* Thus, Algeria and Egypt, for example, have adopted *khol'* divorce, which a woman can request in return for a monetary compensation she pays to her husband. Women's advocates of this type of divorce had argued for the adoption of the practice because it already existed in the classical *shari'a.* Hence there was no legitimate ground, religious or otherwise, for denying women a right, which women had in the remote past. Nevertheless, advocacy for a re-institution of a practice that was already sanctioned by religious law is different from making reform contingent upon a re-interpretation of the Quran and related texts.

In what way does Quranic attributor contextualism foreclose the development of a theory of gender? Theorizing, if it is not to serve narrow interests, needs to be free of constraints to be able to embrace the diversity of social life. I suggest that Quranic attributor contextualism displays a number of features that constrain theorizing:

First, in spite of its attempt at historicizing problematic *suras*, Quranic attributor contextualism re-inscribes women in a pre-political transcendental discourse, which by definition is subject to infinite interpretations to decipher the ultimate meaning of concepts, exhortations, or injunctions. By pre-political, I mean a discourse that by necessity focuses on women as objects of a divine will rather than situated, living subjects. Hence, women's pressing mundane concerns, such as access to work, political participation, or equal pay for equal work are subjected to references to hypothetical discussions of what would constitute gender justice if the text were read properly, or read in the context of invocation of behaviors belonging to historical or mythical Muslim personages. Interpretation becomes the meta-principle to invoke when dealing with women's issues. In the end, such an approach favors idealism (in the Hegelian sense) over the analysis of the material conditions of women's existence. It encloses the feminist discourse in a hermeneutic circle of contextualization–deconstruction–reconstruction–contextualization of the reconstructed ...

Second, by defining progress as a matter of the proper understanding of texts or of divine "discourse", it obscures the notion of rights as well as social change as a force that propels ideas and actions. (The Western experience is a learning experience: even when rights are secured, their implementation is not; rights can also be overturned as attempts at rolling back abortion rights have shown in the USA as well as in MENA.)

Three, in tiptoeing around the idea of revelation, it vitiates its own claim for change. Indeed, if there is a "divine discourse" which by definition cannot be reproduced in its essential truthfulness since it must use a human being to convey it, on what grounds can a woman or a man decide that the (liberatory) message has been conveyed as it was conceived? Who has the ability to read the intention of the Divine? Or who can decipher the intention behind the "discourse." Or, is there an intention? In other words, it is an act of faith to decide that the originary (divine) message was gender-blind in its effects. From a skeptical point of view, "we" women can never know. Noted in passing is the significance of arguing that the divine has a discourse, an act that implicitly questions faith as faith.[28]

Finally, women's Quranic attributor contextualism essentializes and normatively fixes a religious identity that has traditionally been at once more fluid and individual. A woman may be a practicing Muslim in so far as she believes in the goodness of her religion from which she draws spiritual sustenance. However, she may not be convinced that her political, economic, and juridical rights should be dependent on, or read as deriving from her religion. She may insist on her religion as a matter between her and her maker, rather than a process of negotiated interpretations over whether she should be treated equally with men in her life as a working woman. She may prefer to claim change as a worker, mother, or politician in the profane world of everyday life rather than as a "Muslim". Fixing her identity in religion seen as a total institution occludes her other identities, or subsumes them under her beliefs. She is turned into a "believer" whether she is worshipping, trying to discharge her functions as an engineer, or dealing with sexual harassment. This hypothetical woman is not arguing for a "privatized" view of her religion.[29] She is locating herself in her daily life in which she interacts with a plurality of individuals many of whom are Muslims acting according to the norms regulating roles in various social settings. Identities resist fixity even among women contextualists who have been observed to switch from "secular" to "Islamic" feminism and back.[30]

Taken together, these characteristics of Quranic attributor contextualism may not facilitate theorizing about the relationship between women, religion, and social change. They are either assumptions or prescriptions to build an interpretation that has a presumed social purpose. When Quranic attributor contextualism presents itself as *the* solution to gender inequality and defines itself as the *only* appropriate and viable method of advocacy, it becomes a political ideology with hegemonic ambitions using religion as its vehicle. It then appears as the counterpart of the essentialist representation of Islam so common among faith-based groups or parties. They both seek to liberate[31] women, one from masculinist interpretations, the other from assumed deviations from a normative conservative interpretation of Islam. While the difference between the two modes of approaching religion may be substantial, they mirror each other in their doing battle with the spirit and letter of Islam while assuming that individual worshippers, whose experience of their religion is discounted, have no ideas of their own. Neither perspective asks whether women want to be liberated from the way they perceive their faith, or need liberating at all. It is opportune to recall the young researcher I interviewed who, after spending time in mosques to interview Salafi women, found herself in the throes of doubting the existence of God. She was curious about women's Quranic contextualism, but did not see it as the answer to her spiritual quandary. Her relation to her faith was deeply personal; hers was not the attitude of a consumer of religious interpretations, it was that of the skeptical woman, standing on the margins of the religious field, being in it but not of it, even if from her physical appearance she passed for the "passive" believer. This woman's circumstance stands as a metaphor for the myriad of ways in which women live, experience, and relate to their faith. It is a metaphor for the richness and complexity of women's lives, which escapes the reach of the multiplicity of "discourses" about religion. In the thick of a contested Islam caught up in the twirl of liberatory discourses (devoid of a theory of liberation), a woman may not find what she was told was there, liberation. What matters to her is her faith as she understands it, unequivocally.

Building a critical feminist theory in MENA

Conditions of possibility

The need to build a theory that captures the specific as well as universalistic character of gender in MENA is all the more pressing that the intellectual ascendency of Quranic contextualism is aided by its unacknowledged academic postfeminist background knowledge. Since postfeminism is a response to second wave feminist theory, feminist theorizing in MENA would benefit from clarifying its positioning toward this body of theory. A distinction needs to be made between subjecting antecedent feminist theory to critical analysis, and denying or misrecognizing its import. Feminist theory provided a vocabulary that has entered, in translation, the Arabic vernacular.[32] Translation plays a crucial role in the more or less unobtrusive ways in which the transfer of concepts from one language to the next conceals the equation of meanings in different contexts. The result is "the trap of semantic nominalism,"[33] whereby universal categories, such as freedom, are replaced with categories referring to local practices, such as culture.[34] Denial severs feminist values or theoretical concepts from the groups that originated them just as it obscures the circumstances under which they were elaborated.[35] From the perspective of this book, there is room for elaborating a theory that would build on the liberatory ideal of feminist theory, and take it to another level by freeing it of its cultural self-centeredness and its loss of moral compass, which caused it to be complicitous in neo-imperial policies that have harmed women in MENA.[36]

A theory sensitive to the changes that have affected MENA locally and geopolitically requires building a conceptual foundation that avoids three major temptations: (a) the reification of fixed identities. To assert differences in cultural experiences is not the same as accepting local cultural practices steeped in normative conceptions of gender inequality as constitutive of identity. It does not mean justifying them as appropriate, or defending them; (b) the uncritical use of totalizing concepts such as "patriarchy," (which poses a problem and resolves it at the same time), or "agency" where there is none. This means avoiding the use of postmodernist concepts *as* full-fledged theories by understanding their situated character; and (c) suspension of a critique of the political economy of religious policies which appear to align with women's interests. In order words, resisting the conflation of Islam as a lived faith and Islam as an instrument of political control in the age of security. To reiterate, *wasatiya* Islam, born out of security concerns and enmeshed in the "war on terror" reveals the extent to which states compromises the integrity of forms of Quranic contextualism by enlisting some of their proponents as embodiments of the success of their policies.

Radicalizing feminist theory

What would a critical feminist theory conscious of its location in the world be like? It would radicalize elements that had launched feminist theory in the West on its critical path before it became a victim of its own success. It would reclaim the ideal of freedom; rethink the principle of universalism; rekindle critical analysis of self and culture; re-center the struggle for gender equality in the larger (geo)political economy framework.

Freedom is feminist theory's ultimate purpose. Freedom from political, economic, and juridical constraints that would put an end to the justification of violations of women's exercise of their citizenship rights on biological grounds. As a process, freedom is the object of a constant struggle to emancipate one's self from ideologies and policies (such as that of "*wasatiya*" Islam) that present themselves as liberatory but in reality exact a new form of subjection. As Linda Zerilli put it, "freedom is not only freedom from interference from others, what we call 'negative liberty,' but also from politics itself."[37] (Said in passing Zerilli points to the importance of not conflating the social with the political[38], and of emphasizing the "I will" as much as the "I can").[39]

Freedom does not exhaust itself in an amended family code, or the creation of a corps of women *imams*. Freedom also requires being able to decide for one's self between alternatives without incurring sanctions. This is different from the bourgeois conception of choice, of choosing between varieties of the same. Finally, freedom has a psychological emancipatory dimension requiring a perpetual rejection of tutelage whether in the name of the family, polity, state, or interpretations of religion. Most important, freedom is indivisible–a fact postfeminist academic theory rejected–. Freedom is not good for some women and unsuitable to others; it cannot be compromised without turning women into agents of their own exclusion from their own history. Freedom is the single most important goal of feminist theorizing. In this respect, Linda Zerilli rightly argues that freedom is the "abyss" of feminism and also its "lost treasure" that needs to be rediscovered.[40] It cannot be compromised without incurring the risk of lowering women's sights. Yet, it has been given a bad name, as synonymous with rejection of ethical or moral values. Freedom is a constant process of seeing through the layers of justifications of the unjustifiable, of expanding one's autonomy to think for one's self, of ceaselessly raising one's consciousness in order to act as a full agent of one's own life.

Universalism as a principle of theorizing gender equality is not specific to one culture. Rethinking the universalistic character of women's aspirations to equality is imperative. The kind of universalism used by second wave feminism was Euro-centered, unconcerned with its ideological uses, and based on what Foucault called the Western ratio which, in order to define itself as a universal reason, divides the world into "Occident" and "Orient," and denies the rationality of the Orient, perceived as a "limit-experience" for the West.[41] Yet, there is a universal reason that includes Orient and Occident. This is the kind of universalism that movements of decolonization sought to avail themselves of, the kind of universalism which early critics of cultural imperialism such as Aimé Césaire called for, and which is at present driving peoples and movements in a number of MENA countries in their search for political freedoms.

Recapturing and de-localizing universalism is a way of reasserting the common denominator as well as purpose of knowledge: the human being. To gauge the anxiety universalism causes when it becomes contested, one only has to delve into the debates over "multiculturalism." One variant of these debates posed the question whether universalism is ethnocentric?[42] The question denotes the fear that acknowledging the equal value of other cultures is a *problem* that must be dealt with conceptually. Another variant articulated by Judith Butler asks:

> What happens when a disenfranchised group proceeds to claim 'universality', to claim they ought properly to be included within its purview? Does that claim presuppose a broader, more fundamental notion of universality, or is it that the claim is performative … ? Does the new universality appear as if it has been true all along?[43]

Remarkably, the premise of these questions is not questioned: that universalism is Western, it is owned. Universalism becomes problematic when those who were excluded from it claim it. From this perspective, what matters is how to "translate" universality in another cultural idiom without purportedly making its new "subjects" complicitous in its colonial past. What if universalism as practiced in the West emerged as supreme by borrowing as well as suppressing other expressions of universalism? The answer, according to the author is that universality "only means that when we speak its name, we do not escape our language, although we can—and must—push the limits."[44] The circle is closed, Butler joins Foucault who set a "limit" to the Western ratio. However, as she sees it, the "limit" is the uncertainty created by others who are claiming universality for themselves.[45] The assertion of the regional character of universalism obscures the notion of the human-ness of others, above and beyond cultural differences; it further passes over the idea of culture as a path (rather than an imaginary obstacle) towards a universal good.[46] Ultimately, what is passed under silence is the substantive meaning of "universalism" for others.[47] This apparent fossilization of the notion of universalism contrasts with explorations of the commonalities between treatments of the universal in Western as well as non-Western thought undertaken by intellectuals on the Islamic periphery.[48]

Freedom, as an imperative, calls for a relentless critical methodology. Relentless critical analysis applies not only to the questioning of justifications of cultural practices that hamper women's freedom of action, but also to critiques of culture in the region. Although Quranic attributor contextualists use the critical ideas developed by some male Islamicists who reassess Islam from a modernist perspective, they have done so uncritically, preferring instead to rely on them as a sort of legitimation of their own views.[49] More important, critique cannot spare the self. Self-criticism is a corrective to the political discourse that embeds feminist concepts in a discourse of accommodation of gender inequality.

In the end, these foundational principles of an emancipatory critical theory may be summarized as a refusal of the either-or blackmail women intellectuals (including myself) experience when they are expected to either accept a reified "culture" or be defined as "secular," or "Westernized;" either accept the promise of liberation through religion-as-discourse, or acquiesce to illegitimate family codes as well as the political order that sustains them. The temptation is great to dismiss a call to build a theory that radicalizes the promising principles enunciated by others as an academic luxury. Indeed, life under a security state actively engaged in the cultural politics of the "war on terror" is relentless and threatens to mystify the most alert conscience. However, "de-radicalization policies" are fueled by knowledge of Islam as well as of women, both of which need to be demystified through a relentless critical praxis understood as theoretically informed action.

In sum, the point is not to repeat the lapses of antecedent feminist theory, but to move the scholarship forward by developing feminist theory's unrealized potential. For MENA, this means working towards a truly cosmopolitan theory critical of itself, and anchored in the concrete world in which women live, work, and suffer. It is a theory that is oriented toward freedom from all forms of subjection including subjection to ideas that promise change in a supra-rational world, make change dependent on the expansion of an enlightened religious discourse, or conflate faith with knowledge of faith. It's a theory that aims for the expansion of awareness of the mystifying ways in which women's aspirations can become instruments of women's own subjection to politically infused cultural norms and practices on a global scale.

Notes

1 Michel Foucault, "What is Enlightenment?" in Paul Rabinow, ed., *Ethics and Subjectivity: The Essentials Works of Michel Foucault 1954–1984* (New York: The New Press, 1997), 313; Michel Foucault, *Dits et Ecrits*, vol. 2, 1976–1988, edited by Daniel Defert and François Ewald with the collaboration of Jacques Lagrange (Paris: Gallimard, 2001), 1396.

2 The discussion of this author's method in no way implies that her work is typical of the genre, is embraced, or questioned by other women epistemological Quranic contextualists.

3 Asma Barlas, *"Believing Women" in Islam: Unreading Patriarchal Interpretations of Islam* (Austin, TX: University of Texas, 2002), 2.
4 Ibid.
5 Ibid., 3.
6 Ibid., 31.
7 Ibid., 23.
8 The author does not fully explain why she adds the *Sunnah* as an "external" context when she also distinguishes between two *Sunnah*, one prophetic, the other mundane.
9 Ibid., 31.
10 Ibid., 64. Although in the glossary *ahadith* is defined as referring to both *hadith* and *sunnah*, the *sunnah*'s role in misinterpretations of the Quran is treated as autonomous. See 42–50, 63–68.
11 Citing Fazlur Rahman, the author allows for Byzantine, Jewish, and Persians additions to the *sunnah* by generations of legal scholars. Ibid., 64–65. For Rahman, see his *Islam and Modernity: Transformation of an Intellectual Tradition* (Chicago, IL: Chicago University Press, 1982).
12 Ibid., 127.
13 Barlas, *"Believing Women" in Islam*, 34.
14 Barlas's methodology owes a great deal to Farid Esack's. See for instance his interview on video in IDEA, Oct. 17, 2014 at www.idea.int/news-media/media/interview-farid-esack, accessed May 21, 2020. See also Farid Esack, *Qur'an Liberation and Pluralism: An Islamic Perspective of Interreligious Solidarity Against Oppression* (New York: Oneworld, 1997), esp. ch. 2.
15 Ibid., 3.
16 See for example M. A. Amir-Moezzi, *Le Coran silencieux et le Coran parlant: sources scripturaires de l'Islam entre histoire et ferveur* (Paris: CNRS, 2011). For a non-Muslim source, among others, see Helmut Gätje, *The Qur'an and its Exegesis: Selected Texts with Classical and Modern Muslim Interpretations* (Oxford: Oneworld, 1996).
17 Barlas, *"Believing Women" in Islam*, 53–54, reproduces *suras* about veiling but does not discuss their systematic treatment in the *tafsir*.
18 See Marnia Lazreg, *Foucault's Orient: The Conundrum of Cultural Difference, from Tunisia to Japan* (New York: Berghahn 2017), 136–137.
19 Ibid.
20 Wael B. Hallaq explains the role of the state in controlling the *shari'a*. See his *An Introduction to Islamic Law* (Cambridge: Cambridge University Press, 2009), esp. ch. 8. It must be noted that codification involves a process of selecting out parts of classical *shari'a* and articulating them as a series of injunctions presented as "articles."
21 See "Supporter of Gender Equality in Inheritance Resigns from Morocco's Religious Scholar's League," *North Africa Post*, March 21, 2018, https://northafricapost.com/22799-supporter-gender-equality-inheritance-resigns-moroccos-religious-scholars-league.html, accessed May 3, 2020. See also Ursula Lindssey, "Can Muslim Feminism Find A Third Way?" *The New York Times*, April 18, 2018. www.nytimes.com/2018/04/11/opinion/islam-feminism-third-way.html, accessed May 3, 2020.
22 Asma Lamrabet, "Communiqué de presse du Dr. Asma Lamrabet explicitant les raisons de sa démission du centre d'études féminines en Islam au sein de la Rabita Almohamadya des Oulémas du Maroc," n.d. asma-lamrabet.com. The text of the resignation also appears in *Jeune Afrique*, "Maroc: Asma Lamrabet livre les raisons de sa démission de la Rabita des Oulémas," March 26, 2018.
23 Asma Lamrabet, *Women in the Qur'an: An Emancipatory Reading*, trans. Myriam François-Cerrat (Markfield: Square View, 2016), introduction.
24 For an analysis of the movement see, among others, Gustavo Gutierrez, *A Theology of Liberation* (Maryknoll, NY: Orbis Books,1973). Gutierrez is a Peruvian theologian.

25 See Mary Daly's pioneering work, *Beyond God the Father: Towards a Philosophy of Liberation* (Boston, MA: Beacon Press, 1972) *or Gyn/Ecology: The Metaethics of Radical Feminism* (Boston, MA: Beacon Press, 1990). See also Rosemary Radford Ruether, *Sexism and God Talk: Towards a Feminist Theology* (Boston, MA: Beacon Press, 1993).

26 See for example Judith Plaskow, *Standing Again at Sinai: Judaism from a Feminist Perspective* (New York: HarperCollins, 1991).

27 See Kathleen McPhillips, "De-colonizing the Sacred: Feminist Proposals for a Post-Christian, Post-Patriarchal Sacred," in Kathleen McPhillips and Lisa Isherwood, eds., *Post-Christian Feminisms: A Critical Approach* (New York: Routledge, 2016), 129–146.

28 Selami Varlik makes a similar point in examining Fazlur Rahman's (who also inspired women Quranic contextualists) hermeneutic method which privileges knowledge over understanding so that "faith is no longer determinative in the discovery of the moral ends of the Quran." See Selami Varlik, "Le sens objectif du Coran à l'épreuve de l'historicité," *Archives des Sciences Sociales des Religions,* 60ème année, 170, (April–June 2015), 10.

29 Ziba Mir-Hosseini suggests that "the privatization" of religion is the bone of contention between feminists and Islamic feminists. See her "Beyond 'Islam' vs. 'Feminism,'" *IDS Bulletin* 42, no. 1 (2011): 67.

30 Mir-Hosseini (ibid., 70) notes this phenomenon, which she terms "radical identity shifts," with some dismay in Morocco, Egypt, and Iran.

31 It is noteworthy that Barlas adopts Badran's definition of "liberatory in the sense of both being inclusive and being based in notions of justice that cut across spurious unproductive binaries and divisions." Hence this kind of liberation can be achieved through a reasoned theory rather than religion. See Asma Barlas, "Engaging Islamic Feminism: Provincializing Feminism as a Master Narrative," in Anitta Kynsilehto, ed., *Islamic Feminism: Current Perspectives* (Tampere, FL: Tampere Research Institute, 2008), 21.

32 The difficulty of translating feminist terms accurately has sometimes led translators to simply Arabize gender as *djender.* The term *niswan* (derived from *nissa,* women) cannot be used because it is pejorative in many countries. Consider *nis'ai* or *niswi* (for feminist—of women), and *unthawi* (feminine) used as a synonym of *niswi.* Kamel Abu Deeb, the translator of Edward Said's *Culture and Orientalism* used "unuthi" for feminism. See Pernille Arenfeldt and Nawar Al-Hassan Golley, *From Mapping Arab Women's Movements: A Century of Transformation from Within* (Cairo: The American University in Cairo Press, 2012), 10.

33 Jorn Leonhard, "Translation As Cultural Transfer And Semantic Interactions: European Variations of *Liberal* Between 1800 and 1830," in Martin Burke and Melvin Richter, eds, *Why Concepts Matter: Translating Social and Political Thought,* vol 6 *Studies in the History of Political Thought* (Leiden: The Netherlands, 2012), 94.

34 Ibid.

35 A similar process has been termed "cryptomnesia" and its overcoming "conscientization." See Jean-Pierre Vernet, Jorge Vala, Ligia Amâncio, and Fabuzio Butera, "Conscientization of Social Cryptomnesia Reduces Sexism and Rejection of Feminists." *Social Psychology* 40, no. 3 (2009), 125.

36 For a lucid study analyzing feminism's loss of political bearing, see Hester Eisenstein, *Feminism Seduced: How the Global Elites Use Women's Labor and Ideas, to Exploit the World* (New York: Paradigm, 2009).

37 Linda M. G. Zerilli, *Feminism and the Abyss of Freedom* (Chicago, IL: University of Chicago Press, 2015), 9–10.

38 Ibid., 8.

39 Ibid., 16.

40 Ibid., 165–182.

41 For a discussion of how Foucault explained the universalism of the Western *ratio*, see Lazreg, *Foucault's Orient*, 192–196.
42 Seyla Benhabib, *The Claims of Culture: Equality and Diversity in the Global Era* (Princeton, NJ: Princeton University Press, 2002), 25.
43 Judith Butler, "Restating the Universal: Hegemony and the Limits of Formalism," in Judith Butler, Ernesto Laclau and Slavoj Žižek, eds., *Contingency, Hegemony, Universality: Contemporary Dialogues on the Left* (London: Verso, 2000), 38.
44 Ibid., 41. Said in passing, the "Left" affiliation claimed by Butler in the text from which the quotation is derived fails to question the postcolonial vocabulary that defines conscious individuals as "subaltern" or "unknowable" subjects. These are totalizing concepts carrying a baggage of unfounded assumptions about the selfhood and subjectivity of others. See ibid., 36.
45 Ibid., 36.
46 This is part of the heritage of universalism as expressed by Immanuel Kant who, in spite of his unenlightened views of non-Western peoples, still envisioned the human being as "a citizen of the world." See in particular, Immanuel Kant, *Anthropology from a Pragmatic Point of View*, trans. Robert B. Louden (Cambridge: Cambridge University Press, 2009).
47 Butler, "Restating the Universal," 35, appears to consider it an effect of translation.
48 For an analysis of this trend, see Farzin Vahdat, "Religious Modernity in Iran: Dilemmas of Islamic Democracy in the Discourse of Mohammad Khatami, *Comparative Studies of South Asia, Africa and the Middle East* 25, no. 3 (2005), 650–664; Roman Seidel, "Reading Kant in Teheran. Towards a Reception of the Iranian Reception of European Philosophy," *AS/EA* LXIV (March 2010); Norma Claire Moruzzi, "Reading Arendt in Iran/Reading Iran Through Arendt: Speech, Action, and the Question of Street Politics," *Great Cities Institute* (Chicago), Publication Number GCP-10–6, n.d., https://greatcities.uic.edu/wp-content/uploads/2013/08/2010_Moruzzi_Reading_Arendt_in_Iran.pdf; Daniel Postel, *Reading legitimation Crisis* in Tehran: Iran and the Future of Liberalism (Chicago, IL: Prickly Paradigm Press, 2006), especially interview with Ramin Jahanbegloo.
49 Islamic feminists in Iran have gone the farthest in this domain as they were exposed to a rich theological literature from men seeking to theorize an Islamic modernity from Iranian as well as Western philosophical perspectives. The wide-ranging literature includes, among others, Mohammed Khatami, *Islam, Liberty and Development* (Global Academic Publishing, 1998). In his desire to theorize a form of democracy that avoids "the dark side of modernity" as it purportedly exists in the West, Khatami saw as "paradoxical" women as citizens participating in the public life, and their natural role as keepers of the family; and Abdolkarim Soroush, *Reason, Freedom and Democracy in Islam: Essential Writings of Abdolkarim Soroush*, ed. and trans., Mahmoud Sadri and Ahmad Sadri (Oxford: Oxford University Press, 2000). Unlike, Khatami, Sorush advocates a cosmopolitan, multicultural conception of identity in which to resituate Islam. Islamic Feminists in Iran found in his writings an impetus for re-exploring Western feminist theorizing, albeit through a postmodernist lens. See Fereshteh Ahmadi, "Islamic Feminism in Iran: Feminism in a New Islamic Context," *Journal of Feminist Studies in Religion* 22, no. 2 (Feb. 2006), 330–53.

EPILOGUE

Against the backdrop of declarations about the death of God as well as man in European societies,[1] the emergence in the Middle East and North Africa of Quranic attributor contextualism, the most elaborate expression of the cultural turn among women, appears at first glance to hold the hopeful promise of the liberation of women from gender inequality in and through religion. However, the book has shown that the cultural turn among women, whether in its inceptive Algerian form or its more ambitious and formalized expression in the region, is a function of structures that limit the fulfillment of its promise. Crucial among these is the state sponsored establishment of a *wasatiya* Islam, which although intended to promote a national/Maghrebin Islam is also inscribed in the cultural strategy of the global "war on terror." Born out of fear, the objective of *wasatiya* Islam policy is to prevent the occurrence of a "radical" Islam assumed to lead to violence. The convergence between states in predominantly Muslim countries and European states on the definition of Islam as the cause of violence is instructive. It reveals a consensus on the transformation of political as well as socio-economic issues (which frame social strife) into cultural ones. Hence, an Islam made to order and immune to political interpretation is deemed an answer to the very issues that enabled the rise of collective restiveness or individual acts of violence.

However, it is the replacement of one politics by another that informs Quranic attributor contextualism. Claiming to be an alternative to a failed "secular" feminism, this trend purports to re-interpret the Quran in order to bring about change in family law which the politics of "patriarchy" hampers. Indeed, family codes wherever they have been instituted result from a political decision, and contravene Constitutions, which by definition express the political will of the people regardless of sex. But, the political epistemology of Quranic contextualism, grounded in a corrected textual interpretation of religion, implies that once freed of patriarchal control, religion would no longer lend itself to misinterpretation or be used as a brake on change; it would merge with a virtual liberation movement; it would become a sort of civil religion.[2] However, this argument underestimates the significance for the individual of questions of revelation, God, authority, truth, and more important the state as a competitor with religious authorities (including the authority women claim) over religious meaning. Through *wasatiya* Islam policy, the state gives itself the power to create a normative Islam enforced through various channels and techniques, including the revival of popular Sufism, support of quietist Salafism, and management of political Islamism. The stated objective of *wasatiya* Islam policy, deradicalization, consummates the politicization of Islam, ostensibly the very issue which the policy intends to combat; it also makes the incorporation of women inevitable. The degree to which women are enlisted in a normative view of Islam varies. In Algeria *wasatiya* Islam focuses on women's religious literacy supplemented with assistance with their daily problems. The limited, albeit useful, guidance *murshidat*, doubling up as surrogate imams and social workers, reflects the limitation of the very policy of *wasatiya* Islam. In this, the Algerian case reveals the contradiction at the heart of the policy. As a conveyer of customs inimical to women, and pursuing deradicalization objectives, it is not concerned with the juridical advancement of women beyond its 2005 amendment of the family code.

By contrast, the Moroccan *wasatiya* policy harnesses the power of the state to present itself to public opinion as the champion of women's rights. Yet, like Algeria, its policy rests on the revival of popular Sufism on a grander scale, and its packaged and manualized deradicalization program palters with feminism and progressivism. The highly publicized incorporation of women as *murshidat*, intends as in Algeria to increase religious literary and shepherd women. The involvement of women as active participants in the state global *wasatiya* policy shed light on the politics of women's Quranic attributor contextualism, its ethics, and the nature of its critical consciousness. Its liberationalist claim collides with the state's monopoly over the definition of Islam, and its position in geopolitics. It raises the question whether liberation, freedom, is a realizable goal when it is contingent not only upon textual reinterpretation—a field in which the state is also a competitor—but also the dismissal if not suppression of alternatives.[3] As a much-touted alternative to "secular" feminism, women's Quranic attributor contextualism thrives on a conflation of religion and culture, and subsumes the resolution of socio-economic and political issues facing women to a reformed Islam. In so doing, it could only comfort the state in its own view by increasing its *'irshadi* power. Perhaps more important, it reduces Islam to a discourse shorn of its experiential dimension which sustains women's faith. It is noteworthy that where the state was able to bring about juridical change, as happened in Tunisia's inheritance law, it did so at the behest of "secular" feminists.

Women's Quranic attributor contextualism is but one incarnation of a het-erogeneous trend frequently identified as Islamic feminism. In spite of the significance of its occurrence, its claim to be the only alternative path to change goes to the heart of the problematic of Islam made familiar by faith-based groups who have traditionally claimed to have the right interpretation of Islam. It raises the question of its audience. The women most in need of change due to the material conditions under which they live may not be concerned with whether their faith, which they do not question, is liberating or could be liberating. Their liberation lies beyond the sacred book whose sacrality they would defend. Dismissed by contextualists as resisting change or "naïve,"[4] these women reveal the depth of faith that escapes the conception of Islam-as-discourse. Conversely, contextualists dismiss women who doubt their perspective as being so revulsed by Islamic patriarchy that they seek "freedom from [Muslim] tradition."[5] Yet these women are hardly a mono-lithic group. They might include Muslim skeptics, agnostics, or those in the throes of a metaphysical crisis as was the case of the young researcher dis-cussed in Chapter 4.[6]

The tension inherent in the contextualist trend between the retrieval of a progressive message in Islam, and its eventual translation into a socio-eco-nomic and political program of action reflects the ambiguities of its unrecog-nized theoretical underpinnings. An unacknowledged heir to academic postfeminism, it is prone to its drawbacks, particularly its unbridled cultural-ism, and its neglect of the liberatory ideal of the women's movement of the 1960s as it unfolded in the United States. The indivisibility of freedom gave way in the epistemology of Quranic attributor contextualism to a hermeneutic circle in which re-interpretations beget more interpretations. Concrete change for women, not only in family law but in material life is subjugated to an infinite play of interpretation of texts, a search for historical events or perso-nages whose deeds must be collected as evidence that change could occur. These processes of infinite regress in search for arguments to convince gov-ernments to undertake reforms delay rather facilitate change. In the Algerian case, the state does not derive its legitimacy from religious texts but from a revolution in a war of decolonization in which women stepped out of their circumscribed family roles to demand freedom and equal rights. These hardly end with the suffrage but require a constant struggle to preserve them as well as implement them. The Moroccan state in its pursuit of an Islam immune to political interpretation avails itself of profane techniques of dissemination of its apparent and highly mediatized support for women, as exemplified in its de facto promotion of plays and films with explicit sexual contents.

What is at stake is perhaps more than a progressive reading of the Quran, which would help to rewrite or modify Islamic law to bring it up to par with the requirements of equality before the law than what Islam is as an idea, and what the role it plays in people's lives is. Efforts made in different countries as far flung as Malaysia, South Africa, and the United States by scholars to rediscover new or originary meanings in the Quran have two objectives in common: dispel misconceptions of Islam that have existed in Western societies for ages and were aggravated by the event of 9/11; and answer the specific issues that they grapple with as Muslims living in the West. This holds true for the women who live in the Middle East or other predominantly Muslim societies but were either educated in the West, or exposed through the global media to the treatment frequently meted out to Muslims in Europe and North America. In other words, the progressive reading of the Quran is driven as much by a scholar's genuine desire to re-value, even protect her religion, as by a quest for belonging in a society where she is a numerical minority. These various pressures arising from the rehabilitation of one's faith in one's eyes as well in the eyes of the other subtly inflect the message contextualists (and liberation theologians) wish to convey; it may even undermine its intended objectives.

Is women's Quranic attributor contextualism a cultural harbinger of a different or new phase of modernity, one lying between a "compressed modernity"[7] and a "third modernity?"[8] If modernity (a contested term) means a critical attitude towards the world, constituted authority, and the self that may or may not be compatible with faith, it appears that women's Quranic attributor contextualism is an effort to bring Islam up to the "modern" world as constituted, rather than constitute an alternative to it. Furthermore, it is doubtful whether it intends to re-enchant a post-Darwinian "modern" world bereft of mystery or spiritual foundation. This is not to say that Islam is incompatible with "modernity." It means that the integrity of Islam as an idea and an experience, its wholeness as a faith are called into question by women not on purely theological grounds (a welcome move), but in order to convince states to live by a retrieved divine truth.[9] They do not take the state to task for the hypocrisy of violating its constitution and cobbling up its own normative Islam. Unless Islam is equated with its misrepresentations, to make change in family law contingent upon exegesis at the exclusion of other methods is a political decision in its own right born out of a conviction that societies in the Middle and North Africa live in a theological stage from which they cannot escape. This move has an unintended consequence: the actual dissolution of Islam or its supersession by a reformed Islam—an outcome that looms on the horizon of the French policy of deradicalization. What if Islam as an idea is not translatable into any one of the languages that seek to fix its meanings, including feminism, conservatism, and orientalism?[10] Constructed as the cause as well as the solution of juridical and social problems, Islam is singularly subjected to infinite re-interpretations and partial historicizations which in the long run contribute to its dismantling. Far from being conservative, this idea is actually prefigured in the hermeneutics of women's (or men's) Quranic contextualist project: critical knowledge of religion as distinguished from faith is in itself an incipient erosion of faith. Hence, after reading Hela Ouardi's book, *Les derniers jours de Muhammad*, a successful professional woman told me in Algiers, "they sold us a lie for 1,400 years!" Christian feminists have already traveled this road, which led some of them to advocate a religion by and for women. This is not to imply that ignorance in religious matters is bliss. The point is to question the liberatory claim that women's Quranic contextualism makes, when it proposes to supersede the straw woman of "secular" feminism, deemed out of step with Muslim culture. In this sense, (political) liberation within religion is close to liberation from religion. Yet, the choice for women is not between a re-interpreted Islam and change but between the politics of gender and governance according to the constitution. *Wasatiya* Islam highlights the state's *political* will to recompose the religious field while on occasion (as happens in Morocco) dangling its "feminism" as a prize for its traffic in Islam.[11] The Moroccan state, which has up to now shied away from a reform of inheritance law demonstrates, if need be, the competing interests of *wasatiya* Islam and feminism.

The control of Islam through a variety of devices including *wasatiya* policy, or Quranic attributor contextualism, no matter how enlightening and useful, often results in a reinforcement of the very excesses it intends to remedy. For example, in the midst of the Corona virus pandemic during Ramadan 2020, the Algerian Ministry of Religious affairs lodged a complaint with the Authority Regulating the Audiovisual (ARAV) against a private TV chain, *Ennahar*. The host of a program, *Insahouni* ("enlighten me"), Sheikh Chemsou, had taken issue with the Ministry's fatwa enjoining people to give the *zakat* (obligary charity) directly to the poor two to three days in advance of the *Eid al-Fitr*, the day when it is normally due, because of the special circumstance created by the Corona virus pandemic. Chemsou declared the *fatwa* wrong because by changing the date of payment of the *zakat*, it transformed it into a *sadaqa*, simple voluntary charity, which therefore needed to be paid again on the *Eid*. Summoned by ARAV, the manager of the *Ennahar* issued an apology.[12] Whatever the merits of the disagreement over the *fatwa*, the Ministry's action was indicative of the state monopoly over religious meaning, which could neither be questioned nor debated. In another instance, the Fatwa Commission of the Ministry of Religious Affairs declared: "fasting during Ramadan which occurs this year in the midst of a pandemic is obligatory considering that no scientific study has shown a link between fasting and infection by Covid19." Although the fatwa exempts infected people from fasting, it specifically enjoins first line medical personnel to fast.[13] The interweaving of scientific research with a religious pronouncement highlights the state's self-appointed role as the enforcer of a religious precept and enlightened institution mindful of science: people must fast because the state supported by science requires them to do so. Science, which the Tripoli Program had called for to combat Algeria's cultural deficit in 1962, is summoned in 2020 to enforce a normative religion, even during a period of soaring unemployment which made it difficult for vulnerable segments of the population to cope with the additional expenses that Ramadan entails.

As an intervention in Quranic studies, women's Quranic attributor contextualism is invaluable. It brings fresh insights into the field, which it broadens and enriches with new research. However, when it is turned into a purportedly unique method of "liberation" of women, it finds its limitations in its selective suspension of critical analysis, either of the state *wasatiya* policy, the material conditions that hamper change in women's lives, or the geopolitical interests framing deradicalization policies which thrive on its support. Furthermore, it assumes that the avenue of change it promotes is welcome by all. Evidence indicates, that youth, whether in the protest movement in Algeria, Tunisia, or Iran does not share in contextualists' vision of the framework of change.[14] The commodification of Islam through satellite TV,[15] and development of Islamic fashion[16] detract from the assumed autochthonous character of women's Quranic attributor contextualism since the stage on which various interpretations of Islam is played out has expanded in ways that escape integration within a unitary framework.

The Algerian case reveals how the state's *wasatiya* policy has spearheaded a variant of the cultural turn that occupied the religious field in a manner that does not at this time have room for a competing conception of Islam from women acting as Quranic contextualists. The state uses *wasatiya* Islam as a compensatory mechanism that reinscribes women as subjects of religious norms as enunciated in the family code. Research is needed to determine if the state can or will allow women Quranic contextualists to emerge and share its space. The state does, however, tolerate individual men to advance on television a view of Islam similar to that of women contextualists operating in Morocco and elsewhere; it also tolerates conservative preachers. The possibility exists, at least since the rise of the national movement of protest, the *hirak,* that a space in which women can advocate for juridical, political and economic change as citizens regardless of their religious status. In more than one way, it is the subsumption of women as believers that overshadows their status as citizens in the eye of a state that promotes and enforces a normative Islam. Knowledge and critical theory are inevitable in understanding and bringing about change. A liberation praxis, as theoretically informed action, helps to resist the capillary dissemination of a national Islam enmeshed in the advancement of the interests of Western states that have traditionally fought Islam to secure the sustainability of colonial empires. Hence, a decolonial liberatory theory would help to gauge programs or policies denouncing Islam as a problem yet also upholding it as a solution.

Notes

1 The phrase "God is dead" appears in Friedrich Nietzsche, *The Gay Science,* trans. Walter Kaufmann (New York: Vintage, 1974), section on "The Madman," 125. Michel Foucault argues that "what Nietzsche's thought heralds is the end of his [God's] murderer." *The Order of Things*: An Archeology of the Social Sciences (New York: Vintage, 1994), 385.

2 For an instructive study of civil religion, see Robert N. Bellah and Philip E. Hammond, *Varieties of Civil Religion* (New York: Harper & Row, 1980), especially part III.

3 It is noteworthy that in Morocco, the ascendance of Islamic feminism appears to have influenced a "secular" feminist association, the Democratic Association of Women in Morocco (ADFM) in its adoption in 2008 of an Islamic feminist framework to advocate for change in inheritance law. Souad Eddouada and R. Pepicelli, "Morocco: Towards an 'Islamic State Feminism,'" *Critique internationale* 46, no. 1 (2010): 87–100. 11. However, the authors see this move as an example of the complementarity of the two trends in Moroccan feminism, secularist and Islamic. They assume that the two groups came to realize that as members of a rising middle class, they pursue a similar goal albeit they express it differently (ibid., 12).

4 Asma Lamrabet, *Islam et femmes: Les questions qui fâchent* (Paris: Gallimard Folio, 2017), 9–10. Lamrabet refers to the women as "sincerely naïve" and essentially duped by the "patriarchal discourse."

5 Ibid., 10. Lamrabet's attitude contradicts the supra-religious universalism expressed in her resignation statement. See Chapter 7 in this book.

6 There are also Muslim women who in the wake of the aborted revolution in Egypt feel they lost their faith. See Nermin Allam, *Women and the Egyptian Revolution: Engagement and Activism During the 2011 Arab Uprisings* (Cambridge: Cambridge University Press, 2018), 159–160.

7 The terms refer to an accelerated form of socio-cultural, economic, and political development. For an application of the term to South Korea, see Kyung-Sup Chang, "The Second Modern Condition? Compressed Modernity as Internalized Reflexive Cosmopolitization," *British Journal of Sociology* 62, no. 3 (2010) 444–464.

8 See José Mauricio Domingues, "Beyond the Centre: The Third Phase of Modernity in Compared Perspective," *European Journal of Theory* 14, no. 4 (2011): 517–535. The author compares paths to development and social change followed in China, India and Brazil.

9 Mohammed Omar Farooq reports that there may be new accretions to *hadith*; he could not find an original source to a hadith attributed to the Prophet during his last pilgrimage before his death that declared women equal to men. Whether this claim is verified by others or not, it raises the question of the integrity of the Quran as well as related foundational texts in an age of deconstruction. See Mohammed Omar Farooq, "Gender Issues and the Search for a Hadith: A Journey in Islamic Diligence," *Islam and Civilizational Renewal* 11, no. 1 (2020): 94–100. The hadith in question is on pp. 96–97.

10 Joseph A. Massad cogently raises the question of the "comparative untranslatability" of Islam. See *Islam in Liberalism* (Chicago, IL: University of Chicago Press, 2015), 10–11.

11 Souad Eddouada and R. Pepicelli use the felicitous phrase "Islamic State Feminism," in their analysis of Morocco. See their "Morocco: Towards an Islamic State Feminism," 2.

12 "Fetwa sur la zakat: la responsable de 'Ennahar TV convoquée par l'ARAV,'" *TSA* (Tout sur l'Algérie), May 22, 2020, www.tsa-algerie.com/fetwa-sur-la-zakat-la-responsable-dennahar-tv-convoquee-par-larav, accessed May 23, 2020. Under normal circumstances *zakat* is collected by the Zakat Fund managed by the Ministry of Religious Affairs.

13 "Ramadan et Covid19: La commission de la fatwa se prononce," *TSA* (Tout sur l'Algérie), April 26, 2020, www.tsa-algerie.com/ramadan-et-covid-19-la-commission-de-la-fatwa-se-prononce, accessed June 7, 2020.

14 In the Islamic Republic of Iran, a study indicates that young people, men and women, have developed a contradictory "post-ideological character" on feminism as well as religion. Rassa Ghafari and Elisabetta Ruspini, "Locating Millenial

Feminism Beyond the Western Context: The Iranian Case," *Participazione e Conflitto, The Open Journal of Political Studies* 13, no. 1 (March 15, 2020): 670, http://siba-ese.unislento.it, accessed May 23, 2020. Haideh Moghissi, "Islamic Cultural Nationalism and Gender Politics in Iran," *Third World Quarterly* 29, no. 3 (2008): 541–554, argues that the younger generation of women and men demand democratic legal change outside the framework of reformist Islam.

15 Shaima El Naggar found that a popular imam who uses satellite TV (and whom she anachronistically identifies as "televangelists") uses a method of persuasion similar to that of advertisers. "Intertextuality and Interdiscursivity in the Discourse of Muslim Televangelists: The Case Study of Hamza Yusuf," *Critical Approaches to Discourse Analysis Across Disciplines* 6, no. 1 (2012): 78–71.

16 Islamic fashion raises the issue of the "policing" of women's bodies through clothing in the context of European countries, especially France which criminalized the "burkini." See Rumee Ahmed and Ayesha S. Chaudhry, "Their Bodies, Ourselves: Muslim Women's Clothing at the Intersection of Rights, Security, and Extremism," in B. Goold and L. Lazarus, eds., *Security and Human Rights*, 2nd edition (Oxford: Hart Publishing, 2019), 66–71.

GLOSSARY

din	faith
dunya (or *dunia*)	life in daily existence; mundane concerns
fatiha (or *'urf*) marriage	religious marriage
fatwa (or *fetwa*), pl. *fatawa*	formal legal opinion issued by a religious scholar or council of scholars
hadith	sayings attributed to Prophet Muhammad
ijtihad	exercising independent judgment in legal or theological matters
jihad	battle
khul'	divorce a woman can obtain in exchange for a compensation
murshida, pl. *murshidat*	lit. guide; a female equivalent of an *imam*
salafi	member of a group or association of individuals who practice Islam according to the *salaf*, the pious men of the first free generations of Muslims after the death of Prophet Muhammad
shari'a	Islamic law
Sufism	mystical Islam
sunna (or *sunnah*)	behavior and actions of Prophet Muhammad as recorded by his companions
'ulema (*'ulama*)	scholars of religion
wasatiya Islam	lit. Islam of the middle ground, or moderate Islam

BIBLIOGRAPHY

Abdelhaleem, Tariq. *The Counterfeit Salafis: Deviations from the Methodology of Ahl Al Sunnah Wal Jama'a*. Scarborough: Al Attique, 2004.

Abugideiri, Hibba. "Revisiting the Islamic Past, Deconstructing Male Authority." *Religion and Literature*, 42, no. 1–2 (2014): 133–139.

Acherchour, El Mehdiet al. *La révolution du sourire*. Algiers: Editions Frantz Fanon, 2019.

AFP (Agence France Press). "Les imams algériens envoyés en France devront 'dépoussiérer' l'Islam." *Le Point*, January 18, 2015. Accessed April 28, 2019 from www.lepoint.fr/societe/les-imams-envoyes-en-france-devront-depoussiere.l.islam-18-01-2015-189753923.php.

Ahmadi, Fereshteh. "Islamic Feminism in Iran: Feminism in a New Islamic Context." *Journal of Feminist Studies in Religion*, 22 (February2006): 330–353.

Ahmed, Leila. *A Quiet Revolution: The Veils' Resurgence, from the Middle East to America*. New Haven, CT: Yale University Press, 2012.

Ahmed, Rumee and Ayesha S. Chaudhry, "Their Bodies, Ourselves: Muslim Women's Clothing at the Intersection of Rights, Security, and Extremism." In *Security and Human Rights*, second edition, edited by Gold B. and L. Lazarus, 66–71. Oxford: Hart Publishing, 2019.

Allam, Nermin. *Women and the Egyptian Revolution: Engagement and Activism During the 2011 Arab Uprisings*. Cambridge: Cambridge University Press, 2018.

Algerie360. "Guelma: une fillette meurt lors d'une séance de 'roqya' dans l'hôpital Abdelhakim Okbi." Accessed June 15, 2019 from https://algerie360.com/20200529-une=fillette-de-10ans-meurt-lors-dun-exorcisme.

Amhair, Loubna. "Morocco World News." February 23, 2016. Accessed from www.moroccoworldnews.com/2016/02/180479/how-to-prevent-the-radicalization-of-women-the-moroccan-model.

Amir-Moezzi, Mohammed Ali. *Le Coran parlant et le Coran silencieux: nouvelles perspectives sur les origines de l'Islam*. Paris: CNRS, 2011.

Amir-Moezzi, Mohammed. *The Silent Qur'an and the Speaking Qur'an: Scriptural Sources of Islam Between History and Fervor*. New York: Columbia University Press, 2015.

Andezian, Sossie. "L'Algérie, le Maroc, la Tunisie." In *Les Voies d'Allah: les ordres mystiques dans le monde musulman des origines à aujourd'hui*, edited by Alexandre Popovic and Gilles Veinstein, 389–408. Paris: Arthème Fayard, 1996.

Asfaruddin, Asma. *The First Muslims: History and Memory*. Oxford: Oneworld, 2007.

Badran, Margot. "Between Secular and Islamic Feminism/s: Reflections on the Middle East and Beyond." *Journal of Middle Eastern Women's Studies*, 1, no. 1 (Winter 2005): 6–28.

Badran, Margot. "Feminism and a New Mediterranean Culture: A Close-Up in Spain." *Samuykta*, 17, no. 1 (January2017): 142–164.

Badran, Margot. *Feminism in Islam: Secular and Religious Convergences*. Oxford: Oneworld, 2009.

Badran, Margot. "Letter to the Editors." *Journal of Feminist Studies in Religion*, 33, no. 1 (Spring2017): 5–8.

Barlas, Asma. *"Believing Women" in Islam: Unreading Patriarchal Interpretations of Islam*. Austin, TX: University of Texas, 2002.

Barlas, Asma. "Engaging Islamic Feminism: Provincializing Feminism as a Master Narrative." In *Islamic Feminism: Current Perspectives*, edited by Anitta Kynselhto, 14–24. Tampere: Tampere Research Institute, 2008.

Barlas, Asma. "Letter to the Editors." *Journal of Feminist Studies in Religion*, 34, no. 1 (Spring2018): 1–5.

Barlas, Asma. "Secular and Feminist Critiques of the Qur'an: Anti-Hermeneutics of Liberation?" *Journal of Feminist Studies in Religion, 32*, no. 2 (Fall2016): 111–121.

Bayat, Asef. *Post-Islamism: The Changing Face of Political Islam*. Oxford: Oxford University Press, 2013.

Bellah, Robert N. and Philip E. Hammond. *Varieties of Civil Religion*. New York: Harper and Row, 1980.

Benhabib, Seyla. *The Claims of Culture: Equality and Diversity in the Global Era*. Princeton, NJ: Princeton University Press, 2002.

Benzenine, Belkacem and Cherif Driss, "Hirak: an II?" Interview by Amin Allal and Farida Souiah. *La Découverte*, no. 102 (2020): 57–69. Accessed from www.cairn.info/revue-mouvements-2020-2-page-57.htm.

Benzenine, Belkacem and Sonia Sarah Lypsic. "L'accès des femmes aux fonctions religieuses publiques dans le judaïsme et l'Islam." In *Juives et musulmanes de la Méditerranée*, edited by Lisa Antéby and Yemimi. Paris: Karthala/MMSH, 2014.

Berque, Augustin. "Un mystique moderniste, le cheikh Ben 'Alioua." *Revue Africaine*, 79 (1936): 691–776.

Bologh, Roslyn. *Love of Greatness: Max Weber's Masculine Thinking*. New York: Routledge, 2009.

Bonnell, Victoria E. and Lynn Hunt, eds. *Beyond the Cultural Turn*. Berkeley, CA: University of California Press, 1999.

Bouasria, Abdelilah. "Bits and Tits: The Dialectics of Bodily Encounters in Moroccan Politics." In *Trajectories of Change in Post 2011 MENA: Challenges and Prospects*, edited by Joshen Lobah and Hamzah Tayebi. Rabat: Hans Striftung Foundation, 2017.

Boubekeur, Amel. "Salafism and Radical Politics in Post-Conflict Algeria." October 20,2008. Accessed from https://carnegie-mec.org/2008/10/20/salafism-and-radical-politics-in-postconflict-algeria-pub-22293

Boukhars, Anouar. "My Enemy's Enemy." April 18, 2018. Accessed October 27, 2019 from https://carnegie-mec.org/diwan76098.

Boukhars, Anouar. "Quietist and 'Firebrand' Salafism in Algeria." November 24, 2015. Accessed from https://carnegieendowment.org/2015/11/24/quietists-and-firebrand-salafism-in-algeria-pub-62075.

Bourdieu, Pierre. *Acts of Resistance: Against the Tyranny of the Market*. New York: The New Press, 1998.

Bouzghaia, Ilyass. "Gender Relations and Social Values in Morocco." In *Trajectories of Change in Post 2011 MENA: Challenges and Prospects*, edited by Joshen Lobah and Hamza Tayebi. Rabat: Hans Seidel Foundation. Takamul Center for Interdisciplinary Studies and Research, 2017.

Brown, Jonathan. "Salafis and Sufis in Egypt." December 20, 2011. Accessed from https://carnegie-mec.org/2011/12/20/salafis-and-sufis-in-egypt-pub-46278

Butler, Judith. *Gender Trouble: Feminism and the Subversion of Identity*. New York: Routledge, 1999.

Butler, Judith. "Restating the Universal: Hegemony and the Limits of Formalism." In *Contingency, Hegemony, Universality: Contemporary Dialogues on the Left*, edited by Judith Butler, Ernesto Laclau, and Slavoj Žižek, 11–43. London: Verso, 2000.

Chamkhi, Tarek. "Neo-Islamism Post-Arab Spring." *Contemporary Politics*, 20, no. 4 (2014): 207–219.

Chang, Kyung-Sup. "The Second Modern Condition? Compressed Modernity as Internalized Reflexive Cosmopolitization." *British Journal of Sociology*, 62, no. 3 (2010): 444–464.

Chikhi, Lamine. "Hard-line Islam Steps out of the Shadows in Algeria." *Reuters*, August 10, 2010. Accessed October 29, 2019 from www.reuters.com/article/us-algeria-religion-salafism-idUSTRE6791TQ20100810.

CIDDEF. *Connaissance des droits des femmes et des enfants en Algérie*. Algiers: CIDDEF, 2007.

Conrad, Sarah Jane. "Linguistics Meaning and the Minimalism Contextualism Debate." *Logiqie et Analyse*, 54, no. 216 (2011): 53–469.

Daly, Mary. *Beyond God the Father: Towards a Philosophy of Liberation*. Boston, MA: Beacon Press, 1972.

Daly, Mary. *Gyn/Ecology: The Metaethics of Radical Feminism*. Boston, MA: Beacon Press, 1992.

DeRose, Keith. "Contextualism and Knowledge attribution." *Philosophical and Phenomenological Research*, 52, no. 54 (December1992): 913–992.

Diamond, Irene and Lee Qimby. *Feminism and Foucault: Reflections on Resistance*. Boston, MA: Northeastern University Press, 1995.

Domingues, Mauricio. "Beyond the Centre: The Third Phase of Modernity in Compared Perspective." *European Journal of Theory*, 14, no. 4 (2011): 517–535.

Dorsey, James M. 2018. "Algerian Controversy Over Salafism Puts Government Control of Religion on the Spot." *Internal Policy Digest*, April 26, 2018. Accessed from https://intpolicydigest.org/2018/04/26/algerian-controversy-over-salafism-puts-government-control-of-religion-on-the-spot.

Duderija, Adis. "Towards a Scriptural Hermeneutics of Islamic Feminism." *Journal of Feminist Studies in Religion*, 31, no. 2 (Fall2015).

Durkheim, Émile. *The Elementary Forms of Religious Life*. New York: Dover, 2008.

Eisenstein, Hester. *Feminism Seduced: How the Global Elites Use Women's Labor and Ideas to Exploit the World*. New York: Paradigm, 2009.

Elaroui, Rkia. *Rabi'a al 'Adawiyya*. Oxford: Oneworld, 2019.

Elliott, Katja Zvan. "Morocco and its Women's Rights Struggle: A Failure to Live Up to its Progressive Image." *Journal of Middle Eastern Women's Studies*, 10, no. 2 (Spring 2014): 1–30.

Esack, Farid. *Qur'an Liberation and Pluralism: An Islamic Perspective of Interreligious Solidarity Against Oppression.* New York: Oneworld, 1997.

Esack, Farid. *The Qur'an: A Short Introduction.* Oxford: Oneworld, 2014.

Faculté Jean Monet. "Du République et Religions." Accessed April 26, 2019 from www.jm.u-psud.fr/du-republique-religion.

Fadl, Khaled Abou El. *And God Knows the Soldier: The Authoritative and Authoritarian in Islamic Discourse.* Lanham, MD: Rowman & Littlefield, 2001.

Fadl, Khaled Abou El. *Speaking in God's Name: Islamic Law, Authority, and Women.* Oxford: Oneworld, 2001.

Farooq, Mohammed Omar. "Gender Issues and the Search for a Hadith: A Journey in Islamic Due Diligence." *Islam and Civilizational Renewal*, 11, no. 1 (2020): 94–100. Accessed June 16, 2019 from https://ssrn.com/abstract=3628282.

Fawcett, Rachelle. "The Reality and Future of Islamic Feminism: What Constitutes Islamic Feminism and Where it is Headed." *Al Jazeera*, March 28, 2013. Accessed February 18, 2019 from www.aljazeera.com/indepth/opinion/2013/03/20133271558558.

Filali, Kamel. *l'Algérie mystique: des Marabouts fondateurs aux Khwans insurgés, XVI/XX siècles.* Paris: Publisud, 2002.

Foucault, Michel. *The Archaeology of Knowledge.* New York: Vintage, 1972.

Foucault, Michel. *La Sexualité. Cours donné à l'université de Clermont Ferrand, 1964 suivi de Le Discours de la Sexualité donné à l'université de Vincennes, 1969.* Paris: Gallimard, 2018.

Foucault, Michel. "Pastoral Power and Political Reason." In *Michel Foucault, Religion and Culture*, edited by Jeremy Carrette, 135–152. New York: Routledge, 1976.

Foucault, Michel. "Society Must Be Defended." *Lectures at the Collège de France, 1975–1976*, edited by Mauro Bertani and Alessandro Fontana, translated by David Macey. New York: Picador, 2003.

Foucault, Michel. "What is Enlightenment?" In *Ethics, Subjectivity, and Truth: The Essential Works of Michel Foucault*, ed. Paul Rabinow. New York: The New Press, 1997.

Foucault, Michel. "What is Enlightenment?" In *Dits et Ecrits, vol. 2, 1976–1988*, edited by Daniel Defert and François Ewald with the collaboration of Jacques Lagrange, 1381–1397. Paris: Gallimard, 2001.

Fraser, Nancy. *Justice Interruptus: Critical Reflections on the 'Postsocialist' Condition.* New York: Routledge. 1997.

Fraser, Nancy and Linda Nicholson. "Social Criticism Without Philosophy: An Encounter Between Feminism and Postmodernism." *Social Text*, 21 (1980): 83–104.

Frégosi, Frank. *L'Islam dans la laïcité.* Paris: Arthème Fayard, 2012.

Front de libération nationale. "Le Programme de Tripoli." In *Les textes fondamentaux de la révolution algérienne.* Algiers: Editions ANEP, 2005.

Front de libération nationale. "Plateforme de la Soummam." In *Les textes fondamentaux de la révolution algérienne.* Algiers: Editions ANEP, 2005.

Front de libération nationale. *La charte d'Alger. Ensemble des textes adoptés par le congrès du parti du FLN.* Algiers: Front de libération nationale, 1964.

Gatje, Helmut. *The Qur'an and its Exegesis: Selected Texts with Classical and Modern Interpretations.* Oxford: Oneworld, 1996.

Geertz, Clifford. *The Interpretation of Cultures: Selected Essays.* New York: Basic Books, 1973.

Genz, Stéphanie and Benjamin A. Brabon. *Postfeminism: Cultural Texts and Theories.* Edinburgh: Edinburgh University Press, 2009.

Ghafari, Rassa and Elisabetta Ruspini. "Locating Millenial Feminism Beyond the Western Context: The Iranian Case." Participazione e Conflitto. *The Open Journal of Political Studies*, 13, no. 1 (March 15, 2020). Accessed May 23, 2019 from http s://siba-ese.unislento.it.

Ghanmi, Lamine. "Salafists' Rise Triggers Concern in Algeria over Cultural Freedom." *The Arab Weekly*, December 8, 2018.

Golley, Nawar Al Hassan. "Is Feminism Relevant to Arab Women?" *The Quarterly*, 25, no. 3 (2004): 521–536.

Golley, Nawar Al-Hassan and Pernille Arenfeldt. *From Mapping Arab Women's Movements: A Century of Transformations from Within.* Cairo: The American University in Cairo Press, 2012.

Gray, Doris H. *Beyond Feminism and Islamism: Gender and Inequality in North Africa.* New York: I. B. Tauris, 2015.

Guardian. "Women-Led Mosque Opens in Denmark." *The Guardian*, February 12, 2016. Accessed December 17, 2019 from https://theguardian.com/world/2016/feb12/ women-led-mosque-opens-denmark.

Guessoum, Ahmed. "Le rôle social et politique des zaouias: évolution et pratiques sociales." Doctoral dissertation, Université de Paris VIII, Paris, July 2017.

Gustavo, Guttierez. *A Theology of Liberation.* Maryknoll, NY: Orbis, 1973.

Habermas, Jürgen. "Notes on a Post-Secular Society." *Signandsight.com*, June 18, 2020.

Hadjadj, Amel. "Le Hirak et la citoyenneté des femmes: opportunités et obstacles." *Revue du CIDDEF*, no. 40 (November2019): 12–16.

Hafez, Sherene. *An Islam of her Own: Reconsidering Religion and Secularism in Women's Islamic Movements.* New York: New York University Press, 2011.

Haitami, Meriem el. "Women and Sufism: Religious Expression and the Political Sphere in Contemporary Morocco." *Mediterranean Studies*, 22, no. 2 (2014): 190–212.

Hallaq, Wael B. *An Introduction to Islamic Law.* Cambridge: Cambridge University Press, 2009.

Haraway, Donna. "Situated Knowledges." In *The Feminist Standpoint Reader: Intellectual and Political Controversies*, edited by Sandra Harding. New York: Routledge, 2004.

Harding, Sandra, ed. *The Feminist Standpoint Theory Reader: Intellectual and Political Controversies.* New York: Routledge, 2004.

Hassan, Riffat. "Muslim Women and Post-Patriarchal Islam." In *After Patriarchy: Feminist Transformations of the World Religions*, by William R. Eakin, and Jay B. McDaniel, eds. Paula M. Cooey, 39–64. Maryknoll, NY: Orbis Books, 1991.

Hasso, Frances S. *Consuming Desires: Family Crises and the State in the Middle East.* Palo Alto, CA: Stanford University Press, 2011.

Hekman, Susan, ed. *Feminist Interpretations of Foucault (Re-reading the Canon).* Philadelphia, PA: University of Pennsylvania Press, 2007.

Hibri, Azizah Al. "Islamic Herstory or How Did We Ever Get into this Mess?" *Women's Studies International Forum*, 5, no. 2 (1982): 207–219.

Hidayatullah, Ayesah. "Muslim Theology in the United States." In *Muslima Theology: The Voices of Women Theologians*, edited by Ednan Aslan, Marcia Hermansan, and Elif Medeni. Bern: Peter Lang, 2013.

Hoffner, Anne-Bénédicte. "Emmanuel Macron face au défi de l' 'Islam de France'" *La Croix*, November 2, 2018. Accessed May 3, 2019 from www.la-croix.com/rpint/ articl/1200912947.

Hourani, Albert. *Arabic Thought in the Liberal Age 1788–1939*. Cambridge: Cambridge University Press, 2014.

Huffpost Maghreb. "Les imams interdits de pratiquer la Roqia dans les mosquées et écoles coraniques." Accessed September 21, 2019 from www.huffingtonpost maghreb.com/2016/05/20/roqia-interdite-mosquees_n_10061756.html?ncid=other_ email_063gt2jca4&utm_campaign=share_email.

HuffPost Maghreb. "Un député islamiste veut faire reconnaître la roqia." Accessed September 21, 2019 from www.huffpostmaghreb.com/2016/05/10/religion-djinn-sorcellei_n_9888314.html?ncid=other_email_063gt2jcad4&utm_campaign=share_ email.

Inge, Anabel. *The Making of Salafi Women*. Oxford: Oxford University Press, 2019.

Jaggar, Alison and Paula Rothenberg, eds. *Feminist Frameworks. Alternative Theoretical Accounts of the Relations Between Women and Men*. New York: McGraw Hill, 1978.

Kant, Immanuel. *Anthropology from a Pragmatic Point of View*, translated by Robert B. Louden. Cambridge: Cambridge University Press, 2009.

Karam, Azza. *Women, Islamisms and the Sate: Contemporary Feminisms in Egypt*. New York: Palgrave Macmillan, 1998.

Kausar, Zeenath. "The Battle of Books! Diverse Trends in Muslim Thought on Women's Issues." *Journal of International Women's Studies*, 15, no. 2 (2014): 165–181.

Kecia, Ali. *Sexual Ethics in Islam: Feminist Reflections on Qur'an, Hadith, and Jurisprudence*. Oxford: Oneworld, 2006.

Khatami, Mohammed. *Islam, Liberty and Development*. Binghamton, NY: Global Academic Publishing, 1998.

Khatir, Foad. "Le changement politique algérien, de la persécution à la réhabilitation des confréries religieuses musulmanes: le cas particulier de la confrérie 'Alawiyya 1909–2009." Doctoral dissertation, Université de Toulouse-Jean Jaurès, June 26, 2016.

Khemissi, Hamid, Ricardo René Larémont and Taybi Taj Eddine. "Sufism, Salafism, and State Policy," *The Journal of North African Studies*, 17, no. 3 (June2012): 547–558.

Koertge, Noretta. "'New Age' Philosophies of Science: Constructivism, Feminism, and Postmodernism." *The British Journal of Philosophy*, 5, no. 1 (2000): 667–683.

Kuhn, Thomas. *The Structure of Scientific Revolution*. Chicago, IL: Chicago University Press, 1962.

Lalami, Feriel. *Les Algériennes contre le code de la famille*. Paris: Sciences Po, 2012.

Lamptey, Jerusha Tanner. "Toward a Muslima Theology, Constructive, Comparative Possibilities." *Journal of Feminist Studies in Religion*, 33, no. 1 (Spring2017): 27–44.

Lamrabet, Asma. "Communiqué de presse du Dr. Asma Lamrabet explicitant les raisons de sa démission du centre d'études féminines en Islam au sein de la Rabita Almohahadya des Oulémas du Maroc." March 26, 2018. Accessed from asma-lam rabet.com.

Lamrabet, Asma. *Islam et femmes: les questions qui fâchent*. Paris: Gallimard, 2017.

Lamrabet, Asma. *Women in the Qur'an: An Emancipatory Reading*. Markfield: Square View, 2016.

Lauzière, Henri. *The Making of Salafism: Islamic Reform in the Twentieth Century*. New York: Columbia University Press, 2016.

Lazreg, Marnia. "Poststructuralist Theory and Women in the Middle East: Going in Circles?" *Journal of Contemporary Arab Affairs, Special issue, Feminism in the Arab Wold: Four Perspectives*, 6, no. 1 (January2013): 667–683.

Lazreg, Marnia. *The Eloquence of Silence: Algerian Women in Question*. New York: Routledge, 2019.

Lazreg, Marnia. "Feminism and Difference: The Perils of Writing as a Woman on Women in Algeria." *Feminist Studies*, 14, no. 1 (1988): 81–107.

Lazreg, Marnia. "*Theorizing the Median Space Between Power and Feminism in MENA.*" Paper presented at Theory and Feminism in the Arab World, University of Zurich, Switzerland, March 17–19, 2016.

Lazreg, Marnia. *Torture and the Twilight of Empire, From Algiers to Baghdad.* Princeton, NJ: Princeton University Press, 2010.

Lazreg, Marnia. *Foucault's Orient: The Conundum of Cultural Difference, From Tunisia to Japan.* New York: Berghahn, 2017.

Lazreg, Marnia. *The Eloquence of Silence: Algerian Women in Question, second edition.* New York: Routledge, 2018.

Le Matin d'Algérie. "Sans moi, Bouteflika aurait été jeté en prison." October 17, 2012. Accessed September 6, 2019 from https://lematindz.net/9919-3-sans-moi-bou teflika-arait-ete-jetc-cn-prison.

Leonhard, Jorn. "Translation as Cultural Transfer and Semantic Interactions:European Variations of *Liberal* Between 1800 and 1830." In *Why Concepts Matter: Translating Social and Political Thought*, edited by Martin Burke and Melvin Richter, 93–106. Leiden: Brill, 2012.

Le360. "Un raki viole une handicappée à El Hajeb." Accessed September 21, 2019 from https://fr.le360.ma/societe/un-raqui-viole-une-handicapee-a-el-hajeb-181792#.XYYbqLduPds.email.

Les Annales Coloniales. "Le centenaire de l'Algérie." *Les Annales Coloniales*, July 30, 1929.

Lévi-Strauss, Claude. *Structural Anthropology, Vol. 3*, translated by Claire Jacobson and Brooke Grundfest Schoepf. New York: Basic Books, 1976.

Lindssey, Ursula. "Can Muslim Feminism Find a Third Way?" *The New York Times*, April 18, 2018.

L'Obs. "Algérie: Attaque du site gazier de Tiguentourine," January 17, 2013. Accessed September 18, 2019 from www.nouvelobs.com/monde/20130117.OBS5781/infograp hie-algerie-attaque-du-site-gazier-de-tiguentourine.html.

L'Obs. "300 personnalités signent un manifeste contre le nouvel 'anti- sémitisme' en France." *Le Nouvel Observateur*, April 22, 2019.

Luizard, Pierre-Jean. "Le soufisme égyptien contemporain." *Egypte/Monde arabe*, 2 (1990). Accessed October 15, 2019 from http://journals.opneaccess.org/ema/218.

Magout, Mohammad. *A Reflexive Islamic Modernity: Academic Knowledge and Religious Subjectivity in the Global Ismaili Community.* Baden Baden: Ergon, 2020.

Mahmood, Saba. *The Politics of Piety: The Islamic Revival and the Feminist Subject.* Princeton, NJ: Princeton University Press, 2005.

Mahmood, Saba. "Secularism, Hermeneutics, and Empire: The Politics of Islamic Reformation." *Public Culture*, 18, no. 2 (2006): 330–335.

Massad, Joseph A. *Islam in Liberalism.* Chicago, IL: Chicago University Press, 2015.

Mandaville, Peter and Melissa Nozell. "Engaging Religion and Religious Actors in Countering Violent Extremism." Accessed June 20, 2020 from www.usip.org/sites/default/files/SR413-Engaging-religion-and-Religious-Actors-in-Counter ing-Violent-Extremism.pdf.

McDonald, Laura Zahra. 2018. "Islamic Feminism." *Feminist Theory*, 9, no. 3 (2018): 347–354.

McDougall, James. *History and the Culture of Nationalism in Algeria.* Cambridge: Cambridge University Press, 2006.

McLarney, Ellen Anne. *Women in Egypt's Islamic Awakening.* Princeton, NJ: Princeton University Press, 2015.

McPhillips, Kathleen. "Decolonizing the Sacred: Feminist Proposals for a Post-Christian, Post-Patriarchal Approach." In *Post-Christian Feminisms: A Critical Approach*, edited by Kathleen McPhillipas and Lisa Isherwood. New York: Routledge, 2009.

McRobbie, Angela. "Postfeminim and Popular Culture: Bridget Jones and the New Gender Regime." In *Interrogating Postfeminism: Gender and the Politics of Popular Culture*, edited by Y. Takser and D. Negra, 27–39. Durham, NC: Duke University Press, 2007.

Mechouet, Noureddine. "Actualités: Entretien avec M. Mechouet, président de l'association des zaouias 'Les zaouias sont la première institution politique du pays'." *Le Soir d'Algérie*, March 21, 2016. Accessed from https://lesoirdalgerie.com/articles/2016/03/21/article.php?sid=193508&cid=2.

Meddi, Adlène. "Laïcité en France: les vrais défis de Macron." *Middle East Eye*, January 15, 2018.

Meijer, Roel. *Global Salafism: Islam New Religious Movement*. New York: Columbia University, 2009.

Ministère des Affaires Religieuses et des Waqfs. *Al jarida al ra'isiya lil jamhouriya al jaza'iriya*. Algiers: Ministère des Affaires Religieuses et des Waqfs, December 8, 2018.

Mir-Hosseini, Ziba. "Islam and Gender Justice." In *Voices of Islam, Voices of Diversity and Change, vol. 5*, edited by Vincent Cornell and Omid Safi. Westport, CT: Greenwood, 2007.

Mir-Hosseini, Ziba. n.d. "What is Islamic Feminism?" Video. Accessed April 14, 2020 from https://youtu.be/Fzf2D43wcTc.

Mir-Hosseini, Ziba. "Beyond 'Islam' vs. 'Feminism'." *IDS Bulletin*, 42, no. 1 (January2009): 67–77.

Moghadam, Valentin. "Islamic Feminism and Its Discontents: Towards a Resolution of the Debate," *Signs*, 27, no. 4 (2002): 1135–1171.

Moghissi, Haideh. "Islamic Cultural Nationalism and Gender Politics in Iran." *Third World Quarterly*, 29, no. 3 (2008): 541–554.

Moroccan American Center for Policy. "Towards a New Morocco-US Strategic Partnership." November2013. Accessed June 20, 2020 from www.moroccoonthemove.com/wp-content/uploads/2013/11/Briefing-papers-Towards-a-New-Morocco-US-Strategic-Partnership-pdf.

Moruzzi, Norma Claire. *Reading Arendt in Iran/Reading Iran Through Arendt: Speech, Action, and the Question of Street Politics*. Chicago, IL: Great Cities Institute, n.d.

Naggar, Shaima El. "Intertextuality and Interdiscursivity in the Discourse of Muslim Televangelists: The Case Study of Hamza Yusuf." *Critical Approaches to Discourse Analysis Across Disciplines*, 6, no. 1 (2012): 76–95.

National Commission on Terrorist Attacks Against the United States. "What to Do? A Global Strategy." Accessed June 20, 2020 from http://govinfo.library.unt.edu/911/report/911Report_Ch12.pdf. .

Nielsen, Richard A. "Women's Authority in Patriarchal Social Movements." *American Journal of Political Science*, 64, no. 1 (January2020): 52–66.

Nietzsche, Friedrich. *The Gay Science*, translated by Walter Kauffman. New York: Vintage, 1974.

North African Post. "Imam Training, Key Instrument of Morocco's Religious Diplomacy." *The North African Post*, October 21, 2017.

Ouardi, Hela. *Les derniers jours de Muhammad: Enquête sur la mort du Prophète*. Paris: Albin Michel, 2017.

Ozcan, Esra. "Turkish Women in Islamism: Gender and the Mirage of 'Islamic Feminism'." *Samyukta*, 17, no. 1 (January2017): 182–192.

Paret. Peter. *French Revolutionary Warfare, From Indochina to Algeria.* New York: Frederick A. Praeger, 1964.

Parsons, Talcott. *The Social System.* Glencoe, IL: The Free Press, 1964.

Pepicelli, Renata and Souad Eddouada. "Morocco: Towards an 'Islamist State Feminism'." *Critique internationale*, 46, no. 1 (2010): 87–100.

Plaskow, Judith. *Standing Again at Sinai: Judaism from a Feminist Perspective.* New York: HarperCollins, 1991.

Popovic, Alexandre and Veinstein, Gilles. *Les Voies d'Allah: les ordres mystiques dans le monde musulman des origines à aujourd'hui.* Paris: Arthème Fayard, 1996.

Postel, Daniel. *Reading Legitimation Crisis in Teheran: Iran and the Future of Liberalism.* Chicago, IL: Prickly Paradigm Press, 2006.

Rahemtulla, Shadaab. *Qur'an of the Oppressed: Liberation Theology and Gender Justice in Islam.* Oxford: Oxford University Press, 2017.

Rahman, Fazlur. *Islam*, 2nd edition. Chicago, IL: Chicago University Press, 1979.

Rahman, Fazlur. *Islam and Modernity: Transformations of an Intellectual Tradition.* Chicago, IL: Chicago University Press, 1982.

Rabasa, Angel, Cheryl Benard, Lowell H. Schwartz, and Peter Sickle. *The RAND Report: Building Moderate Muslim Networks.* Santa Monica, CA: The RAND Center for Middle East Policy. Accessed June 20, 2020 from www.rand.org/content/dam/rand/pubs/monographs/2007/RAND_MG574.pdf.

Rabasa, Angel, Stacie L. Pettyjohn, Jeremy J. Ghetz, and Christopher Boucek. "European Approaches." In *Deradicalizing Islamist Extremists.* Santa Monica, CA: The RAND Center for Middle East Policy, 2010. Accessed June 20, 2020 from www.rand.org/content/dam/rand/pubs/monographs/2010/RAND_MG1053.pdf.

République française, Sénat, travaux parlementaires, Mission d'Information. *Compte rendus de la MI d'organisation, place et financement de l' Islam en France.* Paris: Mission d'Information, 2016.

Rhouni, Raja. *Secular and Feminist Critiques in the Work of Fatima Mernissi.* Leiden: Brill, 2010.

Rothwell, James. "Morocco Arrests Ten Female ISIL Suicide Bombers Who Planned to Strike on Election Day." *The Telegraph*, October 5, 2016. Accessed July 29, 2019 from www.telegraph.co.uk/news/2016/10/05/morocco-arrests-ten-female-isil-suicide-bombers-who-planned-to-s2/?WT.mc_id=tmg_share_em.

Ruether, Rosemary. *Sexism and God Talk: Towards a Feminist Theology.* Boston, MA: Beacon, 1993.

Rysiew, Patrick. "Epistemic Contextualism." *The Stanford Encyclopedia of Philosophy* (Winter2016 edition), edited by Edward N. Zalta. Accessed July 3, 2020 from https://plato.stanford.edu/archives/win2016/entries/contextualism-epistemology.

Sadiqi, Fatima. *Moroccan Feminist Discourses.* New York: Palgrave Macmillan, 2019.

Sakthivel, Vish. "Political Islam in Post-conflict Algeria." November 2, 2017. Accessed December 1, 2019 from www.hudson.org/research/13934-political-islam-in-post-colonial-algeria.

Salime, Zakia. "The War on Terrorism. Appropriation and Subversion by Moroccan Women." *Signs*, 33, no. 1 (Autumn2007): 1–24.

Seedat, Fatima. "Islam, Feminism, and Islamic Feminism: Between Inadequacy and Inevitability." *Journal of Feminist Studies in Religion*, 29, no. 2 (Fall2013): 25–45.

Seidel, Roman. March 2010. "Reading Kant in Teheran: Towards a Reception of the Iranian Reception of European Philosophy." *AS/EA*, LXIV, no. 3 (2010): 681–706.

Sharmani, Mulki Al. "Islamic Feminism: Transnational Reflections." *Approaching Religion* 4, no. 2 (2014): 83–94.

Sheline, Annelle. "Religious Authority: Morocco's 'Commander of the Faithful'." Accessed March 24, 2020 from www.bakerinstitute.org/media/files/files/02d67a3e/cme-pub-luce-sheline-030719_hvUZDee.pdf.

Shirazi, Faegeh. *Velvet Jihad: Women's Quiet Resistance to Islamic Fundamentalism.* Gainesville, FL: University of Florida Press, 2009.

Silva, Rui. "Hermeneutics and Epistemological Contextualism." *Proceedings of the XXIII World Congress of Philosophy. Philosophical Hermeneutics,* 30 (2018): 55–59.

Smith, Margaret. *Muslim Women Mystics: The Life and Work of Rabi'a and Other Women Mystics in Islam.* Oxford: Oneworld, 2001.

Soroush, Abdolkarim. *Reason, Freedom and Democracy in Islam: Essential Writings of Abdolkarim Soroush,* edited by Mahmoud Sadri and Ahmad Sadri. Oxford: Oxford University Press, 2000.

TSA (Tout sur l'Algérie). "Le business ramadhanesque des imams en France." Accessed May 16, 2020 from www.tsa-algerie.com/societe.

TSA (Tout sur l'Algérie) "Ramadan et COVID19: la commission de la fatwa se prononce." Accessed June 7, 2020 from www.tsa-algerie.com/ramadan-et-covid-19-la-commission-de-la-fatwa-se-prononce.

TSA (Tout sur l'Algérie). "Fetwa sur la zakat: la responsable de Ennahar TV convoquée par l'ARAV." Accessed from www.tsa-algerie.com/fetwa-sur-la-zakat-la-responsable-dennahar-tv-convoquee-par-larav.

United Nations High Commissioner for Refugees. *Country Report on Terrorism 2007—Morocco.* Geneva: UNHCR, 2008.

United States Embassy in Algeria. "Imam Exchange Program." Accessed July 28, 2019 from https://dz.usembassy.gov/…Notice-of-Funding-Opportunity-Imam-Exchange-Program.

Vahdat, Farzin. "Religious Modernity in Iran: Dilemmas of Islamic Democracy in the Discourse of Mohammad Khatami." *Comparative Studies of South Asia,* 25, no. 3 (2005): 650–664.

Varlik, Selami. "Le sens objectif du Coran à l' épreuve de l'historicité." *Archives des sciences sociales des religions,* 170 (April–June2015): 247–265.

Vernet, Jean-Pierre, Jorge Vaa, Ligia Amancio, and Fabuzio Butera. "Conscientization of Social Cryptomnesia Reduces Sexism and Rejection of Feminists." *Social Psychology,* 40, no. 3 (2009): 130–137.

Wadud, Amina. *Inside the Gender Jihad. Women's Reforms in Islam.* London: One World, 2008.

Wadud, Amina. *Qur'an and Woman: Re-read the Scred Text.* New York: Oxford University Press, 2007.

Yadav, Stacey Philbrick. "Segmented Publics and Islamist Women in Yemen: Rethinking Space and Activism." *Journal of Middle Eastern Women Studies,* 6, no. 2 (Spring 2020): 1–30.

Zerilli, Linda M. G. *Feminism and the Abyss of Freedom.* Chicago, IL: Chicago University Press, 2015.

Zoubir, Yahia H. "Algeria and U.S. Interests: Containing Radical Islamism and Promoting Democracy," *Middle East Policy,* IX, no. 1 (March2002): 64–81.

INDEX

Printed in Great Britain
by Amazon

70414284R00104